LIECHTENSTEIN MUSEUM VIENNA
THE COLLECTIONS

LIECHTENSTEIN MUSEUM VIENNA
THE COLLECTIONS

Edited by Johann Kräftner
Essays by Johann Kräftner and Andrea Stockhammer
Academic assistant Stefan Körner

LIECHTENSTEIN M U S E U M

Prestel
Munich · Berlin · London · New York

CONTRIBUTORS

Johann Kräftner
THE PRINCELY COLLECTIONS, THE PALACE, THE DISPLAY

Andrea Stockhammer
GALLERY IV TO X

EDITORIAL AND ACADEMIC ASSISTANT
Stefan Körner

CONTENTS

FOREWORD

The Princely Collections have had a presence in Vienna for three hundred years. Even during the High Baroque period, when the most important works of art were housed on the second floor of the then newly-built Liechtenstein City Palace in Bankgasse, they formed a counterbalance to the Imperial Collections in the Stallburg picture gallery.

The Princely Collections have been open to the general public since 1807 when they were transferred to the Garden Palace at Rossau.

When Austria was annexed by National Socialist Germany in 1938, this success story came to an abrupt end. The princely family moved to Liechtenstein, the museum was closed and its artworks were removed to Vaduz during the last weeks of the war under appalling circumstances.

With the Liechtenstein estates expropriated in the former Czechoslovakia and with political circumstances in Austria so difficult in the immediate post-war era, the family was unable to resume where it had left off in 1938.

Only with the successful restructuring of the family's assets in recent decades did it again become possible to consider re-opening the LIECHTENSTEIN MUSEUM in Vienna. When the Museum of Modern Art moved out to the city's new museum quarter, the opportunity was used to consider the future of the Garden Palace at Rossau.

As part of its re-instatement as the family's museum, comprehensive restoration and modernization finally started in 2001. It is a source of great pleasure for me and my family that the Princely Collections are again accessible to the public through the LIECHTENSTEIN MUSEUM.

Hans-Adam II
Prince von und zu Liechtenstein

PREFACE

The Baroque is crucially important to Austrian art history, to the cultural understanding of the country and also to the Austrian awareness of life, and it is central to the concept of the LIECHTENSTEIN MUSEUM where its fascinating world is revealed to the public. The Baroque and Vienna are almost synonymous. Having secured victory over the Turks in 1683, the city developed from a medieval municipality to a Baroque metropolis. The great Liechtenstein family palaces date from that period, too. The Garden Palace at Rossau, built at the time of a fresh start around 1700, is now again home to the Princely Collections. With the LIECHTENSTEIN MUSEUM and its first-rate collection of international appeal, the Baroque is set to become a new trademark for the City of Vienna, just as twenty-odd years ago "Vienna around 1900" became the city's most important slogan that still continues to attract large numbers of visitors to the city.

Home to exquisite masterpieces from the Princely Collections, the LIECHTENSTEIN MUSEUM is a feast for the senses and a place of Baroque *joie de vivre* in which all the art forms are united in a historical ensemble. Amid the glittering setting of the restored Baroque building, an atmospheric composition of paintings, sculptures, precious objects and furniture breathes new life into the splendour, once feared lost, of the Princely Collections in their original surroundings.

Works from the most important epochs of European art are displayed on the piano nobile in apartments with the finest stucco ceilings and imaginatively patterned, original parquet floors. Visitors can explore works of European art ranging from early Italian religious paintings, Rubens, van Dyck and Frans Hals to the painting of the Dutch Golden Age, hung in the Baroque manner, with Rembrandt's work as its highlight.

Alongside the works of art on display in the palace, visitors can expect a complete Baroque work of art that, together with new, unobtrusive fittings, bridges the gap between the sensibilities and ideas of the present and the brilliant heritage of past generations.

An important element within this complete work of art is the historic garden at the LIECHTENSTEIN MUSEUM. An urban oasis, it offers visitors space in which to relax; with its restaurants and garden facilities, concerts and matinees, it recalls the days of Baroque *joie de vivre*.

The return of the Princely Collections to the refurbished palace at Rossau would have been impossible without the whole-hearted commitment of my colleagues. I should like to take this opportunity to thank them all for supporting me throughout the project and contributing to its realization. My special thanks go to Andrea Stockhammer for her enormous effort in writing all the catalogue essays for our first permanent presentation. Her academic assistant, Stefan Körner, provided essential support. Michael Schweller was a calming influence who kept his eye on the bigger picture during the chaos involved in moving the artworks from Vaduz to Vienna.

The team of restorers – headed by Robert Wald, Helga Musner, the director of the workshop in Vienna, as well as Ruth Weiss-Kiebel, Johannes Weiss and Tanja Neuhorn in Vaduz – have restored the property and objects to a condition that entirely does justice to their extraordinary quality. Prestel Verlag's hard work and flexibility made it possible to include our latest acquisitions and images of the galleries in the catalogue.

Finally, very special thanks are due to my assistant, Alexandra Hanzl. Her creativity, energy and tireless commitment were an essential driving force behind the realization of my idea of seeing a rejuvenated and self-confident LIECHTENSTEIN MUSEUM return to Vienna.

My thanks go to Prince Hans-Adam II von und zu Liechtenstein, Princess Marie von und zu Liechtenstein and their family for allowing us the necessary scope to implement the vision of the return of the Princely Collections to Vienna. The thanks of everyone who has worked on this project, the thanks of the City of Vienna, of Austria – and indeed the whole world – are due to the great patron and collector of the arts, Prince Hans-Adam II von und zu Liechtenstein.

Johann Kräftner
Director of the LIECHTENSTEIN MUSEUM Vienna
and of the Princely Collections, Vaduz

THE
PRINCELY
COLLECTIONS

16 H. 15.

πόνΘ ἐνκλήδς πάχͤ

Carl fürst von Lichtenstein, Hertzog
zu Troppaw

THE HISTORY OF THE PRINCELY COLLECTIONS

With the opening of the LIECHTENSTEIN MUSEUM, the world's most important privately owned art collection that is still extant returns to its original historical location. Until 1938 it was the leading voice in the concert of other noble and royal collections in Vienna, and in competition with the old Imperial Collections that formed the basis of Austria's national museums today.

Almost all these aristocratic collections, and there were very many of them, were in the course of the nineteenth and twentieth centuries lost to the families who owned them. The Lamberg Collection remained in Vienna as a gift and has represented the core holdings of the Akademie-Galerie since 1822. The Kaunitz Collection was auctioned as early as 1820 and 1829, and the key sections (picture gallery, collection of prints and drawings) of the Esterházy Collection were sold to the Hungarian state in 1870. The family moved the collection of the Princes Metternich to Schloss Königswarth in Bohemia after they gave up the palace in Vienna (1873). It was put on show again in Königswarth, and rearranged in recent years. The Rothschild family collections fell victim to the National Socialists, the Czernin family collections were largely broken up after the Second World War, with some of the remaining holdings housed in the Residenzgalerie in Salzburg. The Schönborn-Buchheim Collection was never open to the public, miraculously survived and was recently on display in a monographic exhibition at the Haus der Kunst in Munich. The Harrach family collection is the only one that continues to be open to the public, though not in its traditional home in the family's town house in the Freyung, which was sold long ago, but, still complete, in Rohrau near Vienna. The items from the Esterházy Collection that remained in Austria are still present, above all the treasury, which is on show in Forchtenstein. As well as this, extensive holdings in the form of paintings, prints and drawings and porcelain, especially from the late eighteenth and early nineteenth centuries, and the collections of weapons and Ottoman objects, have also survived, and are shown in Schloss Forchtenstein.

All guides to Vienna written in the nineteenth and early twentieth century mention the importance of these aristocratic collections, which constituted one of the major attractions of the capital and royal seat.

The Princely Collections played a key role in all this. Almost immediately after they were first shown shortly after 1700 in Vienna, in the City Palace in Bankgasse, they were made accessible to the public, even if on a limited basis. The young Georg Raphael Donner came to know international Baroque sculpture here. His *Mercury* was a copy of François Duquesnoy's version, and marked the starting point of independent Viennese High Baroque sculpture. The Liechtenstein gallery at Rossau was one of the first museums in the city to be open to the public. It presented copious holdings of paintings, sculpture, craftwork and furniture, all displayed in close proximity. The works of art in the collection were always on the move. There was not just the one gallery to consider, but also the countless castles and country houses scattered around Austria, Bohemia and Moravia. Objects were sold in their hundreds, and then just as much new material was acquired in entire lots. The collecting activities of the Liechtenstein dynasty were dominated by the personal preferences of a number of individual princes. The result was that entire libraries and collections of prints and drawings might be assembled with remarkable speed – and then broken up again: the collections were always caught up in vigorous activity.

Prince Johann II (1840–1929) gave objects away to half of Central Europe. The painting collection in the Wien-Museum owed its existence to one of his gifts, the painting gallery in the Akademie der bildenden Künste in Vienna was given its early Italian works by him and the Österreichische Galerie im Belvedere the major part of its current Biedermeier painting holdings, with major works by Waldmüller and Amerling. The Kunsthistorisches Museum could afford to acquire the *Gölbasy-Trysa Heroon*, but Prince Johann II paid for its transport. He provided countless important museums in Bohemia and Moravia with major works that are still in their possession today. A passion for collecting ran in the family, and is a tradition that is still alive today. The losses the collections suffered as a result of the Second World War were painful – but in the light of the house's history they are perhaps an event to which too much attention need not be paid, an event that can be seen as a thing of the past. The family is one of the very few who are still able to continue actively building their collection. The thrust of their collecting now aims to close gaps made by selling, gaps that have arisen because of a lack of interest in some fields and gaps that should be filled because things are seen in a different way. The family also wish to enhance the value of the holdings they have accumulated by adding carefully targeted purchases. It is frequently the case that a piece is not as significant in its own right as the ensemble of which it is part. It is often necessary to cast light on certain facets to reveal the full significance of a work.

**WORKSHOP OF CASTRUCCI AND
GIULIANO DI PIERO PANDOLFINI** doc. 1615–1637
Pietra dura work with landscape of tower
and houses on a cliff, between 1622 and 1630

We know relatively little about the early history of the collection. Hartmann II von Liechtenstein (1544 –1585) already owned paintings and tapestries, and Hans Mielich's *Portrait of Ladislaus von Fraunberg, Count of Haag* came into his possession through his marriage to Anna von Ortenburg. As a book collector, Hartmann II von Liechtenstein acquired items that are still in the collection today. The first to be infected with an uncontrollable urge to collect was Karl I (1569 –1627), the first prince in the family. He was an extraordinarily cultivated man, went to school in Geneva and embarked on a study visit to France in 1588. He served Emperor Rudolf II as Master of the Household in Prague, was elevated to the rank of hereditary prince by him in 1608 and finally appointed viceroy of Bohemia in 1620.

Spurred on by Rudolf's activities as a collector, Karl started to collect and to commission art as well. We know from correspondence between the two in 1597 that Karl already had a substantial collection of paintings and cabinet pieces in his Prague residence, and that this had attracted Rudolf's attention: he wanted to swap some pieces with Karl.

There are records mentioning a private Silver Vault: inventories tell us that in the *Guardaroba* he kept tapestries and carpets, costly furniture, gold and silver objects, vessels in carved stone and paintings, making this *Guardaroba* the nucleus of the Princely Collections. Karl was not just an active collector; he also acquired important works of art by commission. Adriaen de Fries was commissioned in 1607 to make the life-size bronze *Christ in Distress* for him; we have no precise archival details for the *St Sebastian*, which Karl was also commissioned from de Fries. The circle of goldsmiths, jewellers and gem-cutters employed by Prince Karl must have been a very wide one. His fondness for precious stones and metals shows in the *pietra dura* works, a chest framed in gilded bronze (for which Ottavio Miseroni in Prague received an honorarium of 1134 florins) and a table-top made at almost the same time (1620 –23). All these chamber pieces are still in the collections and are on show in the LIECHTENSTEIN MUSEUM.

QUENTIN MASSYS *c.* 1465/66–1530

Portrait of a Canon

BENVENUTO TISI called Il Garofalo 1481–1559
Apotheosis of Hercules, *c.* 1539

When an inventory was taken of his Prague residence after Karl died in 1633, 83 pictures were listed, including some pieces by Hans von Aachen, a *Perseus* by Jacopo Palma and *The Moneychangers* by Jan Massys. The inventory of the Silver Vault included over 900 different objects.

His son Karl Eusebius von Liechtenstein (1611–1684) continued as his father had started. He is important not least because he underpinned the collection theoretically with his *Werk über die Architektur und der Prinzenerziehung* (Study of Architecture and the Education of Princes) – instructions on how a prince should live, present himself and collect. Karl Eusebius eschewed public office and so had time to concern himself with his own home. He initiated countless

JEAN DE COURT *c.* 1520–1591
Oval bowl with scene of the iron snake,
3rd quarter of 16th century

PIERRE COURTEYS *c.* 1520–1591
Enamel plate featuring a battle scene outside the walls of Troy,
2nd half of 16th century

RUDOLF VON ALT 1812–1902
The Armoury in Valtice Palace, 1845

building schemes, and was the first prince of the House of Liechtenstein to engage large numbers of architects, stonemasons, stucco artists and painters. He acquired Rubens's monumental *Ascension of the Virgin* as the altarpiece for his new parish church in Valtice as early as 1643 – the foundation stone was laid in 1631. The *Ascension* is also to be seen in the LIECHTENSTEIN MUSEUM.

The history of a large lidded vase (*Maienkrug*) in smoky quartz set in gilded bronze is also precisely documented. It dates from 1640: shortly before, in 1638, a large stone weighing 35 pounds was found and the vase and two columns were carved from it.

While in Florence in 1636, Karl Eusebius bought a second important *pietra dura* table-top from Giuliano Pandolfini, whom he apparently visited in his workshop in the Uffizi.

Made between 1625 and 1630, the bronze group *David with the Head of Goliath*, an independent creation by Giovanni Francesco Susini, was acquired by Karl Eusebius, presumably on the same visit to Florence.

Karl Eusebius was also the first to make systematic use of the art trade to purchase paintings and sculptures. It was he who established links with the Forchoudt dynasty of art dealers, who had a branch on Vienna's Judenplatz. Adriaen van Ostade's *Smoking Peasants* was the first painting Karl Eusebius acquired in this long business relationship. He was offered entire collections, and confidently chose the items that were appropriate for his own gallery. Through the painter Johan(n) Spillenberger, he was able to acquire the wonderful *Portrait of a Man*, now attributed to Barthélemy d'Eyck. He bought Hugo van der Goes's small triptych through the Viennese dealer Regnier Megan in 1684.

As well as being interested in art, he also bred horses. The so-called Schloss der Rosse, a large stables by Fischer von Erlach in Lednice, was the result of this second passion. He swapped the world-famous horses bred there with the second major collector of the day, Archduke Leopold Wilhelm, in exchange – what else could we expect? – for pictures.

NICOLAS BIS doc. 1691–1726
JUAN SANTOS FERNANDEZ doc. 1711–1739
FRANCISCO BAEZA Y BIS doc. 1730–1765
Three Spanish flintlock guns with Miquelet locks
in a case, 1710/3

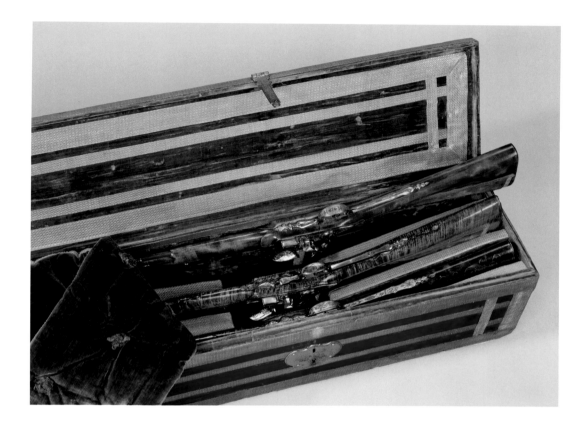

Karl Eusebius's son, Prince Johann Adam Andreas I von Liechtenstein (1657–1712) picked up where his father left off. As luck would have it – the Turks had just been driven out of Vienna, and he acquired the building plot for his summer palace immediately afterwards – he was able to build an enormous number of castles and palaces, and decorate and furnish them exactly as he wished. He was the greatest builder of the Baroque age in Central Europe. Acquiring the plot of land in Bankgasse, on which the magnificent family home was built a little later, meant that he now had the space to realize his dream of a gallery. The famous sculptor Giovanni Giuliani was commissioned to create a brilliant set of sculptures for the main staircase. The stairs leading to the second floor of the house ended in the gallery. Here Prince Johann Adam Andreas was able to present his treasures in an appropriate context; until then most of them had probably been kept in the palace at Valtice. They included some of the key works on which the collection's fame is still based today. For example, in 1693 he was able to conduct

tough negotiations leading to the acquisition of the Decius Mus cycle from Antwerp as the core of an extensive Rubens collection. He commissioned no less an artist than Giovanni Giuliani to make the frames and the cartouches of these works. He also brought the majority of the van Dycks into the collection. Once more it was the agents he employed in the Netherlands and in Italy who kept him informed about what was on the art market. The Forchoudt brothers' business eagerly sought out pictures for him; through them, he acquired the works by Rubens and van Dyck that have already been mentioned, and also drawings by these artists, and craftwork. The *Portrait of Clara Serena Rubens* came into the Princely Collections from one of the most avid collectors of all, Archduke Leopold Wilhelm. The collections in the Kunsthistorisches Museum in Vienna can largely be traced back to him.

Prince Johann Adam Andreas I was also important as a patron. Here he focused above all on Italian contemporaries, whose pictures and sculptures he used to decorate the palaces: Marcantonio

JOHANN GEORG VON HAMILTON 1672–1737
Portrait of a Piebald from the Lednice Stud Farm, 1700

FRANS HALS 1580/1585–1666
Portrait of Willem van Heythuysen, *c.* 1625/30
Bayerische Staatsgemäldesammlung,
Alte Pinakothek, Munich

ANTHONY VAN DYCK 1599–1641
Portrait of James, 3rd Marquess of Hamilton
and 1st Duke of Hamilton

ADAM LENCKHARDT 1610–1661
St Sebastian, post-1642

Franceschini of Bologna and Antonio Bellucci of Venice, the sculptors Giovanni Giuseppe Mazza and Giovanni Giuliani and the stucco artist Santino Bussi should be mentioned here.

One important innovation was the so-called entail: the City Palace in Vienna and the works of art in it were declared to be the permanent, inalienable property of the House of Liechtenstein. This entail stood until 1938, when it was revoked by the National Socialists and replaced by a protection order under the monument protection laws. This was a ruling that was not entirely beyond dispute in law, as there were so many objects in the collection that they were in a state of constant rotation between different properties in several states, while monument protection ended at Austria's border.

On its completion, the City Palace in Bankgasse must have been a veritable temple of the Muses. Apart from the Imperial Collections, which were still shown in the Stallburg at the time, it was without doubt one of the artistic highlights in early eighteenth-century Baroque Vienna.

We cannot put a precise number of the pictures held in the Collections when the prince died in 1712. Vincenzio Fanti's first catalogue of the Princely Collections, printed in 1767, identifies the objects acquired under Prince Joseph Wenzel von Liechtenstein (1696–1772), so that it is possible to form a more or less precise impression of the holdings in 1712. The great Flemish artists, Rubens, van Dyck and Snyders on the one hand, and the Baroque Italians on the other, were dominant even then, with German and Dutch work featuring in addition.

As well as this entailed collection, there were other collections that family members had assembled. Some kept up a lively exchange of items with each other. Emanuel von Liechtenstein (1700–1771) built up a considerable picture gallery in Schloss Loosdorf in Lower Austria, which already had 600 paintings by 1722. His uncle Hartmann (1666–1728) left over 800 pictures in his Schloss Nieder-Absdorf in Lower Austria when he died. Finally, Joseph Wenzel von Liechtenstein also had his own, fine private art collection, which he kept in the palace in Herrengasse; this included the two Batonis he had bought, among others. All these individual collections were brought into the entailed collection in the late eighteenth century. The individual princes had different interests, and so concentrated their collecting activities on different fields. Joseph Wenzel von Liechtenstein had acquired a taste for French art during his visit to Paris, and commissioned some work there and then – including two

of the finest portraits of princes, painted by Hyacinthe Rigaud for Joseph Wenzel, and also the pictures by Jean-Baptiste-Simeon de Chardin that were sold in the post-war period. The enamel panels by Pierre Courteys with the Trojan War cycle are among the best sixteenth-century Limousin enamel work. Not least, Joseph Wenzel commissioned the famous Golden Carriage in Paris. This is the most important surviving French Rococo state coach, not just for its artistic quality, but also for its historical significance.

The pictures commissioned from Bernado Bellotto in 1759 show us what the garden and the palace at Rossau must have looked like then. Joseph Wenzel also took a keen interest in books, and many

DU PAQUIER MANUFACTORY in Vienna
Coffee pot, *c.* 1725/30

of the manuscripts and other precious volumes in the present library were among the items he acquired.

The purchase of the equestrian statuette of Ferdinando I de' Medici indicate how widely Joseph Wenzel's interests ranged, especially in the field of sculpture, to which he felt committed as head of the Austrian artillery and thus head of the imperial foundries. As well as this, Joseph Wenzel commissioned Austrian sculptors like Gabriel Mollinarolo, who produced the almost life-size lead-tin sculptures of *Minerva* and *Apollo* that have only recently been acquired for the collection.

The first printed catalogue of the Liechtenstein gallery, by Vincenzio Fanti, was published in 1767, and was the first printed catalogue for any Viennese gallery. It lists 501 pictures and 186 sculptures; twelve of the pictures are identified as new acquisitions by Joseph Wenzel, the rest of the items he bought must have been housed in

his own gallery in Herrengasse. The catalogue includes the two great equestrian paintings by Johann Georg von Hamilton hung in the first room in Bankgasse, along with the large horizontal formats of Andrea Pozzo's *Church Fathers*, originally intended for the Hercules Hall, and a lot of small landscapes. The centre of this room was occupied by the free-standing sculpture of the *Boy Antinous*, which was later sold to Dresden.

The next room was hung with still lifes, with Renaissance bronzes on the tables. The gallery after that showed a series of small-format pictures by Dutch artists, some Rubens sketches, three Rembrandts, a large number of Florentine *pietra dura* pictures, the *pietra dura* chest, bronze reliefs and Soldani Benzi's *Bacchus* in the centre.

The centrepiece of Gallery IV was Rubens's *Assumption*, with Reni's *Adoration of the Shepherds* as a counterweight, surrounded by a series of landscapes, with two *pietra dura* table-tops in the centre on a base executed in 1711 by Giovanni Giuliani.

Gallery V contained just the entire Decius Mus cycle, only *The Trophy* was in Gallery I; here too numerous Renaissance bronzes were presented on the tables. Portraits by van Dyck and Rubens and Rubens's mythological pictures followed in Gallery VI, followed in Gallery VII by the Italians with Soldani Benzi's bronzes. Gallery VIII housed nothing but portraits of all schools, followed by two more galleries containing pictures, a room with weapons and finally a room for physical experiments, which was not usually open.

The second catalogue for the gallery, much more detailed this time, was published under Prince Franz Josef I (1726–1781). Its author, the gallery director Johann Dallinger, provides short descriptions of the pictures for the first time and mentions their supporting material, which makes them much easier to identify than in Fanti's catalogue.

By the time Prince Alois I (1759–1805) died the pictures had all been brought together in one gallery – after two auctions, held in 1799 and 1800 – including 800 pictures, of which he had personally bought only 306. The gallery was subject to constant change during his reign, but as well as buying and selling he also commissioned paintings from artists. He had his own portrait painted by Lampi, and those of his wife and one of his sisters by Elisabeth Vigée-Lebrun. Works of art by Antonio Canova, Johann Michael Fischer, Heinrich Füger and Franz Anton Zauner came into the collection.

He was especially interested in the collection of prints and drawings and the library. He bought copperplate engravings in large quantities, and Lorenz Janscha and Johann Ziegler dedicated the engraving of *Roman Ruins* in the grounds of Schloss Schönbrunn to the prince. He commissioned a new building for the library in Herrengasse, which meant that it could be displayed in full for the first time. The furniture and content of this library were transferred to the Garden Palace between 1912 and 1914.

Prince Johann I's greatest contribution was that he moved the collection to the Garden Palace (1807), where there was considerably more room to show it than in the cramped space of the Bankgasse. Even so, he must have opted for a way of displaying the pictures that left scarcely a square inch of wall free of paintings, as can be seen from Joseph Bauer's hanging plans, drawn up in 1815, which have survived in their entirety. The prince acquired 711 pictures in the course of his reign; the gallery contained 1613 paintings when he died.

He developed a close working relationship with a number of artists. Joseph Höger should be mentioned here: the prince and he went on their travels together, and he gave the children drawing lessons. He was also in close touch with other artists of the period. A number of pictures came into the collection from the studios of Friedrich Gauermann, Peter Fendi, Josef Kriehuber and Ferdinand Georg Waldmüller. A large number of portraits reveal that the family had a good relationship with Friedrich von Amerling, especially his intimate pictures of the children that are in the collection. The prince met Josef Rebell in Rome, and bought pictures from him, Angelica Kauffmann painted the prince's consort and two of his sisters. Oelenhainz had painted him and his sisters in his youth, and Johann Baptist Lampi was responsible for one of the rare late portraits of him. Finally Rudolf von Alt – at the beginning of the age of photography – was entrusted with the preparation of *vedute* that provide a meticulous record of the family's properties in Vienna – with the exception of the family home in Bankgasse after it was modernized – and in Moravia. After all the changes that have been made, these valuable sheets are often the only records we have of some of the houses. Working with Jacob Falke, whom Prince Alois II (1796–1858) had brought to Vienna to tutor his children and run the library, Prince Johann II (1840–1929) completely rearranged the gallery, with the assistance of Friedrich von Amerling. He weeded out everything he did not feel was up to standard and sent it to his palaces or sold it immediately in order to acquire something else. He was principally interested in the art of the fourteenth, fifteenth and early sixteenth centuries, Gothic and early Renaissance and early Netherlandish masters and the sculpture of the same periods. Eighteenth-century Venetian masters and nineteenth-century painting interested him as well, however. He was guided in his collecting by Berlin art historian Wilhelm von Bode, who also produced the first illustrated catalogue for the gallery in 1896.

Under his aegis, the gallery acquired an independent and personal character that distinguished it from other museums. He deliberately avoided the sober impression given by collections organized to meet academic criteria, and introduced some variety into the interior by the liveliness and wide range of the art objects exhibited. The mixture of furniture, tapestries, applied arts, sculpture and paintings created the refined and warm atmosphere of a family collection that

made the Liechtenstein gallery unique. The Frick Collection in
New York was perhaps a worthy successor over time.
Johann II restored a number of palaces in the same spirit – the art
should always be displayed as an entity – or rebuilt ruined ones.
The Liechtenstein fortress as the family seat and the palace in
Vaduz are two of these major historical reconstructions.
Without this restoration of the palace in Vaduz, it would not have
been possible to emigrate from Vienna in 1938; no prince of Liechtenstein had ever resided in Vaduz before. Prince Franz Josef II von
und zu Liechtenstein (1906–1989) was thus the first to shift his
focus of interest from Vienna and Moravia to the Principality of
Liechtenstein, and he also moved the art collection from its former
location to the palace in Vaduz that has been the base for the
collections since then.
After a turbulent phase during the Second World War and above all
in the last weeks of the war when the collection was brought to
Vaduz, a period of consolidation followed. This was necessary after
the enormous loss of territory in Bohemia and Moravia and the
financial decline in the family's Austrian estates and properties.
Prince Hans-Adam II von und zu Liechtenstein (b. 1945) reorganized
the family's various finances, so as to allow him to pursue an active
collecting policy from the mid-1970s onwards. Some exceptionally
fine pieces have been acquired, particularly in recent years.
The major exhibition at the Metropolitan Museum of Art in New York
in 1985/86 showed the world just how significant the collection is.
The opening of the LIECHTENSTEIN MUSEUM will pick up where that
left off and continue the centuries-old story of one of the most
important private collections in the world in an appropriate fashion.

THE PALACE

PETER VAN ROY 1683 – post 1738
Prince Johann Adam Andreas I von Liechtenstein, *c.* 1706

JOHANN ADAM DELSENBACH 1687–1765
Lednice Palace with the Baroque garden, 1721

THE REBIRTH OF A PRINCELY PALACE

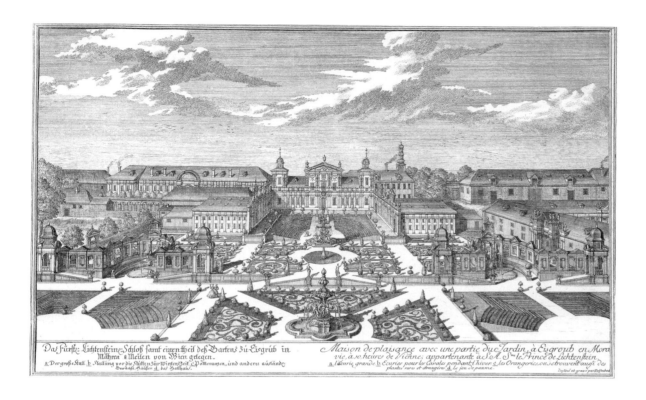

Das Fürstl: Lichtensteine-Schloß samt einen theil deß Gartens zu Eisgrüb in Mähren 8 Meilen von Wien gelegen.
a Der große Stall b Stallung vor die Stütten für Winter Zeit c Pomeranzen und andere ausländc Deutsche Häuser d das Ballhaus.

Maison de plaisance avec une partie du Jardin, à Eisgroub en Moravie, à 10 heures de Vienne; appartenante à S.A.S. le Prince de Lichtenstein
a l'Ecurie grande b Ecuries pour les Cavalex pendant l'hiver c les Orangeries, ou se trouvent aussi des plantes rares et étrangeres d le jeu de paume.

"Money serves only to leave fine monuments to one's eternal and immortal memory."

The foundation stone for his family's mania for building was laid by Karl Eusebius von Liechtenstein (1611–1684) in the form of his wide-ranging treatise on architecture that he addressed to his son and successor, Johann Adam Andreas I von Liechtenstein (1657–1712), who would later build at Rossau. Work started on a palace to the design of Karl Eusebius in Plumlov in Moravia. It was to be his own masterpiece of 'italianità', and was intended to eclipse the monumental quality of the richly columnated Czernin family palace in Prague (built from 1668 to plans by Domenico Egidio Rossi). It was a longing for Italian models, a fascination with the beauty of columnar structures that was to give rise only a short while later in Plumlov to one of the most curious examples of dilettante architecture in Central Europe. This celebration of the Orders clearly follows his treatise which stated "that architecture consists in no other adornment than the five Orders, the Tuscan, Roman Doric, Roman Ionic, Roman Corinthian and Composite … from these, the greatest adornment in the world is drawn … without them adornment cannot be, no altar, no churches, triumphal and other portals, no building can be adorned … without these all building is contemptible, tasteless, without joy, honour, fame."

Johann Adam Andreas I von Liechtenstein was one of the greatest builders and patrons of the Baroque in Central Europe. Educated on an extended grand tour to Germany, Holland, England, France and Italy, he devoted himself above all to the many facets of art and followed his father's wishes by largely abstaining from political and military activity. For him, the great model was "Italy … where the most beautiful buildings in the world are to be seen". He left a legacy in stone throughout Bohemia and Moravia in the form of the palaces at Valtice, Lednice, Aussee, Sternberg, Landskron, Prague, Plumlov, Butschowitz and Kolodej. In Vienna, he had the property at Rossau and the City Palace, a new family home in Bankgasse, built almost simultaneously.

FERDINAND RUNK 1764–1834
Plumlov Palace, *c.* 1825

THE HISTORY OF THE GARDEN PALACE AT ROSSAU: PALACE, GARDEN, BELVEDERE AND THE ESTATE AT LIECHTENTHAL

It all started with the purchase of a plot of land whose dimensions clearly showed the prince's intentions. By 1687, he had acquired the land needed both for a residence and the construction of an ideal community that later came to be called Liechtenthal. Now a suburb of Vienna, it is the only example in the city of large-scale Baroque town planning. Arranged around a horseshoe-shaped court-yard, extensive kitchens and an orangery marked the start of the complex; they were demolished in the early twentieth century. Next came the stables that formed a generously proportioned *cour d'honneur* that terminated in the palace's imposing façade. The Sala Terrena, an open hall of generous proportions, led to the spacious Baroque garden that terminated in a Belvedere. Behind this lay the farming townsmen's and artisans' village laid out on a strict grid with the Liechtenstein family church at its centre. A brewery marked the boundary of the extensive grounds.

The prince's first choice for this project was Johann Bernhard Fischer von Erlach (1656–1723). This Graz-born architect had spent many years working in Rome where he worked under Gianlorenzo Bernini, among others. He was utterly spellbound by Roman Baroque architecture. Fischer presented his client with a design that has not survived; various projects by him for the garden Belvedere and the palace itself are still extant, however. He laid out an expansive garden, probably also designed by him, between the Belvedere and the palace, a spacious building in all design phases. Fischer was able to realize only the Belvedere in the gardens as the prince entrusted other architects with the execution of the other plans. Fischer started to think about the project at the same time as thought was being given to the acquisition of land. His *Princely Pleasure Garden Pavilion* should be seen in the context of the Belvedere and is dated 1687/88. This project bears a hastily sketched coat of arms that is clearly that of the Liechtenstein family. The two buildings engage in direct dialogue with each other despite the distance between them and respond to each other with

SALOMON KLEINER 1703–1761
Bird's-eye view of the Liechtenstein Garden Palace
at Rossau and and the Liechtenthal estate, 1732
Vienna, MAK – Österrreichisches Museum für angewandte Kunst/
Gegenwartskunst, K.I. 5396/1

JOHANN ADAM DELSENBACH 1687–1765
based on Johann Bernhard Fischer von Erlach (1656–1723)
Liechtenstein Belvedere at Rossau, 1721
from Johann Bernhard Fischer von Erlach: *Entwurff einer
historischen Architectur*, Vienna 1721, vol. V, 12

sections curving inwards and outwards, complementing each other as positive and negative forms. Around this time, there were close ties between France and Rome, especially the Accademia di San Luca whose competitions Fischer took part in. As a result, hints of Rome and France are found in his designs. Fischer's design for the pleasure garden pavilion follows Roman models, but for the Belvedere he relied on French ideas that were also to be very important for him in later buildings. In 1688 there must have been a plan for the Belvedere in the grounds of the Liechtenstein Garden Palace. In 1712 he reproduced it in precise and idealized form in his famous *Entwurff einer historischen Architectur* (Designs for Historical Architecture). The design as built is markedly different from the earlier plans; functional reasons seem to have been behind the design changes. In his *Princely Pleasure Garden Pavilion*, Fischer had still intended there to be the essential grotto in the centre, opening directly on to the garden, but after the change of architects for the main building he had to accommodate the grotto in the Belvedere he was designing himself. This change of function also affected the names given to the various sections. The original reference to a "rear building" was replaced by the term *grotta*. In the original plans, this grotto was concealed behind a wide staircase

that lead directly beneath the building's cupola. As the illustration in the *Entwurff einer historischen Architectur* shows, a fountain later became the centrepiece in the space. Building started in 1689, but it is not possible to establish whether the brief was revoked from Fischer as early as 1690/91 when Domenico Egidio Rossi started working on the designs, or until 1692, when Martinelli came on the scene. As reproduced in Salomon Kleiner's engraving, Martinelli gave the building its final form. He created a severe and imposing structure that fulfilled the prince's representative needs; on all sides, shallow terraces afforded access to the garden. Fischer's side terraces were now omitted altogether, and all the architectural development was concentrated in the centre, with the staircases framing the central fountain. The rooms on the main floor opened out on to the terrace and the centre, vaulted room ceased to function as the main access to the whole property. The terrace afforded a most wonderful view of the palace and the city beyond, as Bernardo Bellotto's two *vedute* show. In the opposite direction, the view was of Liechtenthal parish church and village, and it terminated in the princely brewery with its elaborate hexagon shape. From there, the view was of the Danube and its meadows; it terminated in Vienna's two hills, the Kahlenberg and the Leopoldsberg. The arch of the

JOHANN BERNHARD FISCHER VON ERLACH 1656–1723
Drawing for a princely pleasure garden pavilion,
Main façade, 1687/88
Milan, Archivio Civico, Civiche Raccolte d'arte,
Gabinetto dei disegni, Raccolta Martinelli, vol. 9, fol. 33

JOHANN BERNHARD FISCHER VON ERLACH 1656–1723
Drawing for a princely pleasure garden pavilion,
section, 1687/88
Milan, Archivio Civico, Civiche Raccolte d'arte,
Gabinetto dei disegni, Raccolta Martinelli, vol. 9, fol. 23

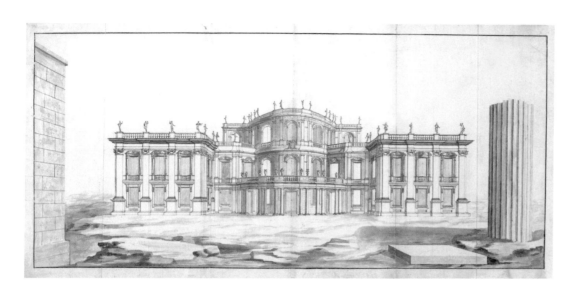

Belvedere framed this view that opened up more and more as one left the garden, with the two towers of Liechtenthal church in the centre of the arch, as shown by Kleiner in his engraving. Fischer's The belvedere is the link between two worlds that were fused into a unity within the princely demesne: the estate workers' homes with the church at their centre and the princely residence centred on the palace.

It is uncertain why Prince Johann Adam Andreas I von Liechtenstein chose not to have the palace built by Johann Bernhard Fischer von Erlach. We have only Fischer's design and the end result from which to draw our conclusions. Fischer designed a piece of architecture that was conceived like a sculpture – to be seen from all sides – with sections curving inwards and outwards, dominated by a dialogue between positive and negative forms, a building that appeared to be without a roof, based on a free treatment of Italian and French models.

ROMAN DESIGNER
Drawing for a pleasure garden pavilion, *c.* 1680
Edinburgh, National Gallery of Scotland, RSA 1322

It cannot have been the prince's intention, however, to build an airy garden complex. What was required was a proper palace somewhere between a city residence and an imposing country seat – something that reflected his power. The genesis of this palace was just as turbulent as that of the Belvedere. Johann Bernhard Fischer von Erlach's final plans were for a *Princely Pleasure Garden Pavilion*, which he published in the fourth book of his *Entwurff einer historischen Architectur*. On the sheet, he named himself as the author of the design. The fact that it was intended for the Liechtenstein family is confirmed by a drawing in Milan's Civiche Raccolte d'Arte, which has close similarities with the engraved reproduction. The drawing found its way to Milan in the estate of Domenico Martinelli and shows the Liechtenstein coat of arms in the cartouche.

A drawing in Edinburgh and another in the Kunstbibliothek Berlin showing the side face are directly linked with the Milan sheet.

The starting point for Fischer's design is the Milan sheet that is signed "Giov. Bernardo Fischer inv. et delin", in other words without his title "von", making it datable to before 1696. In it, the ground-level structure has an inset three-storey oval central section flanked by two two-storey wings, all characterized by pilasters.

Two other drawings from Martinelli's estate show how far Fischer's project had progressed. The first shows the central axis of the middle section with the coat of arms, the second presents a cross-section through the building with a grotto on the ground floor and a double-height domed hall above it as a variant on the original design in which access to the main hall is gained directly from outside, not via a grand internal staircase. This design corresponds with Fischer's other Garden Palaces (Althan, Starhemberg-Schönburg, Mansfeld-Findi), but it was probably the lack of an interior staircase that led the client to reject the design. A scale bar on the drawing of the oval building's central axis enables us to calculate the building's overall dimensions. They correspond approximately to the design as realized with its remarkable side length of almost 80 metres.

SCHOOL OF GIANLORENZO BERNINI 1598–1680
Drawing for a pleasure garden pavilion, side view,
late 17th century
Berlin, Staatliche Museen zu Berlin – Stiftung Preußischer
Kulturbesitz, Kunstbibliothek, Hdz. 1163

In contrast to this first stage of the project, the perspective view published by Fischer in his *Entwurff einer historischen Architectur* reveals a largely modified appearance: a continuous cornice above the second floor now unites the central structure and the side sections that rest upon a rusticated ground-floor base. Only the central section with its two-storey colossal order projects beyond the structure; at the sides, Fischer eschewed columns and pilasters altogether. The central projection rises beyond the cornice, but no longer as part of the main building, but rather as an airy, third-storey gallery entirely in the Roman tradition. As a consequence, the central oval hall appears to consist only of a single storey, the building as a

whole has clearly lost usable space and as such was tending to develop in a way that was not to the taste of Fischer's client. Between the first and last designs of his development – as far as we understand – we find an additional two, one on a sheet in Edinburgh, the other in the *Codex Montenuovo* in Vienna's Albertina. Neither variant has the rusticated ground-floor base of the *Entwurff einer historischen Architectur*, and in both sheets the projecting sections still show the Corinthian Order. With their fenestration, they are an almost perfect quotation of Bernini's Louvre façade. The juxtaposition of monumental pilasters and smaller inserted columns in the central section is reminiscent of Michelangelo's Palazzo dei

JOHANN BERNHARD FISCHER VON ERLACH 1656–1723
View of the façade of one of the pleasure garden pavilions
Vienna, Graphische Sammlung Albertina,
Codex Montenuovo, fol. 15

Conservatori. One difference between the two designs lies in the serlianas of the central section, which in the Viennese design and in a basement storey that Fischer introduced correspond with the design in the *Entwurff einer historischen Architectur* and with the two preliminary Agram drawings of it that have survived.

A sheet of the side view in Berlin has great affinity with the sheet in Edinburgh. In it, too, the side view is dominated by a monumental Order. The orientation of the central section relates to the frontal view. In the side view, the cornice offsets it against the projections. Seen by passers-by, it would scarcely have been noticed.

Another variant of the main view appears in the *Codex Montenuovo*. Here, as in the two preliminary Agram drawings for the *Entwurff einer historischen Architectur* and the published engraving itself, Fischer introduced a basement storey to gain space. The first of the Agram sketches still corresponds with the Edinburgh drawing except for this basement storey, but in the second, the monumental Order of the projecting sections is omitted and the vertical arrangement is replaced with a horizontal one in the form of the rusticated ground floor, thus corresponding largely with the engraving. The ground plan in the *Codex Montenuovo* gives a good impression of

the ground plan of the building. Access is afforded by two oval staircases that – in light of the finished project – are not very imposing, and four tiny servants' staircases in the corners of the recesses in the side flanks.

It is not known what prompted Prince Johann Adam Andreas I von Liechtenstein to abandon this design and to hire other architects. Was the exterior not grand enough for him in the way it was composed of individual elements, or was it because the interior had no representative enfilade? Fischer's single-storey central hall increasingly took shape in later variations on the design, but it was certainly one of its great weaknesses.

Just how very different the Liechtenstein approach was compared with the rest of Vienna's aristocrats is indicated by the fact that Fischer's model for a Belvedere was adopted for many similar sprojects in the city.

Through intermediaries aware of his stated preference for Italian artists, Johann Adam Andreas I quickly came into contact with another architect, Domenico Egidio Rossi (1659–1715), a man who had trained in Bologna. Rossi started to work for the prince as a painter of illusionistic decoration in his Moravian Schloss Valtice,

JOHANN ADAM DELSENBACH 1678–1742

based on Johann Bernhard Fischer von Erlach (1656–1723)

Prospekt eines Lustgartengebäu … vor den N. N. in Vienna, 1721

from Johann Bernhard Fischer von Erlach:

Entwurff einer historischen Architectur, Vienna 1721, vol. IV, 119

a property that was being modernized and transformed from a bulky Renaissance palace into an elegant Baroque residence at the same time as the building work was under way in Vienna.

The most important intermediary between northern and southern Europe was Anton Florian von Liechtenstein (1656–1721), nephew and successor to Johann Adam Andreas. Emperor Leopold I appointed Anton Florian Privy Councillor and delegated him as the first secular figure to the papal court, first as envoy in 1689 and then as plenipotentiary imperial ambassador in 1691. As such, and as Chief Master of the Household and First Minister of King Charles III of Spain, as Chairman of the State Council and Chief Master of the Household to Emperor Karl VI, Anton Florian – from 1712 also the Ruling Prince of the House of Liechtenstein – was able to make the necessary contacts with southern European architects, painters and stuccoists.

With some knowledge of the project's genesis, many elements of Rossi's plan might seem familiar in that Fischer had already used them. Essentially, what we have here, too, is a two-storey complex with a towering central chamber flanked by subordinate rooms. As in one of Fischer's draft stages, a dramatic flight of steps leads from the outside directly into the piano nobile.

Rossi's design has come down to us in an almost complete set of plans that was originally held in the Princely Collections, but which is now distributed across various locations. Three drawings have been held in the Prints and Drawings Collection of Vienna's Akademie der bildenden Künste since 1893; a fourth is in the collection of Budapest's Historical Monuments Office. The 'Wiener Bauhütte' made copies of the complete set of plans and published them in its second volume in 1864. Through a payment made to him on 18 August 1690, it is possible to date Rossi's design; building work started in 1691.

JOHANN BERNHARD FISCHER VON ERLACH 1656–1723

'Faeciata eines Gartten Gebäudtes' (façade of a garden pavilion)

Zagreb, National – and University Library, nr. 70

JOHANN BERNHARD FISCHER VON ERLACH 1656–1723

Unfinished variant of the 'garden pavilion'

Zagreb, National – and University Library, nr. 71

At its heart, beneath a uniform roof, lies the Sala Terrena with a vestibule still open on two sides. The arrangement of two groups of three rooms (*appartimenti*) on the left and right-hand sides of the centre was retained, as were the two recesses in the middle that formed service areas. Like no other Baroque Garden Palace in Vienna, two grand staircases gave access to the piano nobile with its double-height Great Hall and gallery that opened off it. Together, they formed the centrepiece of what had now become a majestic suite of rooms.

Rossi's design was used for the *cour d'honneur* which is formed by the front of the palace and the semi-circle of stables. For the piano nobile, his successor, Martinelli, adopted his ground plan with practically no changes. He merely introduced two spiral staircases for access to all floors at the eastern and western sides as replacements for Rossi's external staircases.

It is not known why Johann Adam Andreas I von Liechtenstein asked Domenico Martinelli (1650–1718) to complete the building. Until he was summoned to Vienna, Martinelli taught at the renowned Accademia di San Luca in Rome – the school that produced Johann Bernhard Fischer von Erlach.

The prince had employed Martinelli at Valtice since 1691 and he came to his attention all the more when the prince unexpectedly found himself facing a second major building project in Vienna. More by chance than design, he was able to acquire one of the best

possible plots in central Vienna, immediately adjacent to the centre of power at the Hofburg. Prince Kaunitz had started to build a substantial palace to plans by Enrico Zuccalli in Schenkenstrasse (now Bankgasse) after his return from Munich in about 1690. He appears to have run into financial difficulties, moved to The Hague for a long period and thus first chose to halt building work before deciding finally in 1694 to sell the land to Prince Liechtenstein. The architect had already been changed under Kaunitz: as Zuccalli was unable to supervise the building works in Vienna, Kaunitz commissioned Martinelli to do so from 1692. To allow construction work to progress on his City Palace as quickly as possible – undoubtedly the most modern and striking palace in Vienna, and the only one fully in keeping with the great Italian models – Johann Adam Andreas I von Liechtenstein delayed work on his Garden Palace for a while. He was able to use this interruption of building at Rossau to have Rossi's plans revised, a task entrusted to Domenico Martinelli from 1692.

There is no doubt that the ideas realized in the City Palace also influenced thinking about the Garden Palace. No secret was made of the fact that Zuccalli's design for the Kaunitz palace was based on Bernini's Palazzo Chigi-Odescalchi in Rome. The building introduced a previously unknown scale and lavishness of style to Vienna. Such an approach would obviously influence the construction of the Garden Palace at Rossau.

DOMENICO EGIDIO ROSSI 1659–1715
Drawing for the Liechtenstein Garden Palace at Rossau,
south façade, 1690
Vienna, Kupferstichkabinett der Akademie der
bildenden Künste, invent. nr. 19.776

DOMENICO EGIDIO ROSSI 1659–1715
Drawing for the Liechtenstein Garden Palace at Rossau,
section, 1690
Vienna, Kupferstichkabinett der Akademie der
bildenden Künste, invent. nr. 19.777

DOMENICO EGIDIO ROSSI 1659–1715

Drawing for the Liechtenstein Garden Palace at Rossau,
Floor plan of the piano nobile, 1690
Vienna, Kupferstichkabinett der Akademie der
bildenden Künste, invent. nr. 19.775

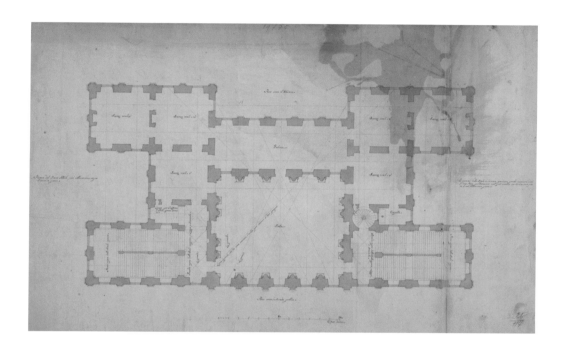

With building work already underway, Martinelli's greatest changes to Rossi's design involved the omission of the outside staircases and the addition of one storey to the side wings. The front elevation of the palace thus acquired the truly Roman dimensions that Rossi had already achieved inside with the height of the rooms. What the Sala Terrena had suggested was now taken to its logical conclusion in the design as a whole. Construction of three storeys, one of the requirements of a prince's country residence, according to Karl Eusebius's treatise, was probably one of the most important points discussed with the architects. Such a possibility had even been mooted in Fischer's first designs.

Inside, Martinelli realized the Sala Terrena in a completely new way, making it an open hall of generous proportions. On the south side, he linked the two symmetrical staircases with a spacious lateral bay whose middle section adjoins the two transparently designed, recessed service areas. On the north side, his transition to the garden became more splendid, with double pillars set in front of the pilasters, aedicules and statues set in niches. All this provided additional accents for the space and drew the garden sculpture inside the house.

Martinelli also substantially modified the design of the façade, not just by raising the side sections, but also by overturning Rossi's aesthetic scheme. The addition of a storey modified the proportions of the base to the façade above it, which had been unsatisfactory in Rossi's design. Its clumsy pilaster arrangement was elongated, thus making it far more elegant. The omission of blind arcades lent the façade a more generous appearance as the overall concept was unified. Moreover, Martinelli avoided the awkward articulation still found in earlier styles of architecture, and which had probably still been used by his client himself for his and his father's amateur creation, Schloss Plumlov in Moravia. From the base of the central section Martinelli removed the deep projections that had been completed before he took over the building work.

The excessive height of the central section in relation to the cornice was not solved satisfactorily. The main cornices of the side wings sit uneasily beside the main cornice of the central section, an error that could be attributed to the prince's frequent changes of mind that in the end led to a breach between him and his architect. It was in the context of designing the façade that Martinelli came to know his client's mercurial temperament. When the prince decided

SALOMON KLEINER 1703–1761
South façade and *cour d'honneur*, Liechtenstein Garden Palace
at Rossau, *c.* 1722

that the palace was too sober and severe, in 1706 he commissioned his sculptor Giovanni Giuliani (1663–1744) to enhance the capitals and window crowns with stucco. The architect had experienced something similar before while working on the City Palace, where in the staircase in particular Giuliani's sculptural decoration had clearly gained the upper hand over the austere architecture. Martinelli put up posters in which he expressly distanced himself from these "variazioni fatta nell'architettura".

THE DECORATION OF THE GARDEN PALACE

The prince's influence on the palace's interior decoration was even greater than on the building's exterior; indeed, the architects were scarcely involved in it. The only exceptions to this were the Sala Terrena, where Martinielli had made crucial interventions in Rossi's plans, and the Hercules Hall, where the ideas Rossi had put forward in his plans were largely retained even after later interventions by Andrea Pozzo.

Departing from the conventional literature, Karl Eusebius in his architectural treatise had not confined himself to the exterior appearance of buildings; he also addressed issues of interior function and furnishings. At Rossau, Johann Adam Andreas I took sole responsibility for them. He was determined to persuade the best Italian artists – above all those from his preferred city of Bologna – to decorate the palace and to create an ensemble of the latest Italian art of the highest calibre. His intention was to create a synthesis of the arts embracing architecture, painting, sculpture and horticulture that would reflect his taste and be passed on to his descendants.

Running like a thread through the planning and construction stages, his frequently changing demands reflect the personal interest he took in the project.

As early as 1693 he wrote to the Bolognese sculptor Giuseppe Mazza (1653–1741) that he was unable to find anyone in Austria with a gift for invention, thereby expressing his dissatisfaction with artists north of the Alps. From 1692 until his death, he corresponded frequently with the Bolognese Marcantionio Franceschini (1648–1729) whose artwork, serene and indebted to early classicism, he preferred above all else. The prince's letters tell us a great deal about his likes and dislikes, but also about the options that were open to him. They represent a unique cultural and historical document of an artist's relationship with his patron. Large-scale cycles on Antique themes are considered first, Johann Adam Andreas I suggesting a story by Ovid, as secular themes were better suited to the location. The prince's first thought was that these

paintings should fill the rooms like tapestries. Franceschini sent his suggestions to the prince by return of post. He felt that a cycle showing Phaeton and Adonis would satisfy the prince's taste for "accidenti bizzari" or, in the second case, a "soggetto vago e delizioso". While erotic themes were among the prince's favourites, Franceschini found it difficult to overcome his initial scruples about "cose lascive": he fought the prince over every centimetre of bare skin, as the pentimenti in many of his paintings show. The fact that the Phaeton cycle was replaced in 1693 by one dedicated to the goddess Diana is obviously related to their discussions and shows how ready Franceschini was to comply with his patron's wishes. With Franceschini's commission, the wall paintings was now at least being addressed, but the issue of the ceiling paintings remained unresolved. Johann Adam Andreas I again looked to Bologna for suitable artists, first enquiring in 1693 about the qualities of Giovan Antonio Burrini. Despite Franceschini's positive response, no com-

BERNARDO BELLOTTO 1720–1780
Liechtenstein Garden Palace in Vienna Seen from the East,
1759/60

mission was placed, possibly because of the very slow progress being made at Rossau, which meant that it was not yet possible to decorate its ground floor rooms. The delays were exacerbated by the construction of the City Palace and were also partly caused because Franceschini himself did not deliver his work on time. His two cycles did not reach Vienna until 1696 and 1700, which must have made the prince realize at last that his approach was impracticable.

It was not until 1702, when building work at Rossau was largely complete, that the question of interior decoration there returned to the top of the agenda. Franceschini was not available to Johann Adam Andreas I at this point, as he was busy painting the Salon del

Maggior Consiglio in Genoa's Palazzo Ducale until 1704. For a change, the prince again turned to Mazza and asked him to recommend a painter who could execute the ceiling frescos.

It may be supposed that the prince still wanted frescos on the ceilings of the ground floor *appartamenti* and smaller inserts in oil in the ceiling panels of the Sala Terrena. A combination of stuccowork, illusionistic architectural painting and inserts in oil on canvas appears also to have been the solution planned for the piano nobile. Antonio Bellucci, who was working on the City Palace at the time, was the artist the prince had in mind for the ceiling paintings. Stuccowork in the Great Hall started in 1703, but it is uncertain if Bellucci was to produce the large ceiling painting there, too. The

BERNARDO BELLOTTO 1720–1780
Liechtenstein Garden Palace in Vienna Seen from its Belvedere,
1759/60

ceiling painting of unknown provenance that was not installed in the western stairwell until the nineteenth century is possibly Bellucci's work that was originally intended for the (now re-named) Hercules Hall.

The Prince took a major step forward in 1704 when he hired Andrea Pozzo (1642–1709), an artist born in Trent who had found fame in Rome. He arrived in Vienna in 1702 to decorate St Peter's, but because its dome was still incomplete, in 1703 he began the frescos in the nave of the Jesuit Church before Johann Adam Andreas I commissioned him in 1704 to decorate the Hercules Hall. Thinking on a large scale, Pozzo modified the hall's design: he cut back on the monumental Order that Rossi had drawn in his longitudinal section through the palace, and took the unfluted half-columns in red stucco up to the now continuous main cornice. This lent the articulation of the walls a monumental quality appropriate to his ceiling fresco. Both longitudinal walls were originally identical, each having five openings at the top and the bottom. One set led downstairs into the Grand Gallery, the other upstairs to the mezzanine, which meant that the hall – and above all the ceiling fresco – was illuminated from another side. In this way, a monumental space was open to an adjacent gallery that was low and long, thereby creating an exciting dialogue. The side openings were originally designed in the same way as the five lower openings in the window wall, and the centre one like the four doorways in the side walls. In 1709 Pozzo

MARCANTONIO FRANCESCHINI 1648–1729
Aurora Abducting Cephalus, 1706–08
Ceiling painting, Gallery V, Liechtenstein Garden Palace
at Rossau

MARCANTONIO FRANCESCHINI 1648–1729
Apollo and Juno, accompanied by Flora, Ceres and Bacchus
and the personifications of Rain and Dew, 1706–09
Ceiling painting in Gallery VII, Liechtenstein Garden Palace
at Rossau

MARCANTONIO FRANCESCHINI 1648–1729

Birth of Adonis, 1692

North wall of the Hercules Hall, Liechtenstein Garden Palace in Rossau, with remains of the frescos by Andrea Pozzo (1642–1709) behind the Neoclassical over-painting
Photo, pre-1900

West wall of the Hercules Hall, Liechtenstein Garden Palace at Rossau, photo, pre-1900

Watercolor of the wall frescos above the central door on the north wall by Andrea Pozzo (1642–1709) in the Hercules Hall, Liechtenstein Garden Palace at Rossau, late 19th century

South wall of the Hercules Hall, Liechtenstein Garden Palace
at Rossau, with remains of the frescos by Andrea Pozzo
(1642–1709) behind the Neoclassical over-painting
Photo, pre-1900

created frescos for the wall areas between the doorways and the windows above them with putti, and added the family coat of arms to the middle of the wall adjacent to the gallery. When the hall was redesigned in the Neoclassical style and painted grey, including the columns' stucco marbling, rectangular panels with lozenges of classical ornamentation were placed over the frescos, thereby completely ruining them; fragments remained visible poking out above and below the Neoclassical panelling. When the hall was restored to its original Baroque design, these final remnants of Pozzo's frescos were removed after being carefully documented in watercolour sketches.

For the narrow sides, Pozzo worked on six horizontal rectangular oil paintings from 1706. Invoices for the work reveal their dimensions and subject matter. In 1709 he put the final touches to four paintings of Church Fathers. A *St Augustine*, a *St Gregory*, a *St Jerome* and a *St Sebastian*, as well as *Noah's Temptation* and *The Mocking of Noah* were still among the pictures on show at Rossau until 1873, but were later sold. The paintings of the saints appear in Fanti's inventory of the gallery's holdings and, corresponding to the rectangular panels on the long sides, hung above the four doorways and above the fireplaces on the narrow sides of the hall.

The fireplace surrounds – like the portals of Untersberg marble – are still original, but the sections above them showing the coats of arms and putti date from the early twentieth century; before that, these sections had undergone many changes. Previously thought to be an overdoor, a bronzed plaster *modello* in the collection of the Stift Heiligenkreuz reveals their original appearance. Hercules is shown on his throne, with his wife Hebe floating above him.

The hall's decorative scheme culminates in the ceiling fresco. Pozzo's monumental painting relates the story of Hercules from his birth and the strangling of the snakes placed in his cradle by Juno, to his fight with the Nemean Lion and other monsters, his defeat of Antaeus and the Amazons, his humiliation by Omphale, his punishment of Nessus to his suicide on a funeral pyre, with Hebe suspended above it, and the allegorical triumph of his translation to Olympus. In between these are bronze-like stucco reliefs showing Hercules and his wife; Mercury presenting a sword to Hercules; and Hercules bidding farewell to Molorchus of Cleonai as he sets off to kill the Nemean Lion. With an illusion of infinity behind them, the Gods inhabit the painting's centre. The intricate stuccowork that had been started before Pozzo's appointment was removed – a sign of

GIOVANNI GIULIANI 1663–1744

Maquette of fireplace piece with scene of Hercules enthroned and
Hebe above him, for the Hercules Hall, Liechtenstein Garden
Palace at Rossau, *c.* 1709

the prince's great trust in him. Pozzo worked on this fresco – his
main work north of the Alps – for four years, and confirmed his final
account on 22 October 1708. He was looking far into the future
with the generous scale of his achievement in which masterly painted perspectives of architecture, the lively frieze of figures from Hercules's adventures and the liberating lightness of the view of the
Olympian gods are effortlessly combined. Pozzo's ceiling is the
work of a virtuoso who in his late work knew exactly how to achieve
his desired effect while making economical use of his resources.
Using charcoal, he applied his illusionistic scheme directly to the
fresh plaster and then developed a palette ranging from intensely
luminous colours for the earthly sphere – the freshness of the
colours in Michelangelo's frescos for the Sistine chapel in Rome
inevitably come to mind – to earthy, muted tones for the heavenly
sphere. As his figures moved further into infinity, Pozzo employed
fewer resources, his most distant figures appearing to be mere
shadows. In many places, we are apparently confronted not with

intricate Baroque fresco, but large-scale, sketch-like watercolour
painting of the late nineteenth century. Detail is not important; the
artist is more concerned with effect, and he deploys his resources
with great virtuosity to achieve it. The figures are painted in broad
strokes, often modelled in light and dark chalk that is hatched over
the ground. It is fortunate that the height of the hall prevented earlier restoration, which would probably have removed much of the
surface that has survived in perfect condition – including hairs from
the artist's brushes trapped in the plaster.

Pozzo had already been associated with the House of Liechtenstein
for some time. Anton Florian von Liechtenstein (1656–1721) had
taken a particular interest in the frescos Pozzo had painted in San
Ignazio in Rome between 1687 and 1694, almost the same time as
the prince arrived in Rome. Anton Florian was so fond of this fresco
that Pozzo explained its details to him in a long and carefully formulated letter that was even distributed in Rome as a description of it.
Pozzo's letter allows us to grasp his fresco as a unique example of
a synthesis of the arts that unites the work of an architect and
painter, a theoretician of perspective and a theologian. Just how
close the artist and the prince were is shown by the fact that Pozzo, through the offices of Anton Florian, dedicated the first part of
his treatise on perspective to the Emperor Leopold; Pozzo again
made use of Anton Florian's connections when dedicating the second part of his treatise. Pozzo's letter and the prince's draft reply
are held in the Liechtenstein family archive. Josef I, whose architecture teacher was Johann Bernhard Fischer von Erlach, not only
accepted the dedication, but expressed his particular pleasure at
it in his reply for the second dedication.

Pozzo's frescos in the Hercules Hall were a hugely difficult act to
follow. Despite his greatest efforts, the prince could not sustain
such a high level and failed to persuade his preferred *quadratura*
painter, Franceschini, to leave Bologna for Vienna, even though a
large number of rooms remained undecorated, including the Sala
Terrena and its adjacent apartments. Johann Adam Andreas I signed
a contract with the stuccoist Santino Bussi (1664–1736) who lent
the ceiling paintings both downstairs and – later – upstairs an appropriate setting with the finest High Baroque stuccowork in Vienna.
When he started work, Bussi did not know who would paint the frescos, so his choice of subject matter had to remain general: Pozzo's
motif of the Deeds of Hercules, and hunting scenes on the garden
side, suggested the direction of his work in the vestibule. Despite

all the convolutions in the history of the decoration work, allusions to the ancient world and hunting and gardening crop up again and again. Reliefs of emperors are effortlessly combined with trionfi in the antique style, fettered Turks, garlands of flowers or hunting trophies. The combination of allegories of agriculture and horticulture with those of architecture, painting, sculpture and poetry in Rottmayr's frescos in the Sala Terrena is no coincidence.

The decoration of the piano nobile remained to be done. On 27 September 1704, the prince wrote to Franceschini, who was now back in Bologna, and enclosed a plan with a sketch. He asked him to come to Vienna the following spring and to bring an able *quadraturisto* with him. Discussions dragged on and it was not until 18 May

1706 that he contracted Santino Bussi to undertake the stuccowork in the gallery and the other six rooms of the piano nobile. The prince had finally dropped the idea of having frescos and *quadratura* painting in these rooms, opting instead for a solution involving stuccowork and ceiling paintings. Bussi's motifs – martial subjects, triumphal processions, busts of emperors – seem to have little in common with Franceschini's paintings. The prince must have found all these problems sobering. In the end, he did not even commission all the paintings he needed for the ceilings from Franceschini, probably well aware that the artist might well not deliver the work. Nevertheless, he refused to allow local artists to work on the piano nobile.

ANDREA POZZO 1642–1709
Ceiling fresco with the Deeds of Hercules and his Apotheosis in the
Hercules Hall, Liechtenstein Garden Palace at Rossau, 1704–08

ANDREA POZZO 1642–1709
Omphale Punishing Hercules
Detail from the ceiling fresco with the Deeds of Hercules and his
Apotheosis in the Hercules Hall, Liechtenstein Garden Palace
at Rossau, 1704–08

ANDREA POZZO 1642–1709

Amazement at Hercules's first heroic deed choking Juno's snakes.
Detail of the ceiling fresco of the Deeds of Hercules and his Apotheosis,
Hercules Hall, Liechtenstein Garden Palace at Rossau, 1704–08

ANDREA POZZO 1642–1709

Diana

Detail of the ceiling fresco of the Deeds of Hercules and his Apotheosis,
Hercules Hall, Liechtenstein Garden Palace at Rossau, 1704–08

ANDREA POZZO 1642–1709

Phoebus with the Hours

Detail of the ceiling fresco of the Deeds of Hercules and his Apotheosis,

Hercules Hall, Liechtenstein Garden Palace at Rossau, 1704–08

ANDREA POZZO 1642–1709

Hebe Hovering above Hercules's Pyre

Detail of the ceiling fresco of the Deeds of Hercules and his Apotheosis,

Hercules Hall, Liechtenstein Garden Palace at Rossau, 1704–08

GIOVANNI GIULIANI 1663–1744
Cleopatra on her Deathbed
Sala Terrena, Liechtenstein Garden Palace
at Rossau, *c.* 1705

GIOVANNI GIULIANI 1663–1744
Dancing Faun
based on Massimiliano Soldani Benzi (1656–1740)
Sala Terrena, Liechtenstein Garden Palace
at Rossau, *c.* 1705

He compromised on this point only on the ground floor and in the stairwells when he employed the Salzburg painter Johann Michael Rottmayr (1654–1730), who then went on to produce one of the most splendid examples of his skill. Shortly before being commissioned on 30 October 1705, Rottmayr had completed his decorative scheme in Schönbrunn's Great Hall, thus establishing his reputation as a fresco painter.

His paintings in the Sala Terrena allude to rural life and the princely house. The *Surrender of the Golden Fleece to Jason* in the Gentlemen's Apartments is a clear reference to the conferral on the prince in 1693 of the Order of the Golden Fleece. The two other ceiling paintings there contain motifs that also relate more to male society (*Sacrifice of Aeneas*, *Alexander's Flight with the Griffins*), while in the

Ladies' Apartments opposite, women are central to events (*Virtue, Ariadne and Andromeda*).

Following water damage, the staircase frescos were covered over in the nineteenth century and elaborately restored only during the recent refurbishment. Martial motifs predominate: a light-flooded *History of the Youthful Military Engineering Corps* contrasts with a dark *Battle of the Gods and Titans*, images intended to illustrate reward and punishment.

In addition to the compositions of artists who worked within the palace, objects – mainly sculpture – acquired by the prince for his residence also contribute to the artistic programme. From 1694 onwards, he placed a large number of orders with Massimiliano Soldani Benzi (1656–1740), Giovanni Francesco Susini (*c.* 1575–

SANTINO BUSSI 1664–1736
Detail of the decorative plasterwork on the theme of Hercules
in the entrance to the Sala Terrena, Liechtenstein Garden Palace
at Rossau, *c.* 1704

Decorative plasterwork in Gallery IX,
Liechtenstein Garden Palace at Rossau, *c.* 1704

Detail of decorative plasterwork with hunting scenes,
north side of the Sala Terrena, Liechtenstein Garden Palace
at Rossau, *c.* 1704

JOHANN MICHAEL ROTTMAYR 1654–1730
Ceiling fresco with Andromeda Being Taken Up into Olympus
Ladies Apartments, Liechtenstein Garden Palace
at Rossau, 1705–08

JOHANN MICHAEL ROTTMAYR 1654–1730
Ceiling fresco with Ariadne Handing Theseus the Thread
Ladies Apartments, Liechtenstein Garden Palace
at Rossau, 1705–08

JOHANN MICHAEL ROTTMAYR 1654–1730
Ceiling fresco with Aeneas's Sacrifice
Gentlemen's Apartments, Liechtenstein Garden Palace
at Rossau, 1705–08

1653) and Giuseppe Mazza (1653–1741) for sculptures for display
in his collection and *bozzetti* as models for local sculptors. The
young Giovanni Giuliani (1663–1744), whom we have to thank for
most of the sculptures on the buildings in front of the palace and in
the garden (now unfortunately lost), used them as reference points
and juxtaposed his ideas of form, which were honed in the Veneto,
with those of Bologna. His pupil Georg Raphael Donner also learned
much about Antique and Italian sculpture from the prince's sculpture
collection, which in turn crucially influenced the development of
Baroque sculpture in Vienna.

In this, too, Johann Adam Andreas I followed his father's advice.
Karl Eusebius's enthusiasm for Classical Antiquity had greatly influenced his son. Using engraved reproductions as their guide, even
the painters employed by Johann Adam Andreas I constantly quoted
Renaissance and early Baroque Italian artists – Reni, Domenichino,
Michelangelo and Raphael – who had assimilated Antique sculpture
in their work. The emphatically physical quality of Franceschini's
paintings revealed the very characteristic that for Karl Eusebius was
a hallmark of the finest painting: "This is now a piece of insight into
good painting … that the painting be well rounded and raised … that
it therefore appear higher and to stand out, as though it could be
grasped, touched and embraced, so that the right shadows fall, so
that it therefore seems outward and round to the eye, as though
something round and graspable were indeed present." Prince
Johannn Adam Andreas I's liking for naked bodies in his paintings
should not be regarded merely as eroticism, but rather as an
expression of his fondness for the Antique and its sculptural quality.
In fact Johann Adam Andreas I expressly asked Franceschini in a letter to paint beautiful naked figures, "belli nudi," which would clearly
demonstrate his art, and praised the Bolognese artist for his depictions of the "belle idea di femine e giovanne".

What was finally created on the exterior of the complex in this long
and intense interplay between various artists and influences is
best revealed by Salomon Kleiner's engraved views and Bernardo
Bellotto's two large-format oil paintings of the palace. Unfortunately,
no pictorial records of the palace interior have survived. Its opu-
lence can only be imagined with the aid of the drawings in some
inventories and our mind's eye.

ANONYMOUS DRAUGHTSMAN
Plan of the Baroque garden,
Liechtenstein Garden Palace at Rossau, pre-1773

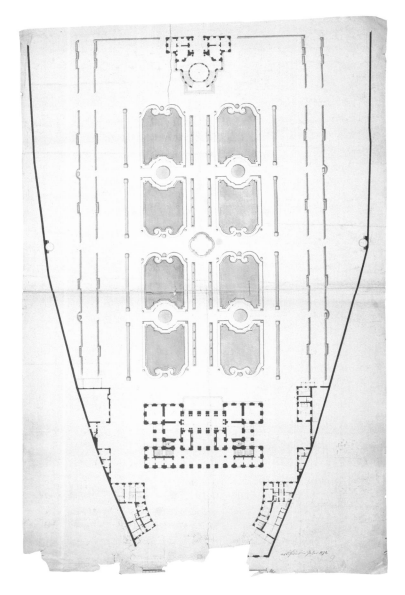

THE BAROQUE GARDEN

The palace garden is also a major attraction. We know its every detail from the two above-mentioned *vedute* by Bellotto and Salomon Kleiner's series of engravings that allow us to form a much clearer picture of the garden's original appearance than that of the palace interior. This fact alone indicates how important the garden was in the original design.

Johann Bernhard Fischer von Erlach produced one of the earliest designs. The French designer Jean Trehet, who worked at Schönbrunn, also had a hand in drawing up plans for it.

Large flowerbeds flanked on both sides by avenues of alternating "chestnuts and little firs" bordered the main axis. Beyond them, and cut into beech hedges, lay pergolas that in summer accommodated orange trees. On the Liechtensteinstrasse side lay a semicircular grove of box trimmed into cones and pyramids, and it terminated in a vast grotto. Small orange trees were placed there, too, in the summer. One of Salomon Kleiner's engravings shows them being carried there. In Bellotto's *vedute*, flowering plants are already visible; they were certainly unusual when the garden was completed, but widespread by 1760 when the *vedute* were painted.

That the garden was one of the prince's chief interests is apparent from the fact that from the earliest planning stages he concerned himself with the sculpture that was to be placed in it. He ordered maquettes for terracotta statues from Giuseppe Mazza in Bologna, for example the *Rape of the Sabine Women, Hercules*, a *Venus* or "whatever might please him, if only he might produce beautiful nudes", which in Vienna were then to be transformed into putti and groups of figures. He also badgered Mazza – in vain – to come to Vienna and work for him there.

The second major Italian sculptor whose services the prince secured was Massimiliano Soldani Benzi of Florence; he, too, was to send maquettes modelled on Classical Antiquity and Michelangelo to Vienna. They were intended in part for the gallery in Vienna, but also as models for Giovanni Giuliani, who had trained in Venice and worked for the prince in Vienna. These origins explain the mix of classical and High Baroque elements that co-exist here, and the synthesis of Venetian and Bolognese influences.

SALOMON KLEINER 1703–1761

Orange grove, garden of the Liechtenstein Garden Palace
at Rossau, *c.* 1738

Prospect des Bosquet mit einer Parterre von Waasen, da im Sommer   Veüe du Bosquet avec une Parterre gasoné ou l'on arrange
Orange-Bäume zu stehen kommen.   le orangers en Eté.

Dess. p. S. Kleiner, G. de S. A. S. V. E. de May.   F. M. Regensius sculps.

JOHANN WILHELM WEINMANN

N. 702. a Malus citria ... b. ... Malus limonia... c. Adam's Apple
from Johann Wilhelm Weinmann's encyclopaedia of plants,
*Phytanthoza iconographia oder eigentliche Vorstellung etlicher
Tausend ... aus allen vier Welt-Theilen gesammelter Pflantzen,
Bäume, Stauden, Kräuter*, Regensburg, 1737– 45, vol. 8,
div. engravings, watercolour

JOHANN WILHELM WEINMANN

N. 52. Aloe tuberosa seu yucca gloriosa major
from Johann Wilhelm Weinmann's encyclopaedia of plants,
*Phytanthoza iconographia oder eigentliche Vorstellung etlicher
Tausend ... aus allen vier Welt-Theilen gesammelter Pflantzen,
Bäume, Stauden, Kräuter*, Regensburg, 1737– 45, vol. 8,
div. engravings, watercolour

JOHANN WILHELM WEINMANN

N.61. Aloe Africana perfoliata glauca non spinosa
from Johann Wilhelm Weinmann's encyclopaedia of plants,
Phytanthoza iconographia oder eigentliche Vorstellung etlicher
Tausend ... aus allen vier Welt-Theilen gesammelter Pflantzen,
Bäume, Stauden, Kräuter, Regensburg, 1737– 45, vol. 8,
div. engravings, watercolour

JOHANN WILHELM WEINMANN

N.778. Peonies
from Johann Wilhelm Weinmann's encyclopaedia of plants,
Phytanthoza iconographia oder eigentliche Vorstellung etlicher
Tausend ... aus allen vier Welt-Theilen gesammelter Pflantzen,
Bäume, Stauden, Kräuter, Regensburg, 1737– 45, vol. 8,
div. engravings, watercolour

JOHANN ZIEGLER 1749–1802
based on Carl Schütz (1745–1800)
Liechtenstein Garden Palace at Rossau
with the English landscape garden, *c.* 1816

As in the City Palace, Giuliani was responsible at the Garden Palace for all the sculptural elements, the building decorations, the free sculpture and the vases, ranging from the attic figures at the front of the building – now extant only as copies made in the 1970s – to those in the garden and the Belvedere that terminates it.
Little of all this is now left, but the *vedute* and the *bozzetti* – of which many are preserved in the collections of the Stift Heiligenkreuz – allow us a glimpse of these past glories.

CHANGES DURING THE EIGHTEENTH AND NINETEENTH CENTURIES: THE COLLECTIONS AT ROSSAU

Changes in the last three hundred years have affected not just the palace itself, but also the complex as a whole including the garden and Belvedere.
Almost nothing remains of the Baroque garden. The views painted by Bellotto before 1760 still show the original garden, with only a few minor changes to its layout, but a short time later, in 1773, under Prince Franz Josef I (1726–1781), its sculptures and vases were sold off. Then between 1797 and 1801, Philipp Prohaska redesigned the grounds in the style of an English landscape garden, work which appears to have concluded with the construction of a small and a large canal, a waterfall and a lake. The prince was probably influenced by a close friend of the family, Count Moritz Lacy, who had been having his estate at Neuwaldegg redesigned as an English landscape garden since 1766. It seems to be no coinci-

(Wien.) PALLAST der GEMÆHLDE-SAMMLUNG S.D. des FÜRSTEN LIECHTENSTEIN   PALLAIS de la GALLERIE du PRINCE LIECHTENSTEIN (Vorstadt Rossau.)
von der Garten-seite anzusehen.   du coté du Jardin.
Vienne chez Artaria et Comp.

PHILIPP PROHASKA

Plan for converting the garden of the Liechtenstein Garden Palace
at Rossau into an English landscape garden, *c.* 1801

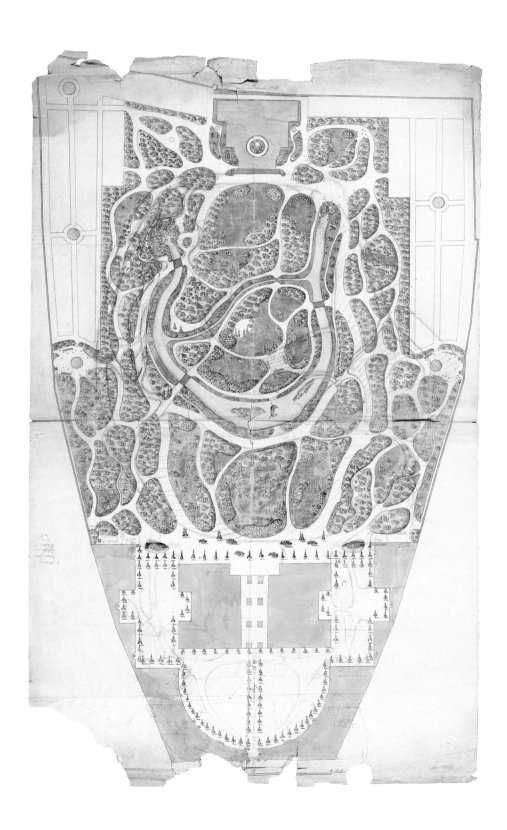

dence that Lacy's portrait is of a quality that stands out among the library's portrait busts that were made a short while later.

The entrance portal, built into the semicircular stable, was also renewed around this time. The plans were drawn up by Joseph Hardtmuth (1758–1816) who replaced the old, spacious portal with a Neoclassical triumphal arch topped with a coat of arms. Its sculptural work was executed by Josef Vogel and Johann Martin Fischer, who was responsible for the coat of arms completed in 1794. This gateway was later changed again by Hardtmuth's successor, Joseph Kornhäusel (1782–1860). In 1814 he opened up the semicircle of stables at its apex and introduced the fence that is still in place today. This dramatically altered the view of the palace, which could originally be seen to its full extent only upon entering the *cour d'honneur*. The shock effect it produced with its monumental size was lost thanks to a Philistine approach even back then. Similarly, the sweeping *cour d'honneur* was replaced by a landscaped area.

Johann Bernhard Fischer von Erlach's Belvedere was not spared changes either. It had already been much redesigned in the late eighteenth and early nineteenth century, and finally found itself flanked by extensive Neoclassical greenhouses. From 1875, the entire complex was replaced by a large, new structure by Heinrich von Ferstel (1828–83). With the ground plans identical, Ferstel adopted the earlier structure in its entirety for the central section of his new building. He thus respected the old Baroque sightline between the buildings, but abandoned the transparency of the main part of the building, which had long since become obsolete as a result of changes in the background in the Liechtenthal estate even at the time the palace was under construction. Then finally, in 1907, the orangery was sold and the former Ministry of Employment, which still exists, was built in its place.

The transition from the eighteenth to the nineteenth century in itself introduced decisive changes into this Baroque cosmos. At the time, most of the prince's collection of paintings hung in the galleries on the second floor of the City Palace in Bankgasse. Over the years, a second gallery had also developed in Herrengasse in another of the family's Baroque palaces that was remodelled by the architect Joseph Hardtmuth in the early Neoclassical style and completed in 1792. Numerous pictures belonging to the Liechtensteins were also to be found in their homes in Bohemia and Moravia, or in Vienna. The majority of the pictures were transferred to Rossau under Prince Johann I (1760–1836) between 1806 and 1810, and made accessible to a wider public there for the first time in the palace and in the Belvedere.

The transfer of the paintings there required substantial alterations to the palace's buildings and furnishings. In the corner rooms on the first floor, some windows were filled in to increase the area available for hanging. In the wall between the Hercules Hall and the gallery, all but one of the doorways and windows that illuminated Pozzo's ceiling frescos were bricked up to make enough room to hang Rubens's Decius Mus cycle, which found a new home in the Grand Gallery.

Other changes affected both the first and second floors and the stairwells, where some of Bellucci's ceiling paintings from Bankgasse, removed from there from 1819 on, were displayed in the museum area. The walls were painted in relatively uniform hues of blue and green, as shown by Raimund Stillfried's 1902 watercolour and early photographs. The floors were renewed as well: the "white

JOSEPH HARDTMUTH 1758–1816

Gateway to the forecourt, Liechtenstein Garden Palace
in Rossau, 1793

JOSEPH KORNHÄUSEL 1782–1860

Gateway to the forecourt, Liechtenstein Garden Palace
in Rossau, 1814

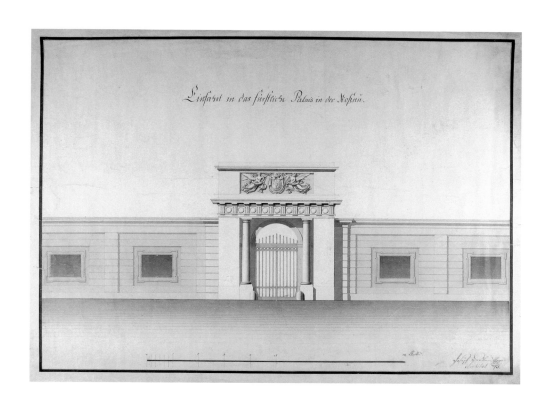

Adapted library from the Liechtenstein palace
in Herrengasse, by Joseph Hardtmuth, installed in the Gentlemen's
Apartments, Liechtenstein Garden Palace at Rossau, 1912–14

marble slabs from Kehlheim" were smashed up and replaced with an imaginatively designed walnut floor that was rediscovered in the course of the refurbishment work.

Entirely in the spirit of a prince's treasury, the objects themselves – judging by photographs – were hung incredibly closely together in a way that no longer accords with current thinking, either in terms of security or aesthetic appeal.

There were changes from time to time throughout the palace's use as a museum: first the Hercules Hall was decorated in the Neoclassical style for its role as a gallery, as shown by photographs taken in the last decades of the nineteenth century. These changes were undone from 1880 to the 1920s, new decorative schemes being adapted to suit the surviving Baroque fireplaces, stucco panels and Franceschini's paintings on the inside long wall of the Hercules Hall. Originally, thought was given to replacing Franceschini's pictures with a cycle of pictures by Hans Canon, who died in 1885. The sketches for it have survived in the Princely Collections. But then on the recommendation of Jacob Falke, the history painter Andreas Groll executed three paintings that were paid for in 1893. There is an invoice dated 1895 for the completion of stuccowork by the sculptor Edmund Rudrich.

A number of plans to "enrich" the stucco ceilings in the stairwells also date from the 1890s, but they were not realized. In keeping with prevailing tastes, the intention was to have the stairwells resplendent in "genuine" Baroque décor; at the same time, attempts were made to embellish the bare walls with Antique spoils, that is, with copies if works from Antiquity. Both were measures taken in most other Viennese Baroque palaces to adapt them to the historicist tastes of the day.

Another major change was the removal to the Garden Palace of the library from the family home, the palace, in Herrengasse that was built by Joseph Hardtmuth under Prince Alois I (1759–1805). Originally the library was housed on the third floor of the courtyard wing of the Herrengasse palace. The room had three aisles, two rows of Ionic columns and was 56 metres long; its feudal interior was one of Vienna's principal attractions. It was completed in 1791 by the cabinet-maker Josef Vogel, with stuccowork by Martin Karl Keller and sculpture by Johann Martin Fischer, among others. The family had lost interest in this palace even by the mid-nineteenth century after the Bankgasse building had been modernized. It was thus cleared out in the early twentieth century, sold and finally released for demolition (the Herrengasse tower block has occupied the site since 1933).

In 1912–14, Gustav Ritter von Neumann installed the library in the wholly differently proportioned Gentlemen's Apartments in the Garden Palace. He skilfully adapted the existing space and created the continuous galleries. The books were arranged according to aesthetic criteria: the first room housed books in white leather bindings, the second housed the gold-tooled leather volumes.

This furnished library is all that remains of one of the most magnificent achievements of early Austrian Neoclassicism. It still forms a unique ensemble with Rottmayr's frescos that both here and in the Ladies' Apartments have survived in a state of remarkable freshness without major restoration.

The comfort of visitors was eventually considered as well when a passenger lift was installed in 1897 to carry visitors to the first and second floors. Events during the Second World War and its aftermath brought about radical changes for the building.

RESTORATION AND THE RETURN OF THE PRINCELY COLLECTIONS

The Princely Collections closed in 1938; at the end of the Second World War, it became possible to evacuate substantial parts of the collection and to take them finally to Vaduz. Lengthy consideration was given to the building's future use; the possibility of re-opening it as a museum was considered. It was first let to the Austrian Building Centre, and then, from 1975, to the Museum moderner Kunst, Stiftung Ludwig Wien. When it moved out on 31 December 2000, a start could be made at the beginning of 2001 on the urgently needed refurbishment of the building. The aim was to re-open the building as the LIECHTENSTEIN MUSEUM in which a substantial part of the Princely Collections from Vaduz would be shown.

To permit the return of the works of art in storage under optimal conditions in the palace at Vaduz, the entire palace at Rossau had to be modernized to meet the security and climate control requirements of modern museums. What was needed above all was air-conditioning in the galleries. In a building of this size, air-conditioning can be installed only with a great deal of effort and expense, but it would have been unthinkable to exhibit the fragile works of the Princely Collections without it.

Not enough side rooms were available, so a new basement that included visitor facilities was created at great expense beneath the Sala Terrena. The restaurant and museum café moved from the palace into the eastern wing of the former stables.

The artistic fabric of the building – in particular the ceiling paintings by Franceschini and Bellucci, Pozzo's and Rottmayr's frescos and Bussi's ceiling stuccowork – has been carefully restored. During restoration work, the main concern was to respect the building's history and to retain as much of its patina as possible while still allowing restoration work to be recognizable as such. Here, too, the aim was to create a modern, up-to-date museum, not an artificial setting. It should be borne in mind that we possess no wholly reliable information about the substance or the appearance of the walls, for example. The interventions carried out in the late eighteenth century were so severe that all evidence in this regard has been lost.

JOHANN MICHAEL ROTTMAYR 1654–1730
The Military Genius Taken Up into Olympus, *c.* 1705
Watercolour sketch for the ceiling fresco in the east stairwell,
Liechtenstein Garden Palace at Rossau (three parts)
Privately owned, Bergamo

139

147

JOHANN MICHAEL ROTTMAYR 1654–1730
The Military Genius Taken Up into Olympus
Inventory photo of the ceiling fresco in the east stairwell,
Liechtenstein Garden Palace at Rossau

JOHANN MICHAEL ROTTMAYR 1654–1730
Mars and Venus
Detail of the ceiling fresco of the Military Genius Taken Up
into Olympus, east stairwell of the Liechtenstein Garden Palace
at Rossau, 1705–08

Pozzo's ceiling fresco in the Hercules Hall and Rottmayr's frescos in the ground floor rooms were fortunately relatively untouched; loose areas had to be secured and the paintings were cleaned to remove layers of dirt. Nineteenth-century restoration work that had been secured with water glass and soaked in linseed oil varnish created problems when restoring Rottmayr's ceiling in the Sala Terrena and new work by Karl Geyger. They required a good deal more attention to restore them to an acceptable condition.

Conservators faced major logistical and restoration challenges with the palace's huge stucco panels that had been treated with dispersing agents during a previous restoration. In places, this meant they were very firmly bonded to the original surface. After being uncovered and carefully retouched using lime milk, the stucco has regained its original sculptural quality that extends from areas that are entirely three-dimensional to sketches incised into the plaster. No decorative scheme of such refinement and virtuosity is found anywhere else in Vienna.

The sheer size of some of the oil paintings posed major problems. Discoloured varnish obscured their original hues; the paintings' appearance was further impaired because of retouching and overpainting. After their transfer from the City Palace in the nineteenth century, Bellucci's paintings in particular were adapted to their new home either by being cut to size, having pieces added or being overpainted. Cleaning was done only if it did no damage to their present condition. Restoration could be completed in time only because most of the pictures could be removed to a warehouse dating from the Austrian Building Centre's occupancy; restorers were thus able to work undisturbed while building work was underway in the palace.

The uncovering of Johann Michael Rottmayr's frescos in the stairwells is particularly interesting. On 30 October 1705, Prince Johann Adam Andreas contracted Rottmayr to paint "two ceilings over two flights of steps". Rottmayr's frescos were almost forgotten after they were concealed by Bellucci's ceiling paintings in the nineteenth century; remaining areas were plastered over. Bellucci's paintings were part of the original decoration of the City Palace in Bankgasse,

JOHANN MICHAEL ROTTMAYR 1654–1730
Minerva Bears the Military Genius Off to the Realm of the Gods
Detail of the ceiling fresco in the east stairwell,
Liechtenstein Garden Palace at Rossau, 1705–08

JOHANN MICHAEL ROTTMAYR 1654–1730
Allegory of Architecture as a Symbol of Princely Munificence
Detail of the ceiling fresco in the east stairwell,
Liechtenstein Garden Palace at Rossau, 1705–08

which was being modernized, but the main picture in the eastern stairwell may have been the ceiling painting by Bellucci that was originally intended for the Hercules Hall.

Adolf Kronfeld's 1931 guide to the gallery still mentioned that there was "a fresco by J. F. M. Rottmayr" behind the ceiling painting showing a scene from the life of Hercules. A sketch by Rottmayr in a private collection near Bergamo was long taken to be a design for the ceiling picture in the Small Hall in Schönbrunn, but was identified by Hellmut Lorenz as a sketch for the ceiling painting in the eastern stairwell of the Liechtenstein Garden Palace. During restoration, Bellucci's oil paintings were removed, and Rottmayr's frescos were uncovered in both. It quickly became clear why they had been covered up: they had suffered water damage. When Bellucci's decorative paintings from Bankgasse became available, they were transferred to the Garden Palace to conceal the damage.

Except where they were plastered over, Rottmayr's frescos have survived like no others in Austria. There is scarcely any dirt on their surface, which, because it was never cleaned, has retained its splendid original colouring that far exceeds any other Baroque fresco painting in Austria.

In the light of this and given the possibility of uncovering and showing the frescos in their original condition, the decision was made to go ahead with restoration and total reconstruction. It will take one more year before work is complete. The most time-consuming task shall be the infilling of the four hundred holes per square metre that will receive the new plaster. Restoration of the artwork is anticipated to take far less time. When work is finally complete, the public will be able to reclaim an unrivalled jewel of Austrian Baroque art.

JOHANN MICHAEL ROTTMAYR 1654–1730

Allegories of Princely Munificence

Detail of the ceiling fresco in the east stairwell,

Liechtenstein Garden Palace at Rossau, 1705–08

JOHANN MICHAEL ROTTMAYR 1654–1730

Retinue of Mars and Venus

Detail of the ceiling fresco in the east stairwell,

Liechtenstein Garden Palace at Rossau, 1705–08

JOHANN MICHAEL ROTTMAYR 1654–1730

Putto with Cornucopeia

Detail of the ceiling fresco in the east stairwell,

Liechtenstein Garden Palace at Rossau, 1705–08

THE DISPLAY

JOSEPH BAUER 1756–1831
Hanging plan for the south wall of the Grand Gallery,
Liechtenstein Garden Palace at Rossau, 1815

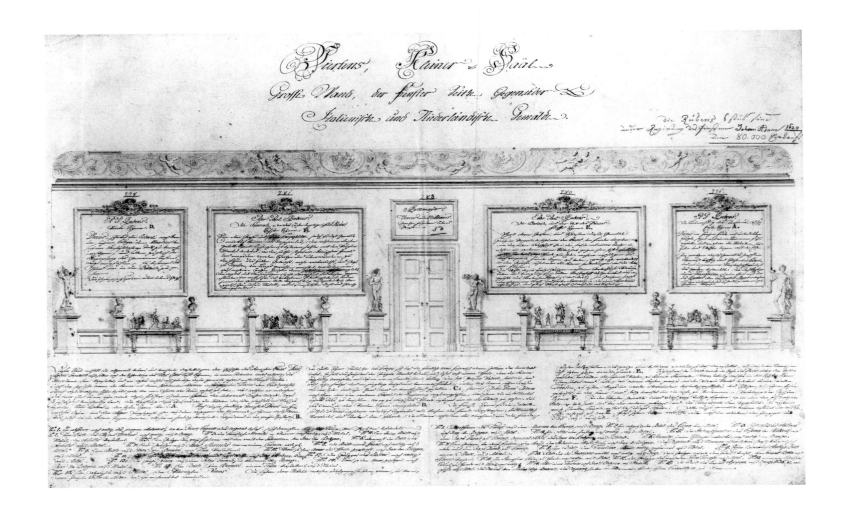

THE PRESENTATION OF THE COLLECTION

We hold only a limited number of documents about how the works in the Liechtenstein gallery, housed there from 1807, were hung historically in the Garden Palace at Rossau. Joseph Bauer's 1815 hanging plan provides some information about the first hanging phase. It draws a very precise picture and also lists the sculptures placed alongside the walls.

Additionally, some photographs and a watercolour by Raimund Still-fried are extant; the watercolour was not painted until 1902 and shows the Grand Gallery. In it is Peter Paul Rubens's Decius Mus cycle, and the collection's large bronzes, which are concentrated here. The walls of the Grand Gallery and the rooms beyond it are in green, a fact that was confirmed by investigations while the building was being converted. Apparently all the rooms in the building were painted a uniform green at the very first stage of its use as a gallery. A historical ground plan confirms that there were still some windows open at this point that were later bricked up. These window niches were opened up during the restoration process. Behind the bricked-up areas were the green niches and remarkably enough the original Baroque windows as well, with their hand-blown glass and hand-crafted ornamental metal fittings. The hanging scheme required the pictures to be hung in close proximity from top to bottom, with the result that there was scarcely any space left free. The colour probably reinforced the impression that the gallery was very dark, but did not make an impact in its own right.

This is confirmed by visitors' accounts, which always describe the gallery as very dark, and also that it was poorly arranged and badly labelled. A fault was that many of the attributions were incorrect. Certainly it is difficult to imagine today – even if some exhibition space on the second floor was used – that 1600 pictures were displayed here. It is also inconceivable in terms of today's thinking that they could be exhibited without the aid of artificial light, especially in the second floor galleries. Even today, despite the rooms having been painted in very light colours, artificial light is essential most of the time because the rooms are so deep, and the windows are relatively small and deep-set. It is particularly noticeable in these galleries that the light is unusual at certain times of the day and year, giving some pictures a very special glow.

The concept behind the new arrangement was to take visitors through the apartments on the ground floor and the piano nobile and offer them a tour that would include all the important areas.

The starting-point is the Sala Terrena, where visitors are welcomed by two masterly Gabriel Mollinarolo sculptures. Apollo and Minerva used to stand on the piers of the bridge leading to the palace in Ebergassing, which had been acquired and extended by Joseph Wenzel von Liechtenstein. Today they stand guard over the latter's Golden Carriage, the centrepiece in the entrance hall.

The route then takes visitors into the library, where they enter a princely setting that has been preserved in every detail. Here, and also in the Ladies' Apartments on the other side of the Sala Terrena, visitors will find one of Austrian High Baroque's finest fresco cycles. This is a major work by Johann Michael Rottmayr, and it will be possible to experience his original concept in its totality once restoration work is completed on the staircase frescos. The library and the Ladies' Apartments offer space for temporary exhibitions; items that are sensitive to light, like prints and drawings, will be shown in the library, which will also house events like chamber music concerts and readings.

Visitors going up the stairs will see the sculpture Elija Increases the Oil of the Widow, another major achievement of Austrian Baroque sculpture, the epoch to which the whole museum is dedicated. The climax of this Baroque experience is undoubtedly the Hercules Hall, Vienna's largest secular space of this period, with its dominant ceiling fresco by Andrea Pozzo.

The seven galleries showing the permanent collection are arranged around this Great Hall. The works of art are arranged according to the most important schools and movements that are represented in the collections and shown using the most significant pictures. It is a concentrated selection: there are about 1600 paintings in the Princely Collections, of which only 180 major works are on show. There is a good reason behind this selection: visitors should be afforded easy access to each picture; it should address them in a way that makes it possible to build up their own personal relationship with the works, and take this away with them.

We have to imagine that originally the collection was on show in the entire building, hung incredibly close together, using the second floor as well at that time. No storage space existed until 1938. If there was no longer room for something, it was taken down and whisked away to one of the palaces or sold.

Grand Gallery, Liechtenstein Garden Palace at Rossau
with the collection as it was in the 19century, photo *c.* 1910

It was not possible to take guidance from an image of one of the historic phases for the present furnishing of the rooms: we know nothing about the original Baroque wall design, except in the Hercules Hall. Anything of the Baroque design that did survive in the galleries, like the original floors that have been uncovered, has been carefully restored. The present colour scheme for the walls draws on historical examples of the period, like the Imperial Chambers at the Stift Göttweig, which have similar, though much stronger, colouring.

The hanging has by and large been done by school, whereby works are arranged to produce a certain tension. The paintings' strong impact had to be brought in line with the nature of the space: this has of course to be respected in an evolved historical ambience, and may even be the more important factor.

The first room of the permanent collection, Gallery IV, shows early Italian painting. The Princely Collections have rich holdings here, leading to a masterpiece of the Renaissance and Giulio Romano's *St John in the Wilderness*, which already points towards Mannerism.

Following the pattern that evolved historically until 1938, a mixture of painting, sculpture, furniture and craftwork has been put together to give an idea of the wealth and diversity of a royal collection. Here, too, though we have not tried to match the nineteenth century's lavish approach: exhibits were presented in showcases, in part constructed from original Renaissance elements, and then crammed full from top to bottom.

Gallery V juxtaposes early portrait painting from the north and the south, with Cranach, Raphael, Barthélemy d'Eyck, Salviati, Franciabigio and Bordone contributing to an exciting dialogue. Painted portraits do not dominate here either: portrait sculpture is accorded the role that is appropriate to it. The pictures are complemented with small bronzes by Antico and Giambologna and craftwork – in this case two of the collection's large works in *pietra dura*.

Gallery VI presents Italian painting in its Baroque heyday in the seventeenth and eighteenth centuries. Pietro da Cortona, Valentin de Boulogne as the principal Caravaggist, Sebastiano Ricci for Venetian painting and Pompeo Batoni as a forerunner of

East stairwell, Liechtenstein Garden Palace at Rossau, with a view of the entrance of the Hercules Hall, photo *c.* 1950

Gallery Room, Liechtenstein Garden Palace at Rossau, with the Decius Mus series of cartoons, photo *c.* 1890

Hercules Hall, Liechtenstein Garden Palace at Rossau, with the collection as it was in the 19century, photo *c.* 1890

burgeoning Neoclassicism represent schools and key points. Soldani Benzi's almost life-size copy of the *Medici Venus* stands proudly in the centre of the gallery, with the furniture and many small bronzes in the space subordinated to it.

There is no doubt that the main attraction of the Liechtenstein Museum is the Grand Gallery (Gallery VII). This houses Peter Paul Rubens's Decius Mus cycle, the most monumental work in the collection. It forms the climax of the tour, along with the *Assumption*, also by Rubens, and Adriaen de Fries's two monumental sculptures, *Christ in Distress* and *St Sebastian*.

Gallery VIII again features Rubens, from the *Lamentation* and *Christ Triumphant over Sin and Death* via major mythological themes including *Venus in Front of the Mirror*, *Mars and Rhea Silvia* and *The Discovery of the Infant Erichthonius*. Rubens's *Satyr and Maid with Fruit Basket* corresponds with Soldani Benzi's large *Bacchus* after Michelangelo's version. Here again the combination of pictures and sculptures tells a particular story.

Gallery VIII contains the best van Dyck paintings from the Princely Collections, Rubens's fascinating portraits of his children and finally also Frans Hals's *Portrait of a Man*, bought from the Rothschild family.

NICOLAS PINEAU 1684–1754
The Golden Carriage of Prince Joseph Wenzel von Liechtenstein, 1738
Sala Terrena, Liechtenstein Garden Palace at Rossau

JAKOB GABRIEL MÜLLER called Mollinarolo 1717–1780
Minerva with the Medallion of Empress Maria Theresia
and Emperor Franz Stephen of Lorraine, *c.* 1764

JAKOB GABRIEL MÜLLER called Mollinarolo 1717–1780
Apollo with the Medallion of Emperor Josef II, *c.* 1764

The last gallery room is devoted to the Dutch School and shows the best still life, genre and landscape painting from the Vaduz holdings, hung in the Baroque style.

The high point of the tour is the Hercules Hall, the culmination of the idea of experiencing the building and the Princely Collections together as a Baroque *Gesamtkunstwerk*. Music is a key feature here, as it is in the library.

The large number of works exhibited is not the main factor here, but the quality of the art on show and the way the individual exhibits relate to each other. Visitors are able to address outstanding works of art, examine them and be moved by them. Being moved is the most important thing for me; art cannot leave you cold, and whether the response sends icy shivers up your spine or elicits pure joy is a matter for the individual. The result of the encounter should not be indifference. Art must burn us, must inflict pain.

FRANZ XAVER MESSERSCHMIDT 1736–1783
Elijah Increases the Oil of the Widow, 1769/70
formerly a fountain in the courtyard of the Savoysches Damenstift in Vienna
Photo 1985

SALA TERRENA, CENTRE

1 / p. 90
Nicolas Pineau (1684–1754)
*The Golden Carriage of Prince Joseph Wenzel I
von Liechtenstein*, 1738
Wood, painted and gilt, steel, bronze gilt, leather,
crystal, velvet with gold embroidery, brocade;
length 610 cm, width 213 cm
Inv. no. SK 1
Provenance: 1738 commissioned by Prince
Joseph Wenzel I von Liechtenstein for proces-
sions as imperial ambassador in Paris

SALA TERRENA, SOUTH

2 / p. 91
Jakob Gabriel Müller, called Mollinarolo
(1717–1780)
*Minerva with the Medallion of Empress Maria
Theresia and Emperor Franz Stephan of Lorraine,*
c. 1764
Pewter; height 149 cm, width 86 cm
Inv. no. SK 915, companion piece to SK 916
Provenance: commissioned with *Apollo with the
Medallion of Emperor Josef II* (SK 916) by Prince
Joseph Wenzel von Liechtenstein for Schloss
Ebergassing (from 1642 to 1788 in the posses-
sion of the Liechtenstein family);
2003 reacquired, by Prince Hans-Adam II
von und zu Liechtenstein

3 / p. 91
Jakob Gabriel Müller, called Mollinarolo
(1717–1780)
Apollo with the Medallion of Emperor Josef II,
c. 1764
Pewter; height 142 cm, width 74 cm
Inv. no. SK 916, companion piece to SK 915
Provenance: with *Minerva with the Medallion of
Empress Maria Theresia and Emperor Franz
Stephan von Lothringen* (SK 915) commissioned
by Prince Joseph Wenzel von Liechtenstein for
Schloss Ebergassing (from 1642 to 1788 in the
possession of the Liechtenstein family); 2003 re-
acquired, by Prince Hans-Adam II von und zu
Liechtenstein

SALA TERRENA, NORTH

4 / not illus.
Giovanni Giuseppe Mazza (1653–1741)
Bust of Apollo with a Lyre, c. 1690/1700
Marble; height 70 cm
Inv. no. SK 13
Provenance: presumably commissioned by Prince
Johann Adam Andreas I von Liechtenstein for the
Garden Palace at Rossau

5 / not illus.
Giovanni Giuseppe Mazza (1653–1741)
Bust of Meleager, c. 1690/1700
Marble; height 67 cm
Inv. no. SK 14
Provenance: presumably commissioned by Prince
Johann Adam Andreas I von Liechtenstein for the
Garden Palace at Rossau

6 / not illus.
Giuseppe Gaggini (doc. 1643–1713)
Bust of Apollo, c. 1690–1700
Marble; height 74 cm
Inscription on hair band: APPOLLO
Signed on the reverse: IOSEPH GAGINO
SCVLPSIT
Inv. no. SK 16
Provenance: before 1712 acquired by Prince
Johann Adam Andreas I von Liechtenstein (pre-
sumably for the Garden Palace at Rossau)

EAST STAIRWELL

8 / p. 92
Franz Xaver Messerschmidt (1736–1783)
Elijah Increases the Oil of the Widow, 1769/70
Formerly as fountain in the courtyard of the
Savoysches Damenstift in Vienna
Pewter-lead alloy; height 173 (excluding socle)
Provenance: 1770 commissioned by Duchess
Maria Theresia Felicitas of Savoy-Carignan, *née*
von Liechtenstein, for the courtyard fountain of
the Savoysches Damenstift

9 / not illus.
Giovanni Giuseppe Mazza (1653–1741)
Bust of Venus, 1692
Marble; height 67 cm
Signed: G. M. F.1692
Inv. no. SK 1365
Provenance: presumably commissioned by Prince
Johann Adam Andreas I von Liechtenstein for the
Garden Palace at Rossau

10 / not illus.
Giovanni Giuseppe Mazza (1653–1741)
Bust of Adonis, 1692
Marble; height 77 cm
Signed: G. M. F.1692
Inv. no. SK 1366
Provenance: presumably commissioned by Prince
Johann Adam Andreas I von Liechtenstein for the
Garden Palace at Rossau

WEST STAIRWELL

11 / not illus.
Giovanni Giuseppe Mazza (1653–1741)
Bust of Ariadne, c. 1695/1700
Marble; height 87 cm
Signed on left edge of bust: GIOSEPPE MAZZA
BOLE (both Zs in mirror writing)
Inv. no. SK 1368
Provenance: presumably commissioned by Prince
Johann Adam Andreas I von Liechtenstein for the
Garden Palace at Rossau

12 / not illus.
Giovanni Giuseppe Mazza (1653–1741)
Bust of Bacchus, c. 1695/1700
Marble; height 85 cm
Signed on left upper arm: GIOSEPPE MAZZA
(both Zs in mirror writing)
Inv. no. SK 1367
Provenance: presumably commissioned by Prince
Johann Adam Andreas I von Liechtenstein for the
Garden Palace at Rossau

13 / not illus.
Giovanni Giuliani (1663–1744)
Allegory of Europa, 1707–09
Sandstone; height 173 cm, width 93 cm,
depth 86 cm
Inv. no. SK918
Provenance: 1709 commissioned by Prince
Johann Adam Andreas I von Liechtenstein as
an Attic figure for the eastern end of the *cour
d'honneur* of the Garden Palace at Rossau

GALLERY IV

GOTHIC AND RENAISSANCE RELIGIOUS ART IN ITALY

PAINTING

The first altarpieces and private devotional pictures in Italy date from the thirteenth century, a period when Byzantine icon painting was a considerable source of inspiration for Western art, and when devotional images from the East were very popular. Painters from Siena in particular drew on Byzantine icon painting both in style and technique, which in Constantinople was highly sophisticated.

PASSION PICTURES

The Man of Sorrows, a depiction of the body of the tormented Christ, was one of the principal themes of medieval painting. The success enjoyed by this image over the centuries reveals its significance. The panel *Christ as the Man of Sorrows* by Naddo Ceccharelli (active 2nd quarter of the fourteenth century) shows the dead Christ as a half-length figure standing in the sarcophagus in a manner also typical of icon painting. This physical position is impossible for a corpse, and explains the divine nature of Jesus Christ, who died as a man: the inconceivable can only be a mystery that the believer accepts in faith. A lavishly embroidered cloth lines the sarcophagus, an allusion to the altar covering, the *corporale*. This equates the sarcophagus with the eucharistic altar at which the faithful receive the body of Christ in the form of the consecrated wafer. The picture expresses the general wish to make Jesus' unimaginable presence in bread comprehensible by transforming it into a visible body.

In his panel, Ceccharelli combines a finely worked gold ground with first attempts at three-dimensional presentation: he places the sarcophagus and the figure in parallel, one behind the other, on shallow spatial planes, although the effect does not yet really create an illusion of depth. The richly ornamented frame contains eight round medallions with portraits of saints that look like miniature icons. Ceccharelli placed his signature conspicuously on the front of the sarcophagus. This reflects the artist's enhanced self-awareness, but also his hope of sharing in the salvation promised by the image. Ceccharelli's panel is dated to *c.* 1347 because the only other work of art that can be attributed to him with any certainty – the *Madonna and Child* (formerly in the Cook Collection, Richmond, VA) – dates from then and is also signed by him.

A passion picture like Ceccharelli's was probably intended for private devotion, a religious practice associated with a gradual transformation within European society over the course of the thirteenth century. The mendicant orders, noted for their preaching, encouraged laymen to become more actively involved in religion. People lacking theological training and language had to be allowed to participate in religious life. Passion paintings thus acquired great significance as tools conveying religious meaning. The image of God suffering and dying as a man speaks to viewers who, through emotion rather than intellect, are better able to grasp what their faith means. In Italy, devastating catastrophes like the plague had increased the tendency towards mysticism. In Siena, where Ceccharelli painted his *Christ as the Man of Sorrows*, and where this type of image was very popular, the 'Black Death' reduced the population by three-fifths between 1348 and 1350.

A MULTIPLICITY OF STYLES

In the thirteenth century, Tuscany took the lead in the development of the panel painting in Italy. It was also there that the most important types of new altarpiece subsequently emerged. They ranged from the polyptych, with many figures, and divided into several fields by architectural elements, to individual panel paintings portraying saints or the Virgin Mary. There was a wide variety of panel forms and arrangements, all tailored to specific requirements. Themes were limited in number, however, the most common being the Madonna.

Attested in the period 1345–1362, Giovanni Baronzio executed the panel *Adoration of the Magi, Crucifixion and Seven Saints* of *c.* 1345 which may have been the centrepiece of a triptych. It was presumably commissioned by an associate of the Franciscan order, the first to adopt this new genre. The choice of saints in the lowest section of the panel, Clara and Francis, identified by the robes of the order, suggests the Franciscans. The Crucifixion of Christ occupies the centre of the painting. Clearly modelled on Giotto (*c.* 1267–1337), it was in fact once attributed to that great innovator in Italian painting. Giovanni Baronzio worked in Rimini where Giotto's fresco cycle, once thought to have depicted scenes from the life of Christ and now lost, strongly influenced the local school of painting. The Adoration of the Magi is inserted in the upper section

are carried into the image, making Peter and Paul appear to be on a stage. This is the first indication of a departure from a two-dimensional gold ground for which spatial connections had no significance. The disc-shaped haloes, the clearly defined outlines of the figures and the even-handed painterly treatment of the figures, as well as the decoration lend the picture an almost ornamental character. As of the fourteenth century, the relationship between the Madonna and Child increasingly gained in significance, especially in small devotional images. In Siena, a portrait type showing the Madonna sitting on the ground in the manner of a courtier emerges as the antithesis of the stately *Maestà*, the enthroned Mother of God. This motif was also known as the *Madonna dell'Umiltà* because the lack of regal trappings such as a throne was thought to express the humility with which Mary accepts her fate. It is rare for the Madonna and Child to be placed on a cloud, as in the panel *Madonna with Child and Two Angels* by Lorenzo Monaco (doc. 1391–1423), one of the major Florentine painters around 1400. Wearing a lapis-lazuli cloak, whose softly flowing folds define her figure, the Mother of God floats on a pink cloud before the eyes of the adoring angels who seem to adopt the same position as the viewer. The mother holds her child so closely to her cheek that the two figures seem to merge into one. Here form emphasizes content, the closeness of mother and child. This approach, marked by a fluidity of line, was a pan-European phenomenon in the period around 1400, and is now known as the Soft Style. A comparison of the altarpiece panels with frescos in the Bartolini Chapel in Santa Trinità, Florence, suggests that the work in the Princely Collections dates from *c.* 1420.

Another type of devotional picture developed from portrayals of Christ wearing the crown of thorns. After having him flogged, crowned with thorns and mocked, Pilate, speaking the words "Behold the Man" (Ecce Homo; John 19, 5), presented Jesus to the waiting crowds. The figure of Christ is now removed from its context and we are shown the moment at which his fate is to be decided. In the nineteenth century, Prince Johann II acquired the painting *Christ in Repose* (Ecce Homo; lit. God's Peace) from the Conte Massa in Ferrara. It was presumably painted there by an unknown master around 1480. The scourged Christ, wearing the crown of thorns, sits on a rock under a baldachin that dominates the picture, its delicate architectural ornamentation already suggesting the Renaissance. Christ is not shown wearing the usual purple robe the sol-

diers mockingly dressed him in, but a simple brown garment. The rope around his neck is a common attribute seen in Ecce Homo devotional paintings, especially in Italy and Spain. The impenetrable black background portends Christ's imminent death, while the baldachin becomes a sign of his majesty, in this instance an allusion to the temple and the triumphal arch. One of the major achievements of Renaissance painting was three-dimensional presentation, achieved here with the aid of powerful central perspective. It is no coincidence that the vanishing point for all lines is Christ's hands; their passive position symbolizes acceptance of the sufferings to come. With no gold ground behind him, the holy figure is transported into the earthly sphere. The baldachin is set against a landscape whose elements are still overlaid in individual registers. This conveys an impression of ornament filling the entire surface, packed evenly with a wealth of detail, right up to the high horizon.

The oeuvre of Marco Palmezzano (1459/63–1539) shows that he was familiar with the work of Giovanni Bellini (*c.* 1430–1516). He places his *Christ as the Man of Sorrows* sitting on his own tomb. The landscape in the background provides a realistic setting, but does not as yet convey any sense of depth. The eye leaps from a rock formation in the foreground – enlivened by highly naturalistic renditions of plants – into a middle ground depicting a cloudy sky. Christ has opened his arms to reveal his stigmata in a gesture reminiscent of his outstretched arms as he was removed from the Cross. In the life of St Bernard, it is interpreted as embracing the faithful. This metaphor recurs in a famous hymn sung at Lamentations of Mary and Passion plays: "Hurry here to be embraced. While he hangs on the Cross, he offers himself with outstretched arms to those who love him in mutual embrace". Palmezzano's *Christ as the Man of Sorrows* is no longer disfigured by open wounds. This already hints at later depictions of Christ's perfect physical beauty as a sign of his divine nature. Even though Palmezzano adopts this innovative approach, his sharp-edged style and handling of plasticity and space show him to be very much still caught up in the late Gothic style.

The *Madonna with Child* by Marco Basaiti (doc. 1496–1530) dates from *c.* 1500. It unites the close-up of the half-length Madonna icon figure with a landscape background. Even though the gold ground has been abandoned in favour of greater realism, the landscape here still remains a flat background, without perceptible depth. Both the figure of the Mother and the Christ Child are still in the tradition

of the Byzantine icon. He stands on a rock slab that suggests his later tomb. Yet triumph over death is also anticipated in the fact that the child is standing, and in his gesture of blessing. The child's sharply outlined shadow and the darker front edge of the slab transform the two-dimensional structure into a plinth leading into the abyss. A degree of sharpness in the modelling and bold light-and-dark contrasts lend the figures a sculptural quality. Basaiti worked in Venice in the workshop of Giovanni Bellini, from whose *Pietà* (*c*. 1470, Pinacoteca di Brera, Milan) he borrowed the structure of the tomb. Basaiti favoured stronger colours than his master, as can be seen clearly in Mary's garments in canonical blue and red.

CONQUERING THE LANDSCAPE

The early Renaissance further developed the theme of the Madonna sitting on the ground and transferred the motif to open countryside. Broad spaces gain in iconographic significance. The mystical devotional picture becomes a Marian idyll. An everyday quality returns to the relationship between mother and child: the Virgin plays with the child, teaches him to read or play music, or has him taught by the angels. The young St John also joins in. Enrichment of genre motifs expresses a desire for intimacy between the viewer and the adored Mother of God, in whose life the believer participates. At the same time, objects acquire a symbolic significance that lends the painting an additional layer of meaning. The earliest examples of this are found in the work of the Venetian Giovanni Bellini.

Piero di Cosimo's (1461/62–1521) panel *Madonna with Child and the Young St John*, probably painted in Florence between 1505 and 1510, shows the Virgin and Child on her lap and the adoring young St John in a hilly landscape that reveals hints of Dutch painting in its effects of breadth and depth. Yet that school's new atmospheric qualities are unwanted here: all the pictorial elements as far as the horizon are drawn sharply and meticulously. On some withered branches, a black cloth of honour hangs behind the Madonna: what was once magnificent brocade is now simple cloth. A book, probably the Bible, lies open for reading on a gnarled tree-trunk. The odd flower is seen in the foreground, the carnations being a reference to Christ's Passion. Mary's delicate face is reproduced with particular precision, and it reflects the light using fine chiaroscuro modelling.

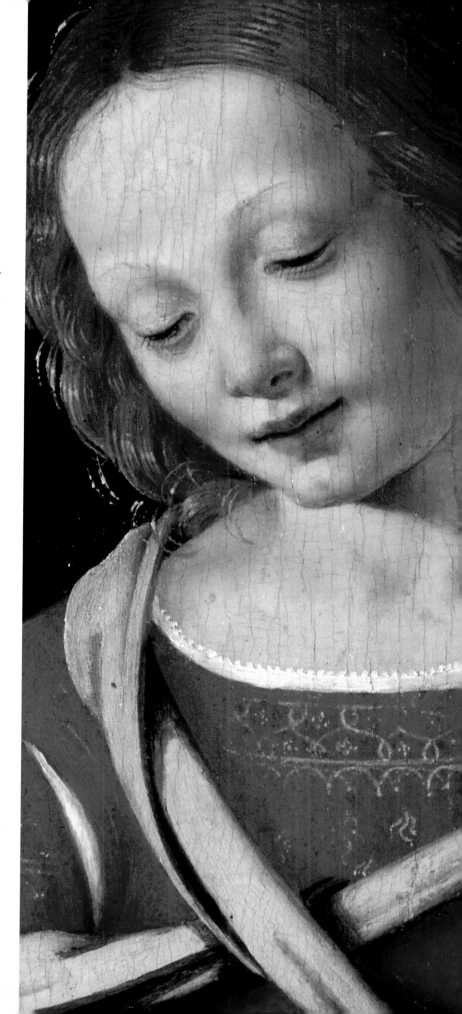

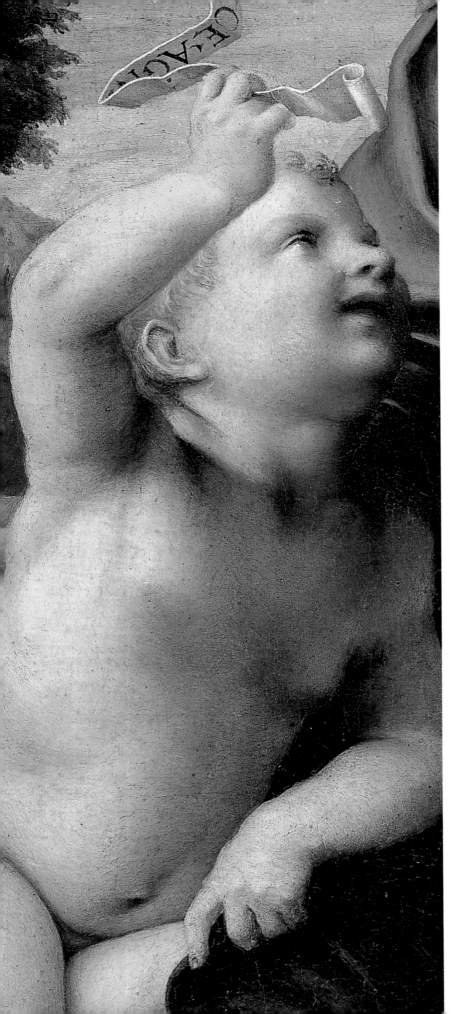

Piero de Cosimo himself provided important stimuli for Francesco di Cristofano, known as Franciabigio (1482–1525), who also worked in Florence. He addressed the popular Renaissance motif of the *Madonna dell'Umiltà* in several paintings. The picture in the Princely Collections, *Madonna with Child and the Young St John*, is a late work dated between *c.* 1518 and 1524. It might be intended to represent a particular event in the life of Jesus: on their return from Egypt, the Holy Family meets the young St John, who has withdrawn to live in the wilderness. The man in the background is probably St Joseph, approaching the gate of a medieval town. The treatment of the theme is related to Raphael's *Madonna in the Countryside* (1505–06, Kunsthistorisches Museum, Vienna). Franciabigio borrowed even more directly from Raphael's *Madonna dell'Impannata*, from which he took John's pose. This explains why in 1805 the work in the Princely Collections was still thought to be by Raphael before Franciabigio's monogram was discovered on the hem of Mary's robe, permitting attribution to the Florentine painter. Franciabigio's response to his eminent predecessor Raphael reveals the new significance of religious paintings during the Renaissance. As they were no longer objects of worship, it was the painter's ability that came to the fore: his invention and skill made a picture admirable.

Franciabigio had his own particular way of integrating Christ's future suffering and death into his image: the Christ Child's strangely unstable pose is explained by a dark fissure in the ground at his feet, a subtle allusion to his rocky tomb. The lettering on the banderole in his hand, "ECCE AG(NUS DEI)" (Behold the Lamb of God; John 1,19) also points to his sacrificial death. Compared with Piero di Cosimo, Franciabigio's colours are more muted, his landscape is more atmospheric and his whole approach to the image is more painterly. Piero's clearly defined plastic forms, which do not reflect any real physical quality, give way here to more fluently shaped garments. They follow the shape of the body more closely but draw it to our attention only in parts, leaving others plunged into the darkness of the space. The soft modelling with light and shade and the blurred transitions, which can ultimately be traced back to Leonardo, make the figures a natural part of their surroundings.

Bernardino Luini's (*c.* 1480/85–1532) *Madonna with Child and the Young St John* is a *Madonna dell'Umiltà* of *c.* 1515 from the Lombardy School. Luini combined Leonardo da Vinci's innovations with the Milanese tradition. In the picture in the Princely Collections, the foreground into the background. The harmonious character of the picture is due to the balanced proportions of its individual elements. A carefully matched colour scheme logically anchors the powerful colouring of the Madonna's robe in the overall design, and has it taken up elsewhere in the picture.

The staff with cross in the boy John's hand anticipates the Passion of Christ. His blossoming wreath is repeated as a victor's wreath in an aureole in the sky. The inscription "HIC ARMIS VICTOR DE ORBE" TRIUMPHABIS (You will triumph over the earth with these weapons, victorious one) alludes to Christ's victory over death. Moretto's authorship is not confirmed by a signature, but the compositional scheme and individual motifs typical of Moretto suggest that attribution to him is justified.

HALF-LENGTH FIGURES OF SAINTS

Moretto's painting *Madonna with Child and St Anthony* is an example of a special type of painting popular in the High Renaissance: a landscape format with half-length figures of saints, usually with the Virgin standing in the centre. This type developed from Giovanni Bellini's still somewhat additively structured panels into Titian's dialogue-like scenes between Mary and the saints, the type Moretto was probably following here. The small format suggests private use as a devotional image. Bonvicino's picture was probably also painted for this purpose between 1540 and 1545. This illustrates another trend that would prove influential in the future: the Madonna is now transferred into the private family sphere, thus engaging the viewer even more closely. In Moretto's picture, the interior is dominated by a heavy, copper-coloured curtain that is still reminiscent of the baldachin motif in pictures of the Madonna enthroned. The red shades in St Anthony's cloak and the Virgin's dress were originally much stronger, meaning the colour scheme – which reveals the work's Venetian origins – was consistent.

A pictorial form involving a tight, dramatic close-up developed in the fifteenth century. It combines movement within a scene with the appellative character of the traditional icon. Vincenzo Catena (c. 1480–1531) also chose a compact view for his picture *Christ Bearing the Cross*, painted in the 1520s: it shows only a half-length figure of Christ with the cross on his shoulder, yet he goes a step further in conveying his meaning. In the mid-fourteenth century,

Christ bearing the cross was removed from Passion scenes involving a large number of figures. He became the subject of a new devotional image symbolizing the suffering of humanity. The concentration on Jesus' face, and its simple presentation, lend Catena's painting the characteristics of a bourgeois portrait. The similarity in structure to portraits by Catena's teacher Giorgione is certainly no coincidence. As a composition, Catena's *Christ Bearing the Cross* takes its inspiration from a painting by Giovanni Bellini (Isabella Stewart Gerdner Museum, Boston, MA), whose late work was an important source for Catena. The calm pictorial structure, based on parallel lines, reinforces the contemplative character of the devotional image. Only the theatrical lighting against a black background relates to the drama of the events. Catena lived and worked mainly in Venice, and was in contact with Giorgione. He was highly regarded in Venetian humanist circles.

Circular images of the Madonna, known as tondi, emerged in Florence in the second third of the fifteenth century. *Madonna with Child, the Young St John and Two Angels* of c. 1500 by Sebastiano Mainardi (c. 1460–1513) is of this type. As though introducing him to her son, the Mother of God tenderly raises the young John's chin. The setting appears to be a room in an Italian palace, its round windows offering a view of the countryside beyond. On the shores of a lake, on which gondolas rock, lies a town, its tall patrician towers reminiscent of those in Mainardi's home town of San Gimignano which have survived to this day. A church can be seen through the window on the left. From early Christian times, a church was a symbol of Mary, who was called the "house of God" as it was through her that Jesus became incarnate. Sebastiano Mainardi worked in Domenico Ghirlandaio's workshop, and largely remained faithful to his master's style. The sharp, almost graphic outlines of his figures are characteristic of Mainardi; despite foreshortening that suggests three-dimensionality, essentially they develop within the picture plane. Strong primary colours, such as red, blue, green and yellow, are arranged in uniform planes of colour. The diffuse light makes the highly delicate faces appear perfectly beautiful but does not produce a convincing illusion of depth.

Perino del Vaga (1501–1547) also began his career in Florence. After training, he went to Rome in 1517/18, where he met Raphael (1483–1520), who influenced the composition of his tondo *The Holy Family*, held in the Princely Collections. Vaga based his composition on Raphael's *Madonna Aldobrandini* (c. 1510, National Gallery,

VINCENZO CATENA *c.* 1480–1531
Christ Bearing the Cross, *c.* 1520/30
IV.14

London) and the *Madonna dell'Impannata* (1513/14, Galleria Palatina, Florence). His painting dates from *c*. 1540, its arrangement of figures yielding to its circular form. The sharpness of its plastic modelling has an almost sculptural quality. Its powerful colours, reminiscent of Michelangelo (1475–1564), are intensified by harsh light that almost transforms them into white highlights. In this spotlight-like illumination, everything else sinks into darkness, including the figure of St Joseph who with some difficulty seems to be forcing his way into the picture from behind. What appears merely to be an everyday scene is – by means of light – lent the significance of a world-changing event: Christ's incarnation.

THE SAINT AS HERO OF ANTIQUITY

Renaissance Christian humanism saw Christ's perfect physical beauty as a symbol of his divine nature. Images showing a naked, increasingly athletic body of Jesus lent Him the aura of an ancient hero. Portraits of saints also took this approach. Since entering the catalogue of the Princely Collections in 1767, *St John the Baptist in the Wilderness* has traditionally been attributed to Giulio Romano (1499–1546). The painting is largely identical to the work of the same name in the Tribuna of the Uffizi in Florence, which is usually attributed to Raphael. St John the Baptist sits on a stony outcrop of a grotto-like rock formation that forms a dark background for his brilliantly lit figure. A leopard skin is slung round his body, revealing more than it conceals. He is pointing with his raised right hand to a wooden cross from which a supernatural light emanates. The spring rising close by can be read as a symbol both of baptism and of the purity of faith. Beams of light issue from the cross, the "light that shines in the darkness" (John 1,5), as mentioned in the Gospel according to St John. The emphatically naked, athletic body and the heroic pose bestow on the saint the appearance of a worldly hero. The rediscovery of ancient models, so crucial to the Renaissance, has at last found its way into religious painting.

SCULPTURE AND APPLIED ART

The Princely Collections own one of the first autonomous bronze statues of the Renaissance in the form of the *Shield Bearer* of *c.* 1473 by Bertoldo di Giovanni (*c.* 1440–1491). Bertoldo, who developed this art form, was a sculptor and medal-worker at the court of Lorenzo the Magnificent in Florence, and he described himself as a successor to Donatello. Bertoldo's shield bearer is a muscular, naked man with a thick beard. The girdle of vine leaves at his hips matches the wreath on his head. He carries a large club as well as his shield. Here the artist combines the attributes of so-called savages with those of Hercules and Bacchus. The same applies to the companion piece to this bronze, the figure of a satyr bearing a club, held in the Frick Collection in New York. These two and a statuette of Hercules on horseback in the Galleria Estense in Modena probably formed a miniature equestrian monument. The motif of Hercules on horseback was known only in Ferrara. It is thus possible that the group was made for Ercole d'Este, the Duke of Ferrara, whose name and immense power led to a whole series of representations of Hercules in his home town; he was also known as a very able horseman. These three figures with their stocky forms are considered to be the earliest statuettes by Bertoldo, and probably date from *c.* 1470.

Andrea Mantegna (*c.* 1431–1506) worked at the Gonzaga court. Written records describe him as a painter, draughtsman, engraver and sculptor. The *Marsyas/St Sebastian* in the Princely Collections, recently attributed to Mantegna, may convey an impression of his qualities as a sculptor. This sculpture of a naked man bound to a tree-trunk with both hands operates on two levels of meaning, one mythological and one religious. It could be the satyr and renowned flautist Marsyas. Greek myth relates how he challenged Apollo to a musical contest, which he lost. To punish him for his pride, Apollo had Marsyas flayed alive. The no less brutal alternative represents the martyrdom of St Sebastian. A bodyguard of the emperor Diocletian, he was executed by archers for protecting Christians from persecution. It is assumed that the holes in his body, which once contained arrows, were a later modification. Perhaps the figure was originally intended to be Marsyas and then reworked as St Sebastian.

The sculpture may have stood in the *grotta* of Isabella d'Este (1474–1539) in Mantua during the sixteenth century. Its 1542 inventory records "a naked figure bound to a trunk". Stylistically, too, it matches the work of the artists active at the Gonzaga court in Mantua. The descriptive naturalism of the pain-racked features and the elegance of the slender body wound around the tree create tension within the figure.

While *St John the Baptist* of *c.* 1540/50 by Jacopo Sansovino (1486–1570) was produced much later, during the middle of the following century, the slender figure and the narrow radius of its movements suggest a certain affinity with Quattrocento sculpture. Sansovino, the major sculptor of his day in Venice, took a keen interest in Donatello's work in the 1530s and 1540s. This is apparent from the bronze in the Princely Collections and also the marble statue of the same figure in Santa Maria Gloriosa dei Frari in Venice (1554), which was placed next to Donatello's John the Baptist there.

ANDREA MANTEGNA (?) 1431–1506
Marsyas/St Sebastian
IV.22

The bronze shows the saint as a penitent in the wilderness, with a shaggy fleece hanging from his half-naked body. The lowered head with furrowed, careworn brow and open mouth, combined with the hand-on-heart gesture, eloquently express his acknowledgement of his own sinfulness and his regret at it. The message of this bronze is thus conveyed not only through the facial features, but also through the convincing, slightly slumped pose adopted by the torso and extending into the figure's left hip. The figure would not, in fact, require the support of the tree-trunk. Perhaps the design, first executed in wax, was intended for a marble sculpture that, for whatever reason, was rejected by the client and was then cast in bronze instead.

BERTOLDO DI GIOVANNI *c.* 1440–1491
Shield Bearer, *c.* 1473
IV.24

JACOPO SANSOVINO 1486–1570
St John the Baptist, *c.* 1540/50
IV.19

Cassone, Siena or Asciano, 14th century
IV.20

Façade cupboard, southern Germany, *c.* 1580
IV.23

PAINTINGS

IV.1 / p. 110
Piero di Cosimo (1461/62–1521)
Madonna with Child and the Young St John,
c. 1505/10
Oil on panel; height 72 cm, width 54 cm
Inv. no. GE 264
Provenance: signed 1733 by seal as entail

IV.2 / p. 105
Ferrara master
Christ in Repose, c. 1480
Oil on panel; height 54 cm, width 35 cm
Inv. no. GE 860
Provenance: before 1883 Conte Massa Collec-
tion in Ferrara; 1883 acquired by Prince Johann II
von Liechtenstein from Guggenheim in Venice

IV.3 / p. 102
Gregorio di Cecco (doc. 1389–1424)
Madonna Enthroned with Angels and Saints
Oil on panel; 45 cm, width 26 cm
Inscription on scroll: FIAT
Inv. no. GE 866
Provenance: 1882 acquired by Prince Johann II
von Liechtenstein as a work by Turino di Vanni

IV.4 / p. 104
Lorenzo Monaco (doc. 1391–1423)
Madonna with Child and Two Angels, c. 1420
Oil on panel; height 68 cm, width 36 cm
Inscription on frame: AVE GRATIA PLENA DMS
TECUM
Inv. no. GE 865
Provenance: 1900 acquired by Prince Johann II
von Liechtenstein from Prof. Constantini in
Florence

IV.5 / p. 101
Giovanni Baronzio (doc. 1345–1362)
Adoration of the Magi, Crucifixion and Seven
Saints, c. 1345
Oil on panel; height 58 cm, width 31 cm
Inv. no. GE 867
Provenance: 1881 acquired by Prince
Johann II von Liechtenstein

IV.6 / p. 100
Naddo Ceccharelli
(active 2nd quarter of the 14th century)
Christ as the Man of Sorrows, c. 1347
Oil on panel; height 71 cm, width 50 cm
Signed at bottom: NADDUS CECCH[ARELLI]
DESENIS MEPINX[IT]
Inv. no. GE 862
Provenance: 1892 by Prince Johann II
von Liechtenstein, possibly in England

IV.7 / p. 109
Marco Basaiti (doc. 1496–1530)
Madonna with Child, c. 1500
Oil on panel cradled; height 64 cm, width 51 cm
Signed at bottom: .BAXAITI. P. (the line above
is no longer legible)
Inv. no. GE 846
Provenance: 1887 acquired by Prince Johann II
von Liechtenstein from Guggenheim in Venice

IV.8 / p. 115
Bernardino Luini (c. 1480–1532)
Madonna with Child and the Young St John,
c. 1515
Oil on panel; height 83 cm, width 66 cm
Inv. no. GE 847
Provenance: 1890 acquired by Prince Johann II
von Liechtenstein from the art dealer Miethke

IV.9 / p. 113
Francesco di Cristofano, called Franciabigio
(1482–1525)
Madonna with Child and the Young St John,
c. 1518–24
Oil on panel; height 121 cm, width 90 cm
Signed on the gown hem with the artist's
monogram
Inv. no. GE 254
Provenance: 1790 acquired by Prince Alois I
von Liechtenstein from the painter Johann Adam
Braun in Vienna

IV.10 / p. 106
Marco Palmezzano (1459/63–1539)
Christ as the Man of Sorrows
Oil on panel; height 91 cm, width 63 cm
Signed bottom left: MARCHVS FOROLIVIENSIS
Inv. no. GE 878
Provenance: before 1909 private Venetian
collection; 1909 acquired by Prince Johann II
von Liechtenstein from Do. Barozzi in Venice

IV.11 / p. 123
Giulio Romano (?) (1499–1546)
St John the Baptist in the Wilderness
Oil on panel; height 178 cm, width 154 cm
Inv. no. GE 22
Provenance: 1712 first recorded in the
collection in Prince Johann Adam Andreas I's
estate inventory

IV.13 / p. 119
Sebastiano Mainardi (c. 1460–1513)
Madonna with Child, the Young St John
and Two Angels, c. 1500
Oil on panel cradled; diameter 82 cm
Inv. no. GE 853
Provenance: 1890 acquired by Prince Johann II
von Liechtenstein in Venice

IV.14 / p.118
Vincenzo Catena (c. 1480–1531)
Christ Bearing the Cross, c. 1520/30
Oil on panel cradled; height 47 cm, width 38 cm
Inv. no. GE 35
Provenance: before 1712 acquired by Prince
Johann Adam Andreas I von Liechtenstein, after
1712 in the possession of his daughter Maria
Theresia Felicitas, Duchess of Savoy-Carignan

IV.15 / S. 114
Alessandro Bonvicino, called Moretto
(c. 1492/1495–1554)
Madonna with Child and the Young St John, c. 1550
Oil on panel; height 38 cm, width 51 cm
Inscription on stone tablet: HIC/ARMIS/
VICTOR/DE OR/BE TRI/VMPHA/BIS
Inscription on other stone slab: O QUAM TE MEM
OREM VIRGO NAMQZ HAVD TIBI PARTUS/MORTALIS
GREMIO ES QUEM AMPLECTERIS O DEA CERTE
Inv. no. GE 879
Provenance: 1895 acquired as a work by Prince
Johann II von Liechtenstein at auction at the
Scarpa Gallery in Milan by Paris Bordone

IV.16/not illus.
Alessandro Bonvicino, called Moretto
(c. 1492/95–1554)
St Jerome, c. 1525
Oil on panel; height 39 cm, width 31 cm
Inv. no. GE 313
Provenance: 1869 acquired by Prince Johann II
von Liechtenstein in Venice

IV.17 / p.116
Alessandro Bonvicino, called Moretto
(c. 1492/95–1554)
Madonna and Child with St Anthony, 1540/45
Oil on panel cradled; height 46 cm, width 58 cm
Inv. no. GE 13
Provenance: probably acquired by Prince Alois I
von Liechtenstein, as first mentioned in
Dallinger's 1805 catalogue of the collection

IV.18 / p.120
Perino del Vaga (1501–1547)
The Holy Family, c. 1540
Oil on panel; diameter 85 cm
Inv. no. GE 24
Provenance: 1822 acquired by Prince Johann I
von Liechtenstein as a work by Raphael from
the dealer Carlo Gamora in Vienna

SCULPTURE AND APPLIED ART

IV.19 / p.129
Jacopo Sansovino (1486–1570)
St John the Baptist, c. 1540/50
Bronze; height 53 cm
Inv. no. SK 20
Provenance: before 1900 Alfred Beit in London;
before 1920 Sir Julius Wernher in London, after
1920 in the possession of his heiress, Lady Alice
Wernher in London; before 1945 Lady Ludlow in
London; 1945 to 1973 Sir Harold Wernher in
London and Luton Hoo, Bedfordshire; 2001
acquired by Prince Hans-Adam II von und zu
Liechtenstein

IV.20 / p.130
Cassone, Siena or Asciano, 14th century
with the coat of arms of the Ospedale de
S. Maria della Scala in Siena
Panel gilded; height 64 cm, width 160 cm,
depth 56 cm
Inscription on the banderoles: SALVE REGINA
MISERICORDIA VITA DVLCEDO/SPES NOSTRA
SALVS AD TE CLAMAMVS EXVLES/FILI EVAE AD
TE SVSPIRAMVS LVENTES EXVLES
Inv. no. SK 779
Provenance: 1896 acquired by Prince Johann II
von Liechtenstein from Stefano Bardini in
Florence

IV.21 / p.125
Circle of Pyrgoteles (d. 1531)
Madonna with Child
Marble; height 40 cm, width 34 cm
Inv. no. SK 87
Provenance: 1882 acquired by Prince Johann II
von Liechtenstein from Guggenheim in Venice

IV.22 / p.126
Andrea Mantegna (?) (1431–1506)
Marsyas/St Sebastian
Bronze gilded; height 35 cm
Inv. no. SK 18
Provenance: 1542 presumably in the inventory
of the *grotta* of Isabella d'Este in the Palazzo
Ducale, Mantua; 2001 acquired by Prince
Hans-Adam II von und zu Liechtenstein

IV.23 / p.131
Façade cupboard, southern Germany, c. 1580
Spruce, solid and veneered walnut;
height 238 cm, width 216 cm, depth 75 cm
Inv. no. MO 1559
Provenance: 2003 acquired by Prince
Hans-Adam II von und zu Liechtenstein

IV.24 / p.127
Bertoldo di Giovanni (c. 1440–1491)
Shield Bearer, c. 1473
Bronze with remains of fire-gilding; height 23 cm
Inv. no. SK 258
Provenance: 1880 acquired by Prince Johann II
von Liechtenstein from the art dealer Stefano
Bardini in Florence

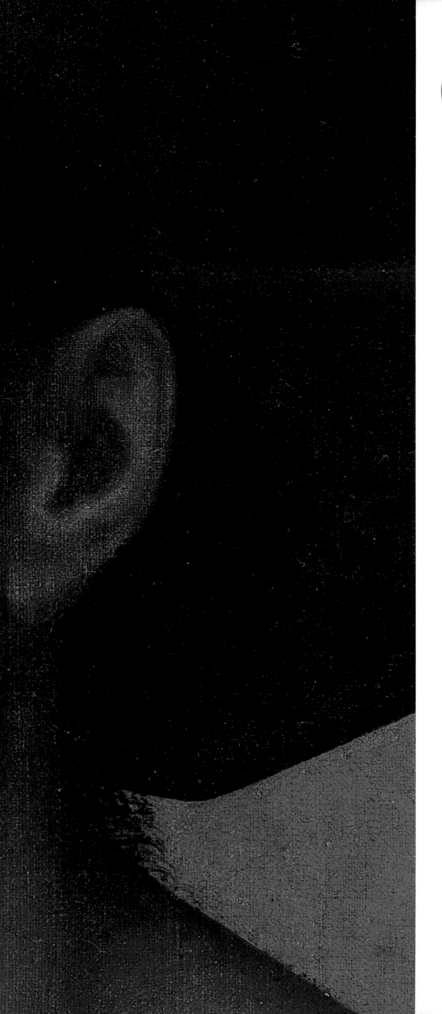

GALLERY V

RIVALRY BETWEEN THE NORTH AND SOUTH: LATE GOTHIC AND RENAISSANCE PORTRAITURE

PAINTING

The Princely Collections hold a wide range of fifteenth and sixteenth-century portraits which reflect the vigorous artistic exchange between the northern and southern countries of Europe. Southern France was an important melting pot for Dutch and Italian influences. It was there that one of the most impressive and mysterious early Renaissance portraits was produced: the *Portrait of a Man* bears the date 1456, the only clear information there is about it, placed prominently in the background. A man dressed in black fixes the viewer with his hypnotic gaze, only his hand protruding a little over the edge of the balustrade that separates one from the other. The composition as a whole, with its carefully painted details in the face and the subtle modelling of light and shade, reveals detailed knowledge of the early Netherlandish portrait, especially the work of Jan van Eyck (*c.* 1390–1441). He and his contemporaries enriched the portrait genre by adopting a style in which reality was reproduced faithfully, almost ruthlessly, and which did not even shy away from ugliness. In its close attention to detail, it traces every feature in a face, regardless of unflattering peculiarities, as is seen here in the portrait in the Princely Collections. Light and shade are not used arbitrarily to achieve three-dimensional effects, but result from a consistent treatment of incident light.

Apart from these aspects, which suggest connections with the north, the picture has a monumental quality that is scarcely found in contemporary Flemish portrait painting. Painters trained in the north preferred a narrow focus, which made a more direct impact on the viewer. A tentative attribution to the French court painter Jean Fouquet (*c.* 1420–*c.* 1480) was certainly a step in the right direction. But it was someone else, a Flemish painter working in the south of France, who combined all the above-mentioned characteristics. Barthélemy d'Eyck (doc. 1440–1470) was related to Jan van Eyck and began his career as a book illustrator in van Eyck's Bruges workshop, a fact that explains his meticulous painting technique. He was court painter to René I, Duke of Anjou and King of Naples, from 1447 to 1470, the period when the portrait in the Princely Collections was produced. Already during the lifetime of Simone Martini, the Anjou kings, from their political stronghold in southern Italy, were a significant factor in the export of the artistic innovations taking place there.

Written records are a good source of information about the lively exchange of ideas between north and south. Paintings were moved around and artists travelled a great deal, so the achievements of Netherlandish artists became common knowledge in Italy as well. In the fifteenth century, early Italian Renaissance artists adopted the three-quarter and front views that were preferred by their northern counterparts.

The brothers Francesco and Bernardino Zaganelli (1460/70–*c.* 1510) shared a workshop in Cotignola in Emilia Romagna. They may both have been pupils of Marco Palmezzano in Forlí, and their painting followed the traditions of the Ferrara school. Stylistically, their work is difficult to distinguish; they worked so closely together, in fact, that they formed the habit of jointly signing their paintings. The only work signed by Bernardino alone is the portrait of *St Sebastian* (1506, National Gallery, London); it is typical of the brothers' almost exclusively religious subject matter. The *Portrait of a Lady* probably dates from *c.* 1500 and is attributed to Bernardino. It shows a young woman in an elegant red dress with a fine hairnet, delicate circlet and an impressive pearl necklace with a pendant jewel. Her light skin tone contrasts effectively with the dark background. It was customary both in the Netherlands and Italy to use a panoramic landscape as a background. In Italy, Zaganelli's contemporary Giovanni Bellini popularized portraits with neutral backgrounds. Albrecht Dürer adopted the idea and helped circulate it in Germany. In such portraits, the viewer concentrates entirely on the sitter's features, which are modelled by subtle shades of grey in the skin tones. The incident light from the direction in which the subject is looking is also shown in the decorative detail; it makes her pearls shimmer and is also caught in the blood-red pendant jewel. This naturalistic approach to art focuses essentially on tangible, three-dimensional details, however; the large, flat areas of the sitter's dress do not reveal similar organic understanding.

The *Self-portrait* of Michael Ostendorfer (after 1490–1559) shows what form a portrait of this type took in northern European painting. Ostendorfer was one of the Regensburg group that succeeded Albrecht Altdorfer. From 1539, he was court painter to the Count Palatine Friedrich in Neumarkt in the Upper Palatinate. In his self-portrait, which is slightly reminiscent of portraits by Joos van Cleve, the artist presents himself in a brocade robe trimmed with wildcat fur – dressed with some distinction, in other words. His palette and paintbrush here acquire the character of attributes. Concealed

BARTHÉLEMY D'EYCK doc. 1440–1470

Portrait of a Man, 1456

V.7

MICHAEL OSTENDORFER after 1490–1559
Self-portrait
V.3

BERNARDINO ZAGANELLI DA COTIGNOLA 1460/70 – *c.* 1510
Portrait of a Lady, *c.* 1500
V.6

clues sometimes reveal that a portrait was painted for a particular reason. Ostendorfer holds a carnation in his hand. In the fifteenth and sixteenth century, this flower was regarded as a symbol of engagement and marriage. There is a written reference to this, albeit added at a later date, on the reverse of the picture: "Michael Ostendorfer, self-portrait as bridegroom". Carnations were said to have medicinal properties and to ward off demons; red and white carnations, it was believed, offered protection from epidemics and sickness. Carnation water was thought to encourage conception, and so the flower also became a fertility symbol. Portraiture flourished in southern Germany following the region's independent examination of Dutch realism and Italian Renaissance painting. A new interest in the individual, and the crisis in religious painting resulting from the Reformation, which ended the veneration of Mary and the saints in many parts of Germany, made the portrait an important genre in the German Renaissance. Innovative ideas flowed from Albrecht Dürer, for instance. He had experienced the esteem in which painters as independent artists were held in Venice where they were emancipating themselves from the constraints of the guilds: the logical consequence of artists' self-confidence was the autonomous self-portrait. At the same time as artists were enjoying enhanced status in society, biographies and autobiographies were becoming fashionable. Published in 1550, Giorgio Vasari's *Vite de' più eccellenti Architteti, Pittori, e Scultori Italiani* (*Lives of the Most Excellent Painters, Sculptors, and Architects)* had a lasting influence. The book was lavishly illustrated with woodcuts based on self-portraits – albeit some of dubious authenticity.

THE PORTRAIT AND LANDSCAPE

A panoramic landscape as a background for portraits was common in the Netherlands, and this type of picture enjoyed great popularity all over Europe in the late fifteenth century. At first the landscape view was added to the composition as if it were a picture within a picture.

A painting attributed to Raphael is also of this type. Together with Leonardo da Vinci (1452–1519) and Michelangelo (1475–1564) with whose works he familiarized himself during a four-year stay in Florence from 1504–08, Raphael (1483–1520) shaped the visual form of the Italian Renaissance. For his *Portrait of a Man* the artist chose the half-length figure that Leonardo had made popular. A bright, extensive landscape above the black wall forms a picture in its own right, framing the subject's head. The portrait was long thought to be of Guidobaldo I di Montefeltro (1472–1508) because a later inscription on the back of the canvas identifies the sitter as the Duke of Urbino. The work is now considered to bear insufficient resemblance to confirmed portraits of Guidobaldo, however, and the subject remains unidentified. It is not even apparent whether the sitter is a ruler or a member of the aristocracy or the patrician classes as most Renaissance portraits did not feature indications of status such as coats of arms; only the type of clothing denoted a superior social position.

The picture has been dated *c*. 1502/04. It shows some similarity with portraits by Perugino, for instance his *Francesco delle Opere* of 1494 (Galleria degli Uffizi, Florence). The Liechtenstein picture was also taken to be Perugio's work for a time. The attribution to Raphael is based on the fact that it corresponds stylistically with his works of this period such as the *Portrait of Agnolo Dono* (1506, Galleria Palatina, Florence). The limited number of mainly strong colours suggests Raphael. They relate consistently to the forms which are based on distinct drawing, and emphasize the clear structure of the composition. Such harmony and balance are among the chief characteristics of the Italian High Renaissance. In the portrait, too, they are associated with a degree of idealization in which the individual becomes an allegory of the universal.

A double portrait by Bernhard Strigel (1460–1528), probably of Dr Georg Thannstetter (1482–1535) and his wife Martha Werusin (or Merusin), shows a similar relationship between portrait and landscape. Once again, a severely geometrical structure underpins the

BERNHARD STRIGEL 1460–1528
Portrait of Dr Georg Thannstetter, *c.* 1510/15
V.4

BERNHARD STRIGEL 1460–1528

Portrait of Martha Thannstetter, *née* Werusin

(also Merusin), *c.* 1510/15

V.5

composition into which the figures are logically integrated. Maximilian I's court painter probably painted the portraits in 1515 to mark his sovereign's visit to Vienna for a double wedding that had important dynastic implications. Dr Georg Thannstetter was a medical doctor, mathematician and cartographer, and he held a chair at the University of Vienna. He had been personal physician to the Emperor Maximilian since 1510. As a humanist, he combined his medical knowledge with astrological research; his role was that of polymath at the imperial court. The artist's choice of a half-length figure in three-quarter profile was the usual form for a scholar's portrait at the time. Strigel also used this format involving the head and shoulders offset against a length of damask with a landscape view to one side in several portraits of Maximilian I. Choice of the same format probably reflects Thannstetter's self-confidence and the respect accorded to humanists by society. On the other hand, it is also typical of the sixteenth century that no typological distinction is made between rulers and the lower social orders.

Strigel uses the background, which forms a uniform space with that in the portrait of Thannstetter's wife, to show that the two paintings belong together. The couple face in towards each other, their gazes focused on the same point. In the portrait of Martha Werusin (or Merusin), the viewer's attention is caught mainly by her subtly characterized and elaborately wrapped headscarf. Its translucent fabric appears to be fastened with a single gold pin, and now allows her dark cloak and then the red brocade in the background to shimmer through, while several overlapping layers on her head give the impression of an opaque bonnet. Usually made of white linen and concealing the head and neck, such headgear had been considered appropriate for a married woman since the early Middle Ages.

The scholar's portrait was a popular Renaissance genre. The academic disciplines that were being revived and promoted at the time attempted an all-encompassing explanation of mankind's relationship with the cosmos. Scholars' training and their fields of activity were thus correspondingly diverse and they enjoyed a great deal of respect in society, which the large number of portraits reflects. Portraits of courtiers or the bourgeoisie were intended to express a sense of belonging to a family dynasty or to legitimize claims, while the scholar's portrait immortalized his intellectual achievements and his conception of himself. Strigel's choice of a marital diptych was not unusual; Luther, too, commissioned a portrait of himself and his wife.

If the landscapes in Strigel's portraits scarcely seemed real, in later work background detail appeared to be authentic, as is the case in a *Portrait of a Man* that has hitherto has been attributed to Jan van Scorel (1495–1562). Jan van Scorel was the first universally educated painter in the northern Netherlands and one of the first Dutchmen to travel to Italy. He took a particular interest in Venetian painting and studied the work of Michelangelo and Raphael. Attribution of this portrait to Scorel is based on its affinity with a group of similar portraits by him that date from *c.* 1520, meaning they were painted while he was in Italy. The relationship between figure and landscape is reminiscent of northern portraits like those of Hans Memling (*Portrait of a Man with a Roman Coin*, *c.* 1480, Koninklijk Museum voor Schone Kunsten, Antwerp). The man's features, which include rather a long nose and a slightly sloping forehead, are reproduced exactly. Yet the painting's monumental quality, the type of clothing depicted in it and the painterly handling reflect an approach derived from northern Italy. Still in excellent condition, the painting reveals subtleties such as the material quality of the sitter's clothes and the soft modelling of his hair, distinguishing between his dark beard and his lighter, longer hair that catches the light – qualities that one would sooner expect to find in Italian painting by Palma Vecchio, for instance. Combining the characteristics of both schools, this work is an apposite example of the dialogue between the two.

The *Portrait of a Youth before a Wide Landscape* is an unambiguously northern painting. A young aristocrat is shown in a panoramic riverside setting whose design elements respond to the lines of his figure. The youth's rank is indicated by the falconry gear hanging in the branches of the tree on the right. His impressive presence, taking up the whole width of the picture in a frontal view, expresses his self-confidence. Like Ostendorfer in his self-portrait, the man holds a carnation in his hand, which here too suggests that the portrait was painted in connection with his marriage. Starting in the late fourteenth century, portraits of young people were often exchanged in the course of matchmaking, and it is not improbable that this picture was part of the wooing process for a future union. Attribution of this painting to "AG", of whom there are no other records, is based on the little panel bearing the initials AG and the date, 1540. In the way its landscape is designed and relates to the figure, the painting in the Princely Collections is reminiscent of work by the artists of the Danube School – Wolf Huber, for example.

MONOGRAMMIST AG active *c.* 1540
Portrait of a Youth before a Wide Landscape, 1540
V.1

PORTRAITS OF RULERS

In the sixteenth century, it was standard for German princes to commission portraits of themselves as expressions of their court's prestige. Looking to the royal capitals of northern Italy for guidance on how to project an image, these men usually commissioned a three-quarter or full-length portrait that was intended to represent the sitter's power and make his presence felt. Such portraits served not only to keep a prince's memory alive, but also had a representative function.

Lucas Cranach the Elder (1472–1553) was one of the busiest portrait painters of his day. His *Portrait of Elector Friedrich III the Wise of Saxony* (1463–1525) from the Schönborn-Buchheim Collection was one of the first major serial painting commissions. As a companion piece to the portrait of Friedrich's brother, the Elector Johann (b. 1468), it was one of the side panels of a triptych. The centre panels showed Cranach's patron and reigning Elector of Saxony, Friedrich the Magnanimous. Sixty electoral portraits were subsequently painted by Cranach in two formats. They were intended to show a regent's loyalty to the Emperor as well as his dynastic legitimacy. The role of the portrait as a strategic medium can also be ascribed to the numerous likenesses of Friedrich's protégé Martin Luther that circulated widely as prints. Here, the Elector presents himself as a patron of artists and scholars, which he actually was as the founder of the University of Wittenberg. The portrait does not feature any insignia of power. In the way it is presented, this painting is no different from scholars' portraits like that of Erasmus of Rotterdam by Hans Holbein the Younger, one of the pioneering portrait painters of the German Renaissance. The figure of Friedrich, intersected by the frame, conveys authority, while his face, with its striking chin, suggests determination. In marked contrast, his delicate hands adopt a sophisticated pose that attests to his sensitivity and mental agility. This new gift of observation was known as the 'invention of character'. In it, a realistic approach not only reproduced facial features, but also helped the artist capture his sitter's personality. Only certain parts of the Elector's body, such as his face and hands, are treated sculpturally; in contrast, his bulky body is reduced to a silhouette-like, two-dimensional form.

The *Portrait of Duke Ludwig X of Bavaria* represents a step in the direction of greater realism in physical appearance and three-dimensional quality. It is by Barthel Beham (1502–1540) who was often cited as Dürer's most talented successor. From 1530 to 1535, Beham worked on portraits of the Wittelsbach dynasty for display in the duke's gallery. Around this time, Ludwig X (1495–1545) had his portrait painted by his court painter, but it was not part of the series intended for the Munich Residence. His 1531 portrait has a companion piece that is now in Ottawa (formerly Princely Collections); it probably shows Ursula von Weichs, the Duke's companion. The *Portrait of Duke Ludwig X of Bavaria* is distinguished by its exceptional quality: the fur and hair are executed with meticulous precision, as are the highlights on his forehead and the lines of his face. This affectionate attention to detail in the portrayal of the different materials enlivens this otherwise simple portrait. The subject has greater physical presence here than in Cranach's portrait, however: not only is the surface appearance of his clothes depicted, but we also get a sense of the body beneath. Ludwig's left hand rests on a parapet that is identical to the picture frame. This establishes a special relationship with viewers for whom the picture frame is a tangible part of reality: Ludwig's hand practically reaches out of it towards them. This trick, the shadow he casts on the wall behind him and the sculptural quality of the curtain are subtle devices that indicate the spatial depth of the interior.

The *Portrait of Ladislaus von Fraunberg, Count of Haag* (1505–1566) by Hans Mielich (1516–1573) is an example of the new type of full-length ruler portrait that much more clearly fulfils representative functions. In his portraits of Duke Heinrich the Pious and his wife Katharina von Mecklenburg (dated 1514, Gemäldegalerie Alte Meister, Dresden), Lucas Cranach the Elder had created the first life-size, full-length portraits. With his *Portrait of Emperor Karl V* (dated 1532, Kunsthistorisches Museum, Vienna), Jakob Seisenegger (1505–1557) established an exemplary form of painting for representative purposes that would influence later generations. Mielich's painting probably came into the possession of the princely family in 1568 on the occasion of the marriage of the sitter's niece to Hartmann II von Liechtenstein. An inventory of 1613 proves that this is the painting held longest in the Princely Collections. Self-governing under the Kaiser, Haag ruled the county of Haag in Upper Bavaria near Wasserburg, and was the last of his line. Shortly before the portrait was painted, Fraunberg had married the niece of Duke Ercole d'Este, Emilia Rovella di Pio, in Ferrara. Yet his mother-in-law had her daughter abducted to a nunnery and hired poisoners and murderers to try to kill the count for so long that he finally

FRIDERICH · DER · DRIT · CHVRFV
· VND · HERTZOG · ZV · SACHSS

LUCAS CRANACH THE ELDER 1472–1553
Portrait of the Elector Friedrich III the Wise
of Saxony, after 1532
V.10

BARTHEL BEHAM 1502–1540
Portrait of Duke Ludwig X of Bavaria, 1531
V.9

returned home without his bride in 1556. The next ten years until his death were marked by Ladislaus's hapless attempts to arrange another marriage to prevent the extinction of his line. After his death, the county of Fraunberg fell to his adversary, Duke Albrecht V of Bavaria. In the year the picture was painted, Albrecht V had the count illegally abducted and extorted a substantial ransom from him. His self-confident portrait, comparable to those of the greatest rulers of his day, expresses Ladislaus's pride and steadfastness. With great authenticity, Hans Mielich successfully captures his subject's aggressive nature and tragic fate. The count is presented wearing lavish Spanish clothes, his hand on his dagger as a sign of his ability to put up a fight. An exotic attribute symbolizing distinction and wealth, the leopard at his side is a reference to his Italian adventures and was a present from his brother-in-law. The painting is richly symbolic. Snow-covered Haag castle, its coat of arms featured prominently above it, is seen through the window. The helmet and shield, sword and coat of mail indicate Fraunberg's military achievements, although they are located in close proximity to symbols of mortality such as an hourglass and a skull. The large number of these elements and the wealth of detail that accords them equal status with the figure lend the composition an ornamental character that prevents the viewer from actively making connections between the sitter and his surroundings. It is remarkable that Mielich had used the same format shortly before in his portrait of Duke Albrecht V. It demonstrates Count Haag's power and the artistic freedom that Hans Mielich, a guild painter not primarily beholden to the court, allowed himself.

FLORENCE: FROM THE RENAISSANCE TO MANNERISM

The Princely Collections hold an outstanding Florentine Renaissance portrait in the form of the *Portrait of a Man* by Francesco di Cristofano, called Franciabigio (1482–1525). It reveals the general tendency towards a psychological approach in portraits, found most markedly in the portraits of Lorenzo Lotto. Franciabigio worked in and around Florence throughout his life. Vasari was one of the first to praise Franciabigio's "many and very beautiful portraits from nature", and indeed they are among the Florentine Renaissance's most sensitive portrayals of the human physiognomy and psyche. This portrait, dated "1517" on a *cartellino*, shows an elegantly dressed gentleman. As the subject is not posing in front of a landscape – which is otherwise usual for Franciabigio – but presented in front of a unified, non-descript background, all attention is concentrated on his face. The impressive features convey an essentially melancholy mood that is seemingly intensified by the dark beard and black garb. Thrust into close proximity to the viewer through its narrow focus, the portrait becomes a psychological study of the sitter. All Franciabigio's portraits are characterized by this sombre tone, yet the sitter's melancholy, slightly lost look also conveys the impression that he is observing his own psychological processes, something we find regularly in Franciabigio's work. The subject's powerfully expressive face is combined with detailed treatment of his facial features to create a work of rare individuality.

The *Portrait of a Young Man* by Francesco Salviati (1510–1563) is also from the Florentine school. Probably dating from Salviati's second Roman period, after 1548, it reveals the essential characteristics of Mannerism, the late phase of the Renaissance. The young man wears a fine leather jerkin over a slit red doublet. His right hand carefully holds the neck of a young deer that is unafraid to lick the back of his other hand. Salviati preferred to paint three-quarter views of his subjects. Combined with the plain background that is differentiated only in terms of light and shade, this adds a new element to his work, a sense of depth and a sculptural quality embracing the whole figure. Venetian painters in particular had a preference for painting sitters in three-quarter length poses, their arms bent and hands visible. Titian's portraits of noblemen from as early as the 1520s illustrate the point.

FRANCESCO SALVIATI 1510–1563
Portrait of a Young Man, after 1548
V.11

The language of Mannerism is revealed in a new, elongated ideal figure and an inclination towards emphatic and often slightly artificial gestures. Salviati's concrete implementation of this shows the influence of Parmigianino. The new sense of unemotional composure accords entirely with Mannerist sensibilities. As a means of expressing character, accessories acquire far greater significance: the tame deer symbolizes shyness, gentleness and vulnerability, qualities that are also reflected in the young man's gentle features and suggest kinship between the two. His delicate hands are another strongly expressive element. A completely different way of expressing psychological characteristics has evolved here. Salviati's portraits are also much admired for their painterly qualities and rich colour that conveys sensuousness. He clearly likes colour contrasts, though he employs them within a harmonious palette that would not have been conceivable during the High Renaissance, for instance in Raphael's work. Salviati was thus often described as the principal exponent of refined courtly Mannerism. His fame extended to France where he worked for Francis I for over a year.

THE COMPETITION: VENICE

Florentine art was driven by a colourful approach that was rich in contrasts and based above all on clarity of drawing, while the Venetian tradition inclined towards a painterly representation of reality: experiencing space and atmosphere through matching colour values was more important than the tangible, sculptural quality of the pictorial elements. In Venice, Titian's art was the chief attraction. His example greatly boosted portrait production both in terms of quality and quantity .

Paris Bordone (1500–1571) painted the *Portrait of Nikolaus Körbler* in the 1530s. Körbler (1495–1541) came from a respected, prosperous merchant family, known to have been in Judenburg since the late fifteenth century. He traded on a considerable scale in medicinal and fragrant plants, and also vitriol for which Venice was a major trans-shipment centre. Charles V rewarded him for his services to the imperial army by raising him to the nobility on 20 November 1532, probably the occasion for commissioning this picture from Paris Bordone, whose earliest dated painting this is. Bordone presents the merchant in simple clothing. The subject's pose and contemplative manner place him in the line of Titian's portraits

from the 1520s. Bordone used muted colours that combined to create a harmonious atmosphere. Through soft modelling, certain graphic details stand out and create emphasis.

In its reserve and elegance, the merchant's portrait is the epitome of distinction. In contrast, the *Portrait of a Bearded Man*, dated 1533, conveys tense energy. Determinedly clutching his dagger, this man has earned the painting the title *Cavaliere Attaccabrighe* (Sir Quarrelsome) on account of his self-confident, almost provocative, pose and the way he challenges the viewer with his gaze. Yet he does not grasp his dagger for aggressive reasons: his action should be regarded rather as a symbol of vigilance and readiness to fight. In this context, the action is a convention in terms of pose and movement. For the background to his painting, Bordone chose a semi-circular niche, a popular motif in Italian art. In reality, such a niche usually contained a sculpture; here, the sitter is equated with a statue in a way that lends his portrait a noble quality. Moreover, a niche is also highly effective as a three-dimensional feature, as Vasari had already pointed out. The lighting has an almost dramatic quality that drives the man's face out of the darkness, a device used by Bordone to accentuate the momentary nature of the painting. The silky sheen of his outer garment looks particularly striking against the background that partly recedes into darkness.

Last attributed to Domenico Rubusti, known as Tintoretto (1560–1635), the *Portrait of a Nobleman with his Son* is an unusual double portrait for Venetian painting of its day. This affectionate portrayal of a respectful relationship between a father and son suggests a humanist environment. It is probably derived from the idea of *monita paterna*, paternal instruction. (In his writings, Erasmus of Rotterdam placed the education of children essentially in their parents' hands). The book is open at Virgil's "Third Eclogue", an ancient pastoral poem praising country life that was also admired in Renaissance Venice. The vine protruding into the picture suggests the rural surroundings of a villa. In loose brushwork and ornamental details such as the star pattern on the boy's doublet are portrayed freely and do not capture the rise and fall of its folds. Visible brushwork lends the work a degree of liveliness. Such a technique placed atmospheric effects above graphic precision and became typical of Venetian painting.

DOMENICO ROBUSTI called Tintoretto (?) 1560–1635
Portrait of a Nobleman with his Son
V.14

PARIS BORDONE 1500–1571
Portrait of a Bearded Man, 1533
V.15

SCULPTURE AND APPLIED ART

It is interesting to juxtapose late Gothic and Renaissance portrait painting with examples of contemporary sculpture that reveal an alternative treatment of the motif of the human face. Two busts by Andrea della Robbia and Antico reveal an idealizing tendency: the form and expression of the face are so much generalized that it becomes almost impossible to speak of a portrait (nevertheless, attempts at identification were made repeatedly). Significantly, only historical and mythological figures were possible candidates. The fact that a figure from history was long dead or that a character was fictitious served to justify the sculptor's treatment of his subject.

Andrea della Robbia (1435–1525) made the *Relief Bust of a Young Man* in his Florence workshop *c.* 1470/80. His uncle, Luca della Robbia (1399/1400–1482), is credited with the invention of tinglazed terracotta sculpture whose smooth, durable white surface preserved the luminous quality of the colours applied to it. A striking garland of leaves, fruit and flowers frames the bust of the youth, its coloured glaze lending it an especially decorative note. While attempts have been made to attribute a particular significance to the work, any individuality in the youth's gentle features is subordinated to perfect proportions that appear to create a symbol of unblemished youth. The boy inclines his head forwards, thus raising it slightly above the background. His sideways glance reaches further than suggested by the turn of his head, which further animates the work. Prince Johann II acquired this tondo from the Palazzo Antinori in Florence in 1899. It is known that the della Robbia workshop worked for the Antinori family: Alessandro Antinori commissioned a cartouche of his family coat of arms from it in 1512.

Probably made for Isabella d'Este *c.* 1520, the *Bust of a Youth* is considered to be one of the most beautiful works by Pier Jacopo Alari-Bonacolsi, known as Antico (*c.* 1460–1528). He was the outstanding sculptor to emerge from the Renaissance court at Mantua. This sculpture is highly regarded due to its formal beauty and exquisite execution; gilding enlivens the work and lends it a hint of sumptuousness. With his gentle, clean-cut features and mouth slightly open, the young man appears lost in thought. His curly hair is skilfully arranged and seems almost ornamental. Various attempts have been made to read meaning into the figure. As Antico dispensed with attributes of any kind, it is impossible to identify the figure,

which may well have been his intention anyway: the bust embodies ideal beauty as perceived by the aesthetic of Antiquity. The youth's timeless beauty forms an effective counterpoint to contemporary portraits by Franciabigio, for example. In contrast to his carefully observed facial features and his impressive depictions of states of mind, the perfect beauty of Antico's forms appears to be removed from reality.

The *Equestrian Statuette of Ferdinando I de' Medici* (1549–1609) of *c.* 1600 is one of the few works signed by Giambologna (1529–1608), who became the most influential sculptor at the Medici court in Florence in the second half of the sixteenth century. The Roman *Equestrian Statuette of Marcus Aurelius* at the Capitol in Rome had been a popular model since its creation. A bronze statuette by Antico in the Princely Collections is a free copy of it. The partially gilded sculpture was possibly a gift from the Gonzagas to the Emperor Karl V during one of his visits to Mantua in the 1530s. The monumental original was also Giambologna's point of departure for his *Monument to the Grand Duke Cosimo I de' Medici*, which was placed in the Piazza della Signoria in Florence in 1594. Cosimo's son Ferdinando finally commissioned his own statue from Giambologna about 1600; it has stood in the Piazza SS. Anunziata since 1608.

Equestrian statues were highly regarded as a form of portraiture as they sympathetically expressed the subject's power and dignity. This explains why miniature versions of them were favoured as diplomatic gifts. The bronze in the Princely Collections may well have been made for this purpose, too. While it is clearly closely related to Giambologna's monumental statue, it differs sufficiently enough from it as not to be regarded as the model for the monument as later executed. In its simplification of individual features, the portrait is akin to the equestrian statue. While the subject should be recognizable, it did not aspire to express character. The demands of representation were such that portraits of rulers must appear unapproachable.

PIER JACOPO ALARI-BONACOLSI called Antico *c.* 1460–1528
Bust of a Youth, *c.* 1520
V.21

ANDREA DELLA ROBBIA 1435–1525
Relief Bust of a Young Man, *c.* 1470/80
V.22

PIER JACOPO ALARI-BONACOLSI called Antico *c.* 1460–1528
Equestrian Statuette of Marcus Aurelius, early 16th century
V.20

GIAMBOLOGNA 1529–1608 and **ANTONIO SUSINI**
doc. 1580–1624
Equestrian Statuette of Ferdinando I de' Medici, *c.* 1600
V.23

GIULIANO DI PIERO PANDOLFINI doc. 1615–1637
Pietra dura chest, 1620/23
with coat of arms and monogram of Karl I von Liechtenstein
V.24

A MAGNIFICENT PIECE FROM THE IMPERIAL GEM-CUTTING
WORKSHOP IN PRAGUE

Castrucci's gem-cutting workshop in Prague was founded by Emperor Rudolf II (1552–1612), who was enthusiastic about the new technique of *commesso di pietre dure*. This technique of composing pictures using cut gemstones dated back to Antiquity, and was taken to new heights of mastery in late sixteenth-century Florence – hence the name 'Florentine mosaic'. The significance of the Prague workshop in the history of *commesso di pietre dure* lay in its development of a special technique of representing its subjects. Typically,

an idealized landscape is reproduced using flecks of colour and the natural markings of the stones as seen here in this splendid princely chest.

Between 1620 and 1623, when Giuliano di Piero Pandolfini (doc. 1615–1637) was the foremost master craftsman during the workshop's last years, a ceremonial chest and a table-top were made for Prince Karl I von Liechtenstein. The chest is on the Venetian model: it consists of a wooden core clad with *commessi* and is finished with gilded bronze. Architectural articulation in three axes imposes order on the differently shaped panels. The *commessi* were not originally all made for this chest, but were crafted over ten years.

Karl I von Liechtenstein had probably started collecting *commessi* a
few years before the chest was commissioned. The front bears his
monogram and coat of arms, meaning that the chest can be dated
between 1620 and 1623.

The coat of arms and monogram on the table-top also indicate the
piece was commissioned by Karl I. It is divided into small fields by
strips of reddish-brown jasper, and the fields are inlaid with landscape images, trophies, coats of arms and geometric forms. The
symbolism of these motifs reflects the influence of the scientists
and philosophers active at the court of Emperor Rudolf II in Prague.
The platonic bodies were equated with elements of cosmology:
tetrahedrons and octahedrons thus stand for the elements fire and
air. Within Baroque society's concept of the hierarchy of nature,
precious stones occupied a similarly outstanding position as
princes did in society. This explains why it was a ruler's prerogative
to possess precious stones.

GIOVANNI GIULIANI 1663–1744
Wooden base for a *pietra dura* table-top by
the Castrucci workshop (V.17), 1711
V.18

CASTRUCCI WORKSHOP
Pietra dura table-top, 1620/23
with coat of arms and monogram of Karl I von Liechtenstein
V.17

Cassone, Siena, 15th century
V.19

PAINTINGS

V.1 / p. 148
Monogrammist AG (active c. 1540)
Portrait of a Youth before a Wide Landscape,
1540
Oil on panel; height 59 cm, width 51 cm
Signed top left on a small panel: 1540 AG
Inv. no. GE 699
Provenance: recorded in the collection since
1805 (as a work by Hans Aldegrever)

V.2 / p. 143
Raffaello Sanzio, called Raphael (?) (1483–1520)
Portrait of a Man, c. 1502/04
Oil on panel; height 48 cm, width 37 cm
Inv. no. GE 36
Provenance: before 1823 Borio Collection in
Bologna; 1823 acquired by Prince Johann I
von Liechtenstein as a work by Raphael from
the dealer Carlo Gamora in Vienna

V.3 / p. 140
Michael Ostendorfer (after 1490–1559)
Self-portrait
Oil on panel; height 41 cm, width 31 cm
Signed on reverse: Michael Ostendorfer
"Self-Portrait as Bridegroom"
Inv. no. GE 1491
Provenance: 1939 from Schloss Leopoldstein
to the gallery in Vienna, probably as part of the
acquisition of the Kalwang estate

V.4 / p. 144
Bernhard Strigel (1460–1528)
Portrait of Dr Georg Thannstetter, c. 1510/15
Oil on panel; height 42 cm, width 29 cm
Inv. no. GE 712, companion piece to GE 714
Provenance: recorded in the collection from 1805
(as a work by Hans Holbein) with the *Portrait of
Martha Thannstetter, née Werusin (also Merusin)*
(GE714)

V.5 / p. 145
Bernhard Strigel (1460–1528)
*Portrait of Martha Thannstetter, née Werusin
(also Merusin)*, c. 1510/15
Oil on panel; height 42 cm, width 28 cm
Inv. no. GE 714, companion piece to GE 712
Provenance: recorded in the collection from 1805
(as a work by Hans Holbein) with the *Portrait of
Dr Georg Thannstetter* (GE 712)

V.6 / p. 141
Bernardino Zaganelli da Cotignola
(1460/70 – c. 1510)
Portrait of a Lady, c. 1500
Oil on panel; height 33 cm, width 25 cm
Inv. no. GE 935
Provenance: 1882 acquired by Prince Johann II
von Liechtenstein in Italy as a work by Anselmo
da Folí, 1950 disposed of from the Liechtenstein
Collections; before 2003 in a Swiss private collec-
tion; 2003 re-acquired, by Prince Hans-Adam II
von und zu Liechtenstein

V.7 / p. 138
Barthélemy d'Eyck (doc. 1440–1470)
Portrait of a Man, 1456
Oil on parchment on panel;
height 51 cm, width 42 cm
Dated on both sides of the subject: 1 4 5 6
Inscription on reverse of wooden panel: No.20 /
Von Mantenio / Erkaufft Vom Spillenberger
Inv. no. GE 729
Provenance: 1677 acquired by Prince Karl Euse-
bius von Liechtenstein from the imperial court
painter Johann Spillenberger in Vienna, as "Ein
sehr alter kopff von Mantenia anno 1426 gemahlt"
(A very old head painted by Mantenia anno 1426)

V.8 / p. 147
Jan van Scorel (?) (1495–1562)
Portrait of a Man, c. 1520
Oil on panel; height 47 cm, width 41 cm
Inv. no. GE 854
Provenance: 1880 acquired by Prince Johann II
von Liechtenstein in Florence as a work by
Giovanni Antonio Licino da Pordenone

V.9 / p. 151
Barthel Beham (1502–1540)
Portrait of Duke Ludwig X of Bavaria, 1531
Oil on panel; height 69 cm, width 59 cm
Dated top left: 1531
Inv. no. GE 927
Provenance: 1880 recorded in Lednice Palace

V.10 / p. 150
Lucas Cranach the Elder (1472–1553)
*Portrait of the Elector Friedrich III the Wise of
Saxony*, after 1532
Oil on panel; height 80 cm, width 49 cm
Schönborn-Buchheim Collection, inv. no. G 079
Provenance: 1746 first recorded in the inventory
of the collection of Count Friedrich Karl von
Schönborn

V.11 / p. 157
Francesco Salviati (1510–1563)
Portrait of a Young Man, after 1548
Oil on panel; height 89 cm, width 69 cm
Inv. no. GE 848
Provenance: probably Guadagni Collection in
Florence; before 1894 in the Torrigiani Collection
in Florence; 1894 acquired by Prince Johann II
von Liechtenstein from the dealer Stefano Bardini
in Florence

V.12 / p. 155
Francesco di Cristofano, called Franciabigio
(1482–1525)
Portrait of a Man, 1517
Oil on canvas; height 55 cm, width 40 cm
Dated on the left on a *cartellino*:
A. D. M. D. XVII D. X S
Inv. no. GE 851
Provenance: 1879 acquired by Prince Johann II
von Liechtenstein from the estate of the Marchese
Gino Capponi in Florence

V.13 / p. 152
Hans Mielich (1516–1573)
*Portrait of Ladislaus von Fraunberg,
Count of Haag*, 1557
Oil on canvas; height 214 cm, width 113 cm
Dated and signed on the wooden cornice: ANNO
DN M.D.LVII. HANNS MIELICH A MONAC. FECIT
Inscription on the arms pane: CVM LABORE ET
DEO IVVANTE LADISLAVS GRAFFE ZV HAG
Inscription on the panther's collar: LS
Inv. no. GE 1065
Provenance: after 1557 or 1566 in the posses-
sion of Ladislaus von Fraunberg's sister,
Maximiliane, Countess of Ortenburg, whose
daughter Countess Anna Maria of Ortenburg
married Hartmann II von Liechtenstein in 1568,
bringing the picture into the Princely Collections

V.14 / p. 160
Domenico Robusti, called Tintoretto (?)
(1560–1635)
Portrait of a Nobleman with his Son
Oil on canvas; height 73 cm, width 96 cm
Signed on the chair arm:
AO.AEtS.XXXIIII.D.co T.tto pix
Inscription on the right-hand page of the book:
EGLOGA
Inv. no. GE 230
Provenance: acquired by Prince Johann I
von Liechtenstein

V.15 / p. 161
Paris Bordone (1500–1571)
Portrait of a Bearded Man, 1533
Oil on canvas; height 98 cm, width 84 cm
Signed bottom left: PARIS B
Dated top right: M.D XXXIII / AETAT. XXXVII
Inv. no. GE 93
Provenance: first mentioned in V. Fanti's
1767 catalogue

V.16 / p. 159
Paris Bordone (1500–1571)
Portrait of Nikolaus Körbler, 1532
Oil on canvas; height 100 cm, width 78 cm
Signed bottom right: PARIS bordon f.
Inscription left on the cartouche: 37 / AETATIS
ANOR / M.D.XXXII.
Inscription at top: NICOLAVS.KORBLER.
DA.JVDENBVRG. /
ARMIRAGLIO.DI.CAROLO.V.A.TVNISE.15.32.
Inv. no. GE 1128
Provenance: 1872 acquired by Prince Johann II
von Liechtenstein from Countess Adriani-Widmann-
Rezzonico in Venice

SCULPTURE AND APPLIED ART

V.17 / p. 171
Castrucci workshop
Pietra dura table-top, 1620/23
with coat of arms and monogram of Karl I
von Liechtenstein
Commessi di pietre dure, garnets, and gilt bronze;
height 93 cm, width 89 cm
Inv. no. SK 1401
Provenance: c. 1623 comissioned by Prince
Karl I von Liechtenstein

V.18 / p. 170
Giovanni Giuliani (1663–1744)
Wooden base for a *pietra dura* table-top by the
Castrucci workshop (V.17), 1711
Carved limewood, in 1847 the original gilt bronze
was heavily gilded and silver gilt; height 81 cm,
width 81 cm, depth 86 cm
Signed: Johann … k. k. Hof und Leib (?) Vergolder
im Jahr 847 Salzburg
Inv. no. MO 1565
Provenance: 1711 commissioned by Prince
Johann Adam Andreas I von Liechtenstein for
the *pietra dura* table-top (SK 1401)

V.19 / p. 172
Cassone, Siena, 15th century
Wood gilded; height 64 cm, width 186 cm,
depth 63 cm
Inv. no. SK 780
Provenance: 1883 acquired by Prince Johann II
von Liechstenstein from Stefano Bardini in
Florence

V.20 / p. 166
Pier Jacopo Alari-Bonacolsi, called Antico
(c. 1460–1528)
Equestrian Statuette of Marcus Aurelius, early
16th century
Bronze, partly fire-gilded, silver incrustations;
height 39 cm
Inv. no. SK 19
Provenance: possibly 1530 or 1532 as a gift from
the Gonzagas to Emperor Charles V (inventory
number of the King of Spain's collections survives
on the object); 1999 in the possession of the
Nimesis Fine holdings in Geneva; 2001 acquired
by Prince Hans-Adam II von und zu Liechtenstein

V.21 / p. 164
Pier Jacopo Alari-Bonacolsi, called Antico
(c. 1460–1528)
Bust of a Youth, c. 1520
Bronze with olive-brown patina covered with black
lacquer; height 57 cm
Inv. no. SK 535
Provenance: probably commissioned for the
collection of Isabella d'Este in the Palazzo Ducale,
Mantua; recorded from 1807 in the Princely
Collections

V.22 / p. 165
Andrea della Robbia (1435–1525)
Relief Bust of a Young Man, c. 1470/80
Terracotta, coloured glaze; diameter 70 cm
Inv. no. SK 116
Provenance: 1899 acquired by Prince Johann II
von Liechtenstein from Dr Volpi in Florence and
from the Palazzo Antinori in Florence

V.23 / p. 167
Giambologna (1529–1608) and
Antonio Susini (doc. 1580–1624)
Equestrian Statuette of Ferdinando I de' Medici,
c. 1600
Bronze with remains of red-gold paint;
height 64 cm
Signed on the girth: IOAN.BOLO.BELG.
Inv. no. SK 575
Provenance: acquired by Prince Joseph Wenzel I
von Liechtenstein in the mid-18th century

V.24 / pp. 168–69
Giuliano di Piero Pandolfini (doc. 1615–1637)
Pietra dura chest, 1620/23
with coat of arms and monogram of Karl I
von Liechtenstein
Commessi di pietre dure, garnets, gilt bronze and
ebony; height 56 cm, width 88 cm, depth 49 cm
Inv. no. SK 599
Provenance: c. 1623 commissioned by Prince
Karl I von Liechtenstein

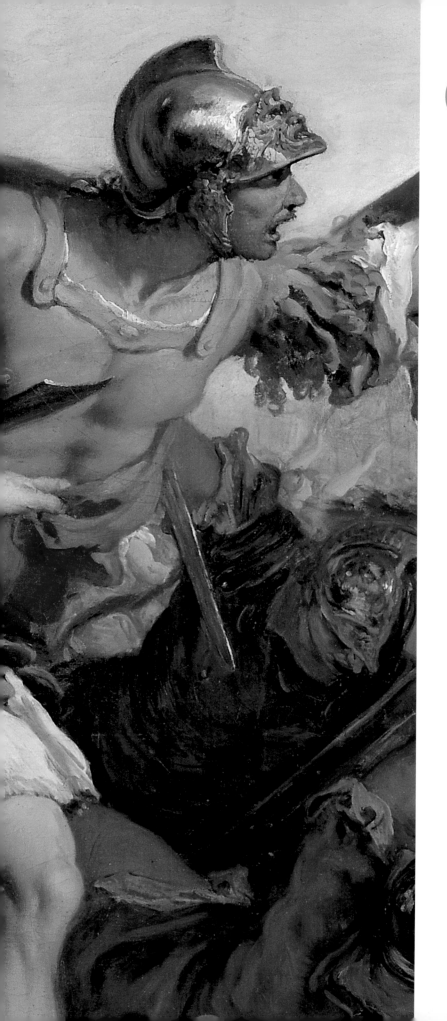

GALLERY VI

THE GREAT SCHOOLS OF THE ITALIAN BAROQUE

There are two trends within Italian Baroque painting, each taking a different view of the relationship between nature and art: the classical approach was modelled on the work of Raphael, and inclined towards stylized and largely idealized representation. In the naturalistic approach, realism took precedence over ideals of beauty, and typical scenes employed dramatic light effects. Caravaggio was the most influential artist in this context.

NATURALISM AND THE CARAVAGGISTI

Jean Valentin de Boulogne (baptized? 1591–1632), who was born in Coulommiers en Brie, was an exponent of the naturalistic school. He lived and worked in Rome from about 1612/14, and was famed for his paintings, often half-length portraits, of fortune-tellers and musicians and guardhouse scenes, which he painted as private commissions. *Cheerful Company with Fortune-teller* is a typical subject for him. A wealth of information is available about how this late work came into being. A Sicilian aristocrat living in Madrid, Fabrizio Valguarnera, when on a visit to Rome in 1631, placed a commission with Valentin for a "picture of people featuring a gypsy, with soldiers and other women playing instruments". Clients were thus able to specify requirements. The crowded inn scene thus contains all the elements that were popular in this genre: loud music is being played at one table, hardly anyone pays attention to a fight that is developing at the next one; only one soldier tries to intervene. A little girl takes the opportunity to steal the purse of one of the brawlers. Amid all this confusion, a fortune-teller reads a young man's palm. Themes and figures were interchangeable in these scenes. They all appealed differently to the perception of viewers, which is why such images were often regarded as allegories of the senses, hearing first and foremost in this case. Valentin's achievement lies not so much in inventing a suitable pictorial form for the theme as in his artfully varied poses and painterly treatment. He demonstrates his skill in his subtle handling of light that gives structure to the work and defines the positions of the figures in the space.

These strong contrasts of light and shade, known as chiaroscuro, are modelled on Michelangelo Merisi, known as Caravaggio (1571–1610). He introduced a completely new way of handling light, with strong highlights making figures stand out against a dark, indeterminate background and casting hard shadows. Caravaggio inclined towards violent subject matter and propagated a naturalism that could be alarming and was generally regarded as a challenge to the prevailing taste in art. The dramatic light and shade effects in his work had a lasting influence on all European Baroque painting up until Rembrandt's time. Young painters of various nationalities who felt drawn to the art of Caravaggio, who had already died, established themselves in the area around the Piazza di Spagna about 1615. They included Simon Vouet, Bartolomeo Manfredi, Nicolas Tournier and also Jean Valentin de Boulougne, who may be regarded as the most important French Caravaggist. Typical features of his work are simply composed pictures and half-length figures, as favoured by Caravaggio himself in his early work. Valentin's work is based on the secular scenes of Caravaggio's early period, but he combined them with the dark, highly contrasting colours of the master's late style. The edge has been taken off the moral undertones that were inherent in sixteenth-century scenes of this kind, however. Caravaggio's admirers in Rome also included a number of Dutch artists, who traditionally went there as part of their training. Most of them arrived in Rome in the early 1610s so did not meet the master in person. Nevertheless, Caravaggio was still a major presence through his work and the reputation he gained for his eccentric lifestyle.

Theodoor Rombouts (1597–1637) was one of the most original of the Flemish Caravaggisti. He concentrated mainly on paintings of drinking scenes, musicians and gamblers. His preferred a wide and horizontal format in which his dramatically gesturing figures and contrary movements provided cohesion, as exemplified by *The Denial of St Peter*. Rombouts set this religious scene in an inn, and gave Peter such realistic, indeed crude, features that he is indistinguishable as a saint from the common folk around him. This genre-like treatment sets Peter on a par with the congregation, a subtle device that calls upon the faithful to follow Christ. Rombouts' picture captures the moment when Peter first betrays Christ after he has been taken prisoner (Gospel according to Luke [22, 54 ff.]). Peter had followed Jesus from some distance behind, mingling with the crowds and awaiting the events that were to unfold in the High Priest's courtyard. When a maid recognized him as one of Jesus' disciples, Peter vehemently denied it.

JEAN VALENTIN DE BOULOGNE 1591–1632
Cheerful Company with Fortune-teller, 1631
VI.3

The motif reflects the Baroque's fondness for representations of moments of insight that also contain an element of surprise. Matthew's calling from among the gamblers is one such moment. In fact, Rombouts' composition and figures are based on a version of this theme by Caravaggio, which the Dutch artist would have been able to see in the church of San Luigi dei Francesi in Rome. In it, too, recent arrivals interrupt a group in conversation. The significance of the scene is accentuated by dramatic lighting that impressively illuminates the moment of sudden insight.

Outside Italy, the foremost exponent of Caravaggio's art was Gerrit van Honthorst (1592–1656). In his native Netherlands, he was a member of the Utrecht group of Caravaggisti who specialized in dramatic candlelit scenes. A typical painting in this style is *St Jerome*. It was painted by a successor to Honthorst, and is presumably modelled on a picture by him (whereabouts unknown). Concealed behind a beam, the light source in this picture creates a dramatic mood that is further heightened by the fact that the saint is illuminated from below. All our attention is focused on the body of

THEODOOR ROMBOUTS 1597–1637
The Denial of St Peter
VI.6

the ascetic saint who in the quiet of the night is engaged in acts of penance. They have obviously already taken their toll on his ageing body: every wrinkle and every vein bulging with the effort are meticulously depicted by the artist.

St Jerome had been a widespread subject since the sixteenth century. The Italians liked to portray him in the open air, but northern painters preferred to show the Church Father at work in his study. The Dutch Caravaggists combined the two concepts: in his portrayals of Jerome in the desert, Honthorst included a wooden shack, a table, books, a crucifix and skull that are all reminiscent of a scholar in his study. Carravagio's interpretation of the saint as the translator of the Bible (c. 1605, Galleria Borghese, Rome) was a major source of inspiration for his successors, as was his choice of a horizontal format and the half-length figure, which subsequently characterized their compositions on this theme.

During the Renaissance, in keeping with humanist ideals, St Jerome was portrayed as a hermit so as to emphasize his role as a learned Church Father, the translator of the Bible and author. As the painting in the Princely Collections shows, in the seventeenth century, Jerome became an ardent penitent beating his naked breast with a

stone to draw blood in acknowledgement of his sinful nature. This should be seen in connection with the Council of Trent, which stressed the need for the active penitential practice.

One of the last artists to adopt Caravaggio's style directly was Honthorst's pupil Johannes von Bronchorst (1627–1656). He was remarkably faithful to his model, as artistic taste since the mid-1620s in the north had clearly favoured Rubens, and Dutch taste Rembrandt, while Caravaggio's followers in Rome had already disappeared by mid-century. Dated 1652, the *St Bartholomew* in the Princely Collections is considered to be Bronchorst's earliest attributed work. Painted either while he was still in Italy or shortly after his return to the Netherlands, its Caravaggesque style is astonishing for the middle of the century.

The apostle Bartholomew was one of the first disciples to be called by Jesus. Bronchorst uses the slanting light entering from the right to emphasize his bare shoulders, which is explained as follows: though there is no other mention of the subject's saintliness, the knife he holds in his hand is a reference to his imminent martyrdom. According to legend, one of the places in which Bartholomew preached the gospel was Armenia. Having converted its monarch to

Detail
VI.6

JOHANNES VAN BRONCHORST 1627–1656
St Bartholomew, 1652
VI.7

Christianity, the king's hostile brother had Bartholomew flayed alive. In contrast to the Dutch Caravaggists, who described every detail with graphic precision as it were, and lent bodies sharply delineated shadows, Caravaggio's influence in Venice engendered a more painterly treatment that is seen in *David with the Head of Goliath* of c. 1670 by Girolamo Forabosco (1605–1679). It is probably one of the late paintings by this artist who worked in Venice and Padua, and shows the kind of soft surface modelling that blurs outlines and atmospherically blends together the figure and its surroundings. The victory of the shepherd boy David over the giant Goliath is seen in the Old Testament as an example of the power of God overcoming an apparently greater evil (1 Samuel 17). Forabosco's painting does not show the triumphal aspect of David's victory, but illustrates the Old Testament account almost literally: "And David took the head of the Philistine and brought it to Jerusalem" (1 Samuel 17, 54). The enormous head, wounded by a stone from David's sling, weighs heavily upon the boy. It also symbolizes the weight of a bloody deed that contrasts starkly with the boy's dreamy features. Like the image of carrying, the animal skin he has wrapped around his body is reminiscent of images of Hercules. Here, then, the Old Testament hero and founder of the kingdom of Israel, David, is associated with the mythological hero and founder of civilization. The fluent curves of the boy's body still echo the northern Italian Mannerism of Forabosco's first teacher, Padovanino. He introduced Forabosco to Titian's impasto style, reflected here in open, loose brushwork. Moreover, Titian's legacy is clearly revealed in the painterly manner in which the theme is handled: light and colour, rather than line and perspective, define the painting.

Just how long chiaroscuro remained significant is seen in *St Jerome* by Paolo Pagani (1655–1716) that dates from c. 1685/90. Pagani worked mainly in Venice, Milan and Central Europe as a painter of historical scenes. His Jerome is set in the desert, but contains no elements that suggest an interior. Pagani's reputation rests on his dynamic representation of the human body: here the saint swings his right arm back in a dramatic gesture as he prepares to strike his breast with a stone as an act of penitence, the range of his movement reflecting the violence of his emotions. His powerful body is wedged into a narrow horizontal space that further reinforces the fierceness of his emotional outburst. In the tradition of Caravaggio, Pagani has the saint's naked body gleam in the dark without any visible source of light, thus emphasizing the drama and

realism of the setting. The consequences of Jerome's existence as a hermit are apparent in his dirty fingernails and tangled, greasy hair that lend him human qualities to which the viewer can easily relate. Here naturalism in the manner of Caravaggio is coupled with a highly painterly treatment.

THE CLASSICAL MOVEMENT

The other important movement that shaped Italian Baroque is best defined as 'classical'. It culminated first in the work done in Rome by Annibale Carracci (1560–1609), who was from Bologna. In it, beauty springs from the imitation of nature, the Antique and Raphael. The ideal form, appropriate to the classical formal canon, is derived in a slow process from all the diversity found in nature, the sculpture of Antiquity and Raphael's clearly articulated, lucid compositions serving as models in association with a sense of colour rooted in the Lombard-Venetian tradition.

Pietro Berettini, known as Pietro da Cortona (1597–1669), was another representative of the classical movement. His frescos represent the high point of Baroque ceiling painting in Rome. *The Punishment of Hercules*, recorded from 1746 in the Schönborn-Buchheim Collection, was probably painted in the mid-1630s for a client in the entourage of the Barberini Pope Urban VIII. Andrea Sacchi painted a companion piece in the form of *Hephaestus Handing Achilles' Weapons to Thetis*. Cortona's encounter with the reliefs and sculptures of ancient Rome was a defining moment for him. In his painting, the hero adopts the much-loved pose of the *Apollo Belvedere* (now in the Vatican Museum). This seated Hellenic figure of a muscular naked man, with its anatomically precise delineation of the limbs, its harmonious proportions and complicated shift of the body axis, became a much-studied and varied motif in both painting and sculpture. The sweeping, tense pose accorded with Baroque design principles. In Cortona's case, it was well suited to illustrating the difficult and conflicting situation in which Hercules is presented here. According to Ovid, as punishment for a murder he had committed, Hercules was bound to serve Queen Omphale for a year, wearing women's clothes and doing women's work. The moment when the ancient hero is disarmed is shown here: putti rob him of his lion-skin and club, and equip him with a distaff and a red dress with a costly girdle. Another putto touches the humiliated

GIROLAMO FORABOSCO 1605–1679

David with the Head of Goliath, *c.* 1670

VI.5

PAOLO PAGANI 1655–1716

St Jerome, *c.* 1685/90

VI.2

PIETRO BERETTINI called Pietro da Cortona 1597–1669
The Punishment of Hercules, *c.* 1635
VI.1

hero with the weakening arrow of love. Cortona's practice in handling the monumental dimensions of frescoes shows in the completely natural way the figure of Hercules dominates the painting.
His expression is one of effortless power, achieved in particular
through the skilful modelling of the torso with the light striking it
from the side. The strong, bright colours correspond to the even
distribution of light in the painting.

With these qualities, Cortona's Hercules takes its place in the classical Baroque style established by Annibale Carracci. The so-called
Accademia degli Incamminati (Academy of the Initiated) grew out of
the Bolognese workshop he set up with his cousins Agostino and
Lodovico. Theory and artistic practice were closely linked in this
association of artists and scholars who set new standards in the
training of artists. Systematic teaching above all encouraged life
drawing. Nude models were used to reconstruct Antique and
Renaissance works so as to allow comparison between the ideal
and the real.

Cortona's sympathetic treatment of Hellenistic sculpture brings to
mind the Paragone, a sixteenth and seventeenth-century debate
that questioned whether painting or sculpture was superior. Some
favoured sculpture for its permanence, grandeur and multiple
viewpoints. *The Rape of the Sabine Women* by Sebastiano Ricci
(1659–1734) certainly looks as if it could challenge sculpture in
terms of multiple viewpoints. Ricci was a famous itinerant artist
who again won recognition for Venetian art throughout Europe. In
1701–02, he painted ceiling frescos in Vienna's Schönbrunn
palace, and thus marked the start of Italian artists' dominance in
the imperial capital. *The Rape of the Sabine Women*, like its companion piece the *Battle of the Romans and the Sabines*, was probably painted *c.* 1700 and depicts an episode from Roman history:
by false pretences, Romulus lured the daughters of the Sabines to
Rome and had them raped by his soldiers to secure the continued
existence of the newly founded city. The men of Rome, it seems,
had been unable to find any women willing to marry them!

The story of the rape is told essentially through five couples,
arranged symmetrically as if on a stage. Rather like in a study of
movement, the same motif is shown from various viewpoints. Ricci
modelled his central couple on Gianlorenzo Bernini's marble group
Pluto and Proserpina (Galleria Borghese, Rome). With his variation
on the theme, the artist showed himself to be a match for that
sculpture's multiple viewpoints. His classical view of art placed

SEBASTIANO RICCI 1659–1734

Battle of the Romans and the Sabines, *c.* 1700

VI.8

beauty of pose above the realistic expression of pain. The women's helplessness is translated into graceful gestures, exaggerated in a way that harks back to Mannerist painting of the late sixteenth century. The glowing colours reveal Ricci's examination of the work of Paolo Veronese, while the pastel illumination of his palette already anticipates the Rococo. Ricci marked the start of developments in seventeenth-century Venetian painting: where his brushstrokes become sketchy, they employ thick impasto. With the paintings in such excellent condition, all their painterly subtleties can still be enjoyed.

The *Battle of the Romans and the Sabines* continues the legend of Rome's foundation. Three years after the rape of the Sabines, their fathers and brothers attempt to avenge the injustice. Battle is engaged before the gates of Rome, but the women do not simply stand and watch. Not prepared to lose their next of kin from whatever side in a self-righteous bloodbath, they throw themselves into the battle to separate the combatants.

The dynamism that events confer on these figures is not just a characteristic of Baroque painting, but of sculpture, too. Ricci's paintings can thus be readily compared with contemporary sculptures such as *Diana and Callisto* by Massimiliano Soldani Benzi. Their graceful gestures appear choreographed, their bodies captured in

mid-movement. Both artists express this fleeting quality through erratic poses created by markedly shifting the figures' centres of gravity outwards. The fluttering garments take up the movement and further reinforce it.

Ricci's painting also derives part of its inner tension from the contrast between the men's raw violence and the women's idealized, vulnerable beauty despite their fear and terror. This typically Baroque preference for striking contrasts in form and content is something else painting shares with contemporary sculpture: Soldani Benzi's bronzes, based on Bernini's busts of the *anima beata* and *anima dannata*, and Filippo Parodi's allegories of Virtue and Vice epitomize these contrasts with the same intensity and,

indeed, even the same roles. The beauty of woman here represents the redeemed soul and virtue, while uncontrolled male anger signifies damnation and vice.

After Rome and Bologna, Naples was the most significant centre of Italian painting in the eighteenth century. After the city was conquered by Austrian troops in 1707, Central European art lovers also came to discover Neapolitan Baroque painting, the most influential representative of which was Francesco Solimena (1657–1747). Prince Joseph Wenzel von Liechtenstein (1696–1772) also appears to have valued this painter highly. A portrait, probably dating from *c.* 1720, shows the prince as a young man, and is correctly attributed to Francesco Solimena. Joseph Wenzel may rightly be described as the most brilliant figure in the centuries-long history of the House of Liechtenstein. He started his military career under Prince Eugène of Savoy. In his role as director-general of artillery, his reform of the imperial artillery was of great military significance. Besides his soldierly and organizational abilities, he was also notable for his confident manner and keen sense of style in keeping with his station. His diplomatic career took him to Berlin as imperial ambassador in 1735 and to Paris in the same role from 1738 to 1741. In 1760, Prince Joseph Wenzel acted as marriage broker to the later Emperor Joseph II in Parma, and he also arranged his coronation as Roman Emperor in Frankfurt in 1764.

Already evident in Solimena's painting, Wenzel's pride and his need to demonstrate his social and official status are both expressed even more forcefully in Hyacinthe Rigaud's two portraits from 1740. The baton, armour and sword lying to one side are references to Joseph Wenzel's military career. In typical portrait style, the prince poses in surroundings that are lent imperial character by the two monumental columns in the background. A beam of light illuminates only Wenzel; his presence is that of a man on a stage that here has the appearance of a balcony. The gleaming reflections of harsh light combined with blackish patches of shadow create strong light and dark contrasts that impart tension to the portrait.

THE FORERUNNERS OF NEOCLASSICISM

Joseph Wenzel I von Liechtenstein probably also acquired *Hercules at the Crossroads* and *Venus Presenting Aeneas with Armour Forged by Vulcan* which Pompeo Girolamo Batoni (1708–1787) painted in 1748. Along with Anton Raffael Mengs, Batoni was the outstanding Roman painter of the late eighteenth century. In *Hercules at the Crossroads*, two women appear to the young hero and try to persuade him to follow opposite paths in life. Voluptas, in the figure of Venus, tries to tempt him into a life of pleasure and indulgence, while Virtus, in the figure of Minerva, commends the hard-working, laborious path of virtue. Hercules chooses responsibility and fame, and so this parable is seen as a paradigm for an ethical decision. Batoni captures the moment when Hercules stops to think and weighs up the arguments for and against what is on offer, while putti play with his club and lion-skin. The painter places him at the centre of the composition, heroically naked, between the goddesses.

Minerva, bearing her helmet, shield and lance, points to the temple of fame in the background, at the end of a stony path. Venus sits at Hercules' feet and seductively offers him a rose. Dice, musical instruments and a theatrical mask symbolize the world of pleasure. The figure of Hercules is a standard feature in the iconography of rulers. During the Baroque period, the myths surrounding him were much used by princes for purposes of self-promotion, which probably explains why Prince Joseph Wenzel von Liechtenstein was so interested in the subject.

Batoni's painting tends towards Neoclassicism, for example in the way it strives for clarity in its narrative presentation. The figures were to be intelligible in outline and in three-dimensional form, and at the same time appropriate to their role in the narrative. In examining the ancient Classical canon of the human figure, the beauty of the body was idealized, but beauty of line was also required. The significance of the outline both in terms of aesthetics and meaning begins to emerge in Batoni's picture: the contours of Minerva and Hercules himself show up effectively against the background. The figure of Minerva also demonstrates the other insight that Batoni and his contemporaries applied to Classical Antiquity: the painter may have been guided by a sculpture like the *Medici Venus*, whose harmonious proportions and idealized form embodied the aesthetic ideal of Classical Antiquity. Batoni's Minerva reveals a similarly elegant and organic standing leg – trailing leg motif, equally clear handling of line and concentration on one side. In alluding to the *Apollo Belvedere*, Batoni not only borrowed the pose, but also adopted the design criteria that characterize the Classical sculpture. Formal clarity is encouraged by an even intensity of light, which entails a rejection of comprehensible lighting conditions. Batoni was admired for his delicate use of colour, although his liking for strong local hues provides a suggestion of Neoclassicism.

Venus Presenting Aeneas with Armour Forged by Vulcan is the companion piece to *Hercules at the Crossroads*, and is very similar to it in composition. The blue-clad, armed figure, the putti and Venus are constants in terms of both form and content. The goddess is now central to the composition, in a pose similar to that of Hercules. Following the story in Virgil's *Aeneid*, she offers her mortal son Aeneas weapons forged by Vulcan so that she can be at his side in his imminent and crucial battle against Mezentius. The loving detail in Aeneas' shield is a reminder of Batoni's training as an artist in his father's gold workshop. The meticulous style and the importance of

POMPEO GIROLAMO BATONI 1708–1787

Venus Presenting Aeneas with Armour Forged by Vulcan, 1748

VI.10

POMPEO GIROLAMO BATONI 1708–1787
Hercules at the Crossroads, 1748
VI.11

drawing clearly show that Batoni was originally a miniature painter. Remarkably, he never attempted the monumental dimensions of a fresco, which was highly unusual for a major eighteenth-century painter. He preferred a manageable format, which he handled with care and a profoundly painterly quality, as he does here. This and the lyrical expressiveness of his elegant figures make his compositions decorative in the best sense of the word.

SCULPTURE AND APPLIED ART

GIAMBOLOGNA AND ANTONIO SUSINI

Antonio Susini (doc. 1580–1624) was the most important collaborator of Giambologna (1529–1608), who went to Italy in 1550, where he became one of the most influential sculptors at the court of the Medici in Florence in the second half of the sixteenth century. Susini worked until 1600 in Giambologna's studio. He specialized in bronze casting, particularly of Classical models and after designs by Giambologna. At his death Giambologna left countless designs to Susini, after which bronzes were cast in the latter's own workshop for many years. Giovanni Francesco Susini (c. 1575–1653) learned the art of bronze casting from his uncle Antonio and took over the workshop after Antonio's death.

Antonio Susini's *Rape of a Sabine Woman* draws on Giambologna's large three-figure marble group of the same subject in the Loggia dei Lanzi in Florence, which had been enthusiastically received when placed there in 1583.

Giambologna had worked on the motif for over ten years, first choosing a two-figure format. The figure of the defeated Sabine man adds another facet to the group's multiple viewpoints, and provides a base from which the composition spirals upwards, hence its name of "figura serpentinata": heroically naked, the figure of the Roman soldier rises above the Sabine man cowering on the ground; the Sabine woman tries to wrest herself from the soldier's grasp. He raises her over his shoulders and presents her to the viewer. From whichever angle the group is approached, none seems like a neglected rear view. The counterforces at work here lend the composition a sense of tension that is rapidly transmitted to the viewer. The fact that Gianlorenzo Bernini used this approach for his marble group *Pluto and Proserpina* (Galleria Borghese, Rome), which in its turn inspired Sebastiano Ricci's version of the *Rape of the Sabine Women*, proves the success of this device.

Deianeira Abducted by the Centaur Nessus of c. 1600 is one of the finest casts to a design by Giambologna. He devised the composition in 1577 and entrusted its execution to his most important collaborator, Antonio Susini. This was an unusually popular bronze, as the large number of castings proves: owners of copies included Emperor Rudolf II and the French King Louis XIV. Karl Eusebius, too, delighted in the composition and acquired a cast from Giovanni

Francesco Susini. The older casting, made by his uncle Antonio and of better quality, was acquired for the Princely Collections by Prince Hans-Adam II von und zu Liechtenstein in 2003.

It represents another of the exploits of Hercules: on his way to visit Ceyx, Hercules and his wife had to cross the river Evenus. The centaur Nessus usually helped travellers across, but on this occasion he tried to abduct Deianeira. This is the moment captured by the sculpture. Contemporaries were probably particularly impressed by the formal clash of forces that are pitted against each other. Dashing forward, the centaur turns back to keep hold of Deianeira, who tries to wriggle out of his arms. It is no coincidence that this creates a pose that advantageously presents the woman's beauty to the viewer. The delicate patina lends her skin a soft glow that brings the perfect forms to life.

A PATRON AND COLLECTOR OF ITALIAN BAROQUE SCULPTURE: PRINCE JOHANN ADAM ANDREAS I VON LIECHTENSTEIN

Massimiliano Soldani Benzi (1656–1740) was court artist to the Medici in Florence and one of the best bronze founders in Europe in the late seventeenth century. Domenico Martinelli, architect to Johann Adam Andreas I von Liechtenstein and creator of the Liechtenstein palaces in Vienna, probably introduced the prince to the Florentine artist with whom Martinelli maintained friendly relations. Thus began fourteen years of collaboration. In the 1690s, the prince was preoccupied with the construction of his two palaces in Vienna. Soldani Benzi furnished designs and models for the Garden Palace at Rossau, which local sculptors then executed in monumental format. For the gallery that was planned for the Vienna palace, Johann Adam commissioned the artist to produce a series of bronzes that he was obliged to make personally. From 1694 Soldani Benzi sold the prince copies of masterpieces in the grand duke's gallery in Florence as well as bronzes he had designed himself.

One of Rome's most famous antiquities, rediscovered there in the 1530s, was the *Medici Venus*, named after its later owners. The marble figure is a second-century copy of a bronze original dating from the first century BC. It was taken from Rome to Florence in 1677 and set up in the Tribuna, where it sensuously embodied the outstanding quality of the Medici collections. In 1695, Johann Adam

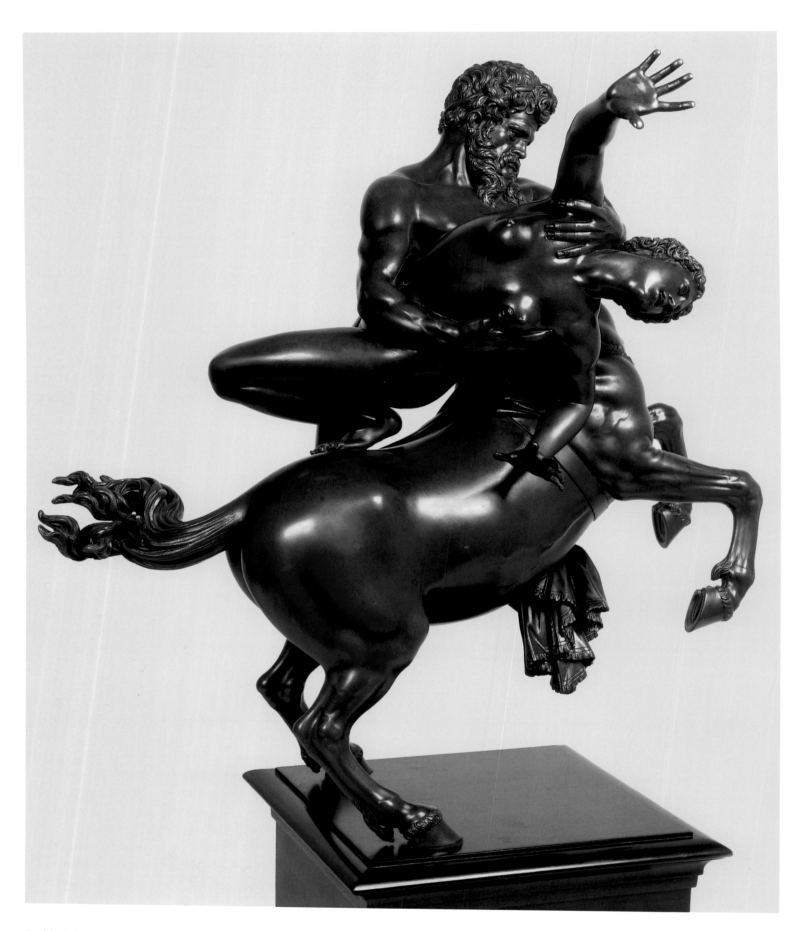

had Soldani Benzi cast a bronze copy the size of the original. It was intended as a companion piece to the *Dancing Faun*, another copy of an Antique piece, and was to be displayed in his City Palace new gallery. According to legend, Venus, the goddess of love and beauty, sprang from the foam of the sea. The dolphin, a symbol of the sea, is thus one of her attributes. Baroque artists modelled representations of the nude body on the *Medici Venus*. "To represent flesh as real flesh" meant animating sculptures. Soldani Benzi worked on his Venus from 1699 to 1702 and paid particular attention to chasing and smoothing its surface so as to lend the body the softness typical of human skin. She was to be "delicata, e mor-

bida come se fusse carne", and this effect was probably better realized in bronze than in stone. The surface sheen enhances the sculpture's sensual appearance. All this effort to produce painterly qualities is reminiscent of the old competition between the art forms. Here sculpture tries to compete with painting's particular qualities. The *Medici Venus*'s harmonious proportions and idealized form embody the aesthetic ideal of Classical Antiquity. They are further distinguished by a subtle balance of mass in the pose, clear lines and concentration on a frontal view. Batoni may have modelled his figure of Minerva in *Hercules at the Crossroads* on a sculpture with similar qualities.

ANTONIO SUSINI doc. 1580–1624
Rape of a Sabine Woman, model, 1581/82
after Giambologna (1529–1608)
VI.14

MASSIMILIANO SOLDANI BENZI 1656–1740
Medici Venus, *c.* 1699–1702
VI.13

MASSIMILIANO SOLDANI BENZI 1656–1740

Diana and Callisto, *c.* 1695/1700

VI.25

In 1702, Massimiliano Soldani Benzi offered to sell Prince Johann Adam Andreas I of Liechtensten two bronze groups he had designed himself: *Diana and Callisto* and *The Judgement of Paris*, dating from *c.* 1695/1700. Johann Adam probably declined, as no more is said about these pieces in subsequent correspondence between the prince and Soldani Benzi. Three hundred years later, the two bronzes found their way into the Princely Collections through the good offices of Prince Hans-Adam II.

Diana and Callisto is a typical Baroque theme in that it captures the moment of a crucial discovery: Diana, the chaste goddess of hunting, notices that one of her companions, all sworn to chastity, is pregnant. Callisto had allowed herself to be seduced by Zeus. The goddess sees this as treachery, and disowns Callisto. Half-naked and bewildered, she attempts to conceal what has long since been revealed. Another companion is clearly very curious and wants to assure herself that the reproof is justified, and tries to push away the arm that Callisto has placed protectingly over her stomach. Yet another companion realizes the seriousness of the situation: she raises her hand on Callisto's behalf to fend off the devastating

judgement pronounced by Diana. This revelation of a secret is strikingly underlined by Diana herself as she lifts her own veil. By pointing conspicuously, she exposes Callisto's nakedness all the more vividly. Soldani Benzi has skilfully captured the narrative context of this particular moment.

Some time later, in 1705, Soldani Benzi offered the prince casts of two busts by Gianlorenzo Bernini, the outstanding sculptor of the seventeenth century who crucially contributed to the development of the Italian Baroque style with his talents as an architect and painter. The busts of the *Anima Beata* and *Anima Dannata*, dating from 1619, are expressive studies of two psychological states: the redeemed and the condemned soul. The representation of an extreme psychological state is as typical of Baroque art as is the representation of opposites in paired works. Bernini rose to the challenge with great intuitive power; indeed, his fame rests on it. The redeemed soul raises its head and looks towards heaven as a sign that it has found grace with God. Its gentle features become an external image of inner beauty. There is also a sense of innocence in the large eyes and parted lips. While Bernini's originals stood in a church, San Jacopo degli Spagnoli in Rome, Soldani Benzi's busts were intended for a secular space, Adam's City Palace in Vienna. The charm of the bronze lies not merely in its expressive face, but also in the decorativeness of its curly hair and floral wreath. Soldani Benzi produced his own version of the model. He was more concerned with details that he chased meticulously. Compared with the softness of the stone version, Soldani Benzi lends his bronze a sharper sculptural quality.

For the *Anima Dannata*, Bernini chose the distorted face of a man staring at the floor, his mouth gaping, his eyes wide open, his brow deeply furrowed. His clearly visible teeth and curled-up tongue reinforce his aggressive expression; his state of damnation causes his hair to stand on end. Terror is expressed in these features. The inspiration for Bernini's facial study was the naturalism of Caravaggio whose successors return again and again to the unbridled power of aggression in their work, as in Valentin de Boulogne's *Cheerful Company with Fortune-teller* where in a similarly expressive way rage distorts the faces of the brawlers.

Bernini's *Anima Dannata* was also the source of inspiration for the *Allegory of Vice* by Filippo Parodi (1630–1702). Prince Johann Adam Andreas I held the sculptor in particularly high regard, and acquired several marble busts from him. The *Allegory of Vice* shows

MASSIMILIANO SOLDANI BENZI 1656–1740
The Judgement of Paris, *c.* 1695/1700
VI.26

MASSIMILIANO SOLDANI BENZI 1656–1740

Bust of the Anima Beata, 1705–07

after Gianlorenzo Bernini (1598–1680)

VI.21

MASSIMILIANO SOLDANI BENZI 1656–1740

Bust of the Anima Dannata, 1705–07

after Gianlorenzo Bernini (1598–1680)

VI.22

FILIPPO PARODI 1630–1702
Allegory of Virtue, 1684/94
VI.19

FILIPPO PARODI 1630–1702
Allegory of Vice, 1684/94
VI.20

a man bound at the chest and arms, writhing in his chains and shouting loudly. Parodi takes Bernini's allegory further and sets the figure in a narrative context. The figure represents the giant Tityus, the traditional personification of vice punished. According to Homer (*Odyssey* 11, 576ff.), Tityus, a son of Zeus, assaulted the goddess Leto, and was hunted down by her children Apollo and Artemis. After his death, he had to atone for his crime in the underworld: he was chained to the ground while a pair of vultures tore at his liver that always grew back. Parodi's sculpture casts a spell on the viewer with its realistic portrayal of tormented suffering. With his face distorted with pain, his mouth open wide and tearing at his hair, Tityus rages against his fate. He becomes a symbol of lack of self-control, kept in check only by chains. The plinth takes on the function of a pillory, giving the impression that vice is quite literally being pilloried here.

Parodi also made a companion piece to this bust, albeit one not associated with Bernini: with the luxuriant laurel wreath in her hair, the sun-disc at her breast and the small spear under her right arm, this woman represents an *Allegory of Virtue*. Her closed lips make her face seem serious and calm in one. Her upward gaze from pupil-less eyes suggests the timelessness of her power. Parodi's bust is modelled on High Baroque portrait busts like those of Bernini or Algardi in which the lavish folds of a garment envelop the torso, concealing the transition between plinth and bust. Two attested dates are crucial when dating Parodi's busts: in 1684, Prince Johann Adam Andreas I von Liechtenstein started to expand his family collection, while in 1694, he wrote enthusiastically to his favourite painter, Marcantonio Franceschini, that he would never have found better sculptors than Parodi and Mazza. The busts must have been produced within this ten-year period.

Console table, Italy, *c.* 1730
VI.15

PAINTINGS

VI.1 / p. 191
Pietro Berettini, called Pietro da Cortona (1597–1669) *The Punishment of Hercules*,
c. 1635
Oil on canvas; height 300 cm, width 200 cm
Schönborn-Buchheim Collection, inv. no. G 067
Provenance: 1746 listed in Friedrich Karl von Schönborn's gallery catalogue

VI.2 / p. 189
Paolo Pagani (1655–1716)
St Jerome, c. 1685/90
Oil on canvas; height 118 cm, width 149 cm
Inv. no. GE 3
Provenance: 1812 acquired by Prince Johann I von Liechtenstein from Georg Radl in Vienna

VI.3 / p. 180
Jean Valentin de Boulogne (baptized? 1591–1632)
Cheerful Company with Fortune-teller, 1631
Oil on canvas; height 190 cm, width 265 cm
Inv. no. GE 2131
Provenance: 1631 commissioned by Fabrizio Valguarnera of Madrid; 1675 exhibited in the church of Sta. Maria di Constantinopoli; 1713 in the sales catalogue of the collection of William III of Orange; 1719 in the collection of Lothar Franz, Count of Schönborn, from the 1970s on permanent loan to the Art Gallery of Ontario; 2003 acquired by Prince Hans-Adam II von und zu Liechtenstein

VI.4 / p. 185
Follower of Gerrit van Honthorst (1592–1656)
St Jerome
Oil on canvas; height 109 cm, width 139 cm
Inv. no. GE 292
Provenance: acquired by Prince Johann I von Liechtenstein

VI.5 / p. 188
Girolamo Forabosco (1605–1679)
David with the Head of Goliath, c. 1670
Oil on canvas; height 121 cm, width 97 cm
Inv. no. GE 38
Provenance: 1733 identified by seal as entail

VI.6 / p. 183
Theodoor Rombouts (1597–1637)
The Denial of St Peter
Oil on canvas; height 94 cm, width 206 cm
Signed bottom left: T ROMBOVS.
Inv. no. GE 628
Provenance: 1789 acquired by Prince Alois I von Liechtenstein from Herr Roys

VI.7 / p. 186
Johannes van Bronchorst (1627–1656)
St Bartholomew, 1652
Oil on canvas; height 137 cm, width 94 cm
Signed and dated right on column base: Johan van Bronchorst F 1652
Inv. no. GE 119
Provenance: 1805 first recorded in the Princely Collections

VI.8 / p. 192
Sebastiano Ricci (1659–1734)
Battle of the Romans and the Sabines, c. 1700
Oil on canvas; height 197 cm, width 303 cm
Inv. no. GE 243, companion piece to GE 245
Provenance: 1819 acquired by Prince Johann I von Liechtenstein from Johann Querci with the *Rape of the Sabine Women* (GE 245)

VI.9 / p. 195
Sebastiano Ricci (1659–1734)
The Rape of the Sabine Women, c. 1700
Oil on canvas; height 197 cm, width 303 cm
Inv. no. GE 245, companion piece to GE 243
Provenance: 1819 acquired by Prince Johann I von Liechtenstein from Johann Querci with the *Battle of the Romans and the Sabines* (GE 243)

VI.10 / p. 198
Pompeo Girolamo Batoni (1708–1787)
Venus Presenting Aeneas with Armour Forged by Vulcan, 1748
Oil on canvas; height 99 cm, width 74 cm
Signed and dated bottom right: P.B. 1748.
Inv. no. GE 163, companion piece to GE 161
Provenance: presumably acquired by Prince Joseph Wenzel von Liechtenstein with GE 161, as it is listed in Dallinger's 1805 inventory, with reference to a lost 18th-century inventory, in which the pictures are mentioned as being privately owned by Joseph Wenzel in the Herrengasse palace

VI.11 / p. 199
Pompeo Girolamo Batoni (1708–1787)
Hercules at the Crossroads, 1748
Oil on canvas; height 99 cm, width 74 cm
Signed and dated bottom right: P.B. 1748
Inv. no. GE 161, companion piece to GE 163
Provenance: presumably acquired by Prince Joseph Wenzel von Liechtenstein with GE 163, as it is listed in Dallinger's 1805 inventory, with reference to a lost 18th-century inventory, in which the pictures are mentioned as being privately owned by Joseph Wenzel in the Herrengasse palace

VI.12 / p. 197
Francesco Solimena (1657–1747)
*Portrait of Prince Joseph Wenzel von
Liechtenstein, c. 1720*
Oil on canvas; height 126 cm, width 101 cm
Inv. no. GE 1209
Provenance: probably commissioned by Prince
Joseph Wenzel von Liechtenstein

SCULPTURE AND APPLIED ART

VI.13 / p. 207
Massimiliano Soldani Benzi (1656–1740)
Medici Venus, c. 1699–1702
after the antique bronze, with red-brown lacquer
patina; height 158 cm
Inv. no. SK 537, companion piece to SK 541
and SK 573
Provenance: 1695 commissioned from the artist
with *Dancing Faun* (SK 541) by Prince Johann
Adam Andreas I von Liechtenstein; both acquired
1702

VI.14 / p. 206
Antonio Susini (doc. 1580–1624)
Rape of a Sabine Woman, model, 1581/82
after Giambologna (1529–1608)
Bronze, red-yellow paint darkened by oxidization
to opaque brown; height 59 cm
Inv. no. SK 115
Provenance: before 1963 Baron Gustave de
Rothschild in Paris; 1963 auction at Christie's in
London; before 1980 in the collection of Baron
Paul Hatvany; 1980 acquired by Prince Franz
Josef I von und zu Liechtenstein at auction at
Christie's in London

VI.15 / p. 215
Console table, Italy, *c.* 1730
Lime, coniferous wood, gilded, marbled;
height 92 cm, width 184 cm, depth 74 cm
Inv. no. MO 908

VI.17 / not illus.
Giovanni Francesco Susini (*c.* 1575–1653)
Hercules and Antaeus, 2nd quarter of
17th century
after Giambologna (1529–1608)
Bronze with golden-red lacquer patina;
height 40 cm
Inv. no. SK 559
Provenance: listed in Prince Karl Eusebius von
Liechtenstein's Quardaroba inventory of 1658

VI.18 / pp. 204–05
Antonio Susini (doc. 1580–1624)
Deianeira Assaulted by the Centaur Nessus, c. 1600
after Giambologna (1529–1608)
Bronze; height 43 cm (excluding socle)
Inv. no. SK 914
Provenance: 2003 acquired by Prince
Hans-Adam II von und zu Liechtenstein

VI.19 / p. 212
Filippo Parodi (1630–1702)
Allegory of Virtue, 1684/9
Marble; height 77 cm
Inv. no. SK 15, companion piece to SK 11
Provenance: commissioned with the *Allegory of
Vice* (SK 11) by Prince Johann Adam Andreas I
von Liechtenstein

VI.20 / p. 213
Filippo Parodi (1630–1702)
Allegory of Vice, 1684/9
Marble; height 77 cm
Inv. no. SK 11, companion piece to SK 15
Provenance: commissioned with the *Allegory of
Virtue* (SK 15) by Prince Johann Adam Andreas I
von Liechtenstein

VI.21 / p. 210
Massimiliano Soldani Benzi (1656–1740)
Bust of the Anima Beata, 1705–07
after Gianlorenzo Bernini (1598–1680)
Bronze with golden-red patina;
height 39 cm
(excluding socle)
Inv. no. SK 516, companion piece to SK 517
Provenance: 1705 suggested as a subject by
Prince Johann Adam Andreas I von Liechtenstein
with *Anima Dannata* (SK 517), 1707 acquired

VI.22 / p. 211
Massimiliano Soldani Benzi (1656–1740)
Bust of the Anima Dannata, 1705–07
after Gianlorenzo Bernini (1598–1680)
Bronze with golden-red patina; height 40 cm
(excluding socle)
Inv. no. SK 517, companion piece to SK 516
Provenance: 1705 suggested as a subject by
Prince Johann Adam Andreas I von Liechtenstein
with *Anima Beata* (SK 516), 1707 acquired,
1920 disposed of from the Princely Collections;
1929 auction in Berlin; 1993 re-acquired,
by Prince Hans-Adam II von und zu Liechtenstein

VI.23 and VI.24 / not illus.
Nicolaus Pacassi (1716–1790)
Two console tables, Vienna, *c.* 1740
Oak, partly gilded, marble (top);
height 77 cm, width 152 cm, depth 88 cm
Inv. nos. MO 20, MO 21
Provenance: from the Savoy Damenstift in Vienna
(foundation of Countess Theresia Anna Felicitas
von Savoy-Carigan, *née* von Liechtenstein),
1902 recorded in the Garden Palace at Rossau

VI.25 / p. 208
Massimiliano Soldani Benzi (1656–1740)
Diana and Callisto, c. 1695/1700
Bronze with dark-brown lacquer patina;
height 41 cm
Inv. no. SK 910
Provenance: 1702 offered to Prince Johann Adam
Andreas I von Liechtenstein with the *Judgement of
Paris* (SK 911) by Soldani Benzi, but not bought;
2002 acquired by Prince Hans-Adam II von und zu
Liechtenstein at auction at Christie's in London

VI.26 / p. 209
Massimiliano Soldani Benzi (1656–1740)
The Judgement of Paris, c. 1695/1700
Bronze, dark brown painted patina; height 38 cm
Inv. no. SK 911
Provenance: 1702 offered to Prince Johann Adam
Andreas I von Liechtenstein with *Diana and Callisto*
(SK 910) by Soldani Benzi, but not bought; 2002
acquired by Prince Hans-Adam II von und zu
Liechtenstein at auction at Christie's in London

PRINTS AND DRAWINGS

VI.27 / not illus.
Matthäus Günther (1705–1788)
Diana and Actaeon
Pen and brown ink on paper, blue and grey wash
on black chalk; height 27 cm, width 42 cm
Inv. no. GR 2022
Provenance: 1863 acquired in Leipzig; Venato
auction in Cologne; 1983 acquired by Prince
Franz Josef II von und zu Liechtenstein

GALLERY VII

PETER PAUL RUBENS, ADRIAEN DE FRIES AND MASSIMILIANO SOLDANI BENZI

PETER PAUL RUBENS'S DECIUS MUS CYCLE

The prince of Liechtenstein who had the Viennese Garden Palace built, Johann Adam Andreas I (1657–1712), in 1693 succeeded – with the help of the Antwerp dealer Marcus Forchoudt – in acquiring the monumental Decius Mus cycle by Peter Paul Rubens (1577–1640). A gallery was built for this sequence of pictures in the Vienna City Palace shortly afterwards, with no less an artist than Giovanni Giuliani commissioned to carve ornate cartouches for the matching frames. When the Garden Palace at Rossau opened as a picture gallery in 1807, the monumental cycle became the centre-piece of the collections exhibited there. It is now returning to the large gallery in which it was on show for almost 150 years.

The name Peter Paul Rubens has become synonymous with Flemish Baroque. It is rare for a painter to be so highly esteemed as he was, even in his lifetime. He worked for kings and princes, export-ing Flemish Baroque across Europe in an operation that required a large, well-organized workshop. Rubens also undertook delicate diplomatic missions on behalf of the courts of Mantua and Brussels, and was thus able to draw on new ideas from other European gal-leries. He backed the Catholic Church's religious mission in Flanders with the altarpieces he created. Rubens was a multi-talented artist: he worked as a sculptor and architect as well as a painter, and also produced book illustrations, engraved reproductions and even tap-estries. He was considered one of the greatest connoisseurs of his day as a collector of art and antiquities, and this also lent his depic-tions of historical scenes a high degree of authenticity.

Rubens went to Italy in 1600, shortly after being accepted as an independent master in the Guild of St Luke in Antwerp. Vincenzo I Gonzaga, Duke of Mantua, an outstanding connoisseur and patron of painting, recognized the then 27-year-old's talent, appointed him court painter and had him travel all over Italy for study purposes. Drawings of statues and sarcophagi reveal that Rubens took a close interest in Antique sculpture. His work as a painter was influenced by Carracci, Caravaggio and Michelangelo, and by the way Venetian painters handled colour.

On his return to Antwerp, Rubens became court painter to the gov-ernor of the Spanish Netherlands, Archduke Albert and his wife, the Infanta Isabella Clara Eugenia. In the same year, 1609, he set up his workshop, which expanded rapidly in the extremely productive period that followed. This studio became a highly profitable com-mercial enterprise, selling pictures all over Europe. Rubens con-tributed in no small way to the development of art through the mass distribution of his work in the form of copperplate engravings.

The cycle of paintings covering all aspects of the victory and death of the Roman consul Decius Mus is the earliest of Rubens's cycles. He happened to feel that complex, substantial works of this kind were appropriate to his talents: "I confess that my heart calls me to create great works, rather than small curiosities. Each to his own. My talent is such that no enterprise, be it ever so large and mani-fold in its object, could possibly have been greater than my confi-dence in myself", Rubens wrote to William Trumbull in 1621. The artist's wide-ranging humanistic education was clearly very useful to him in his artistic analysis of ancient history. Rubens was a member of a circle of scholars around Justus Lipsius, a classical philologist and exponent of Neo-Stoical philosophy. Rubens's study of Antique art, and of Roman sculpture in particular, clearly left traces in his formal language.

Rubens created the Decius Mus cycle, which consists of eight pic-tures, as cartoons for tapestries. It was natural that he became involved in this field as well, as the most costly and virtuoso weav-ing was produced in his native Flanders. Other than the information that Rubens provided himself, nothing else is known about the patrons who commissioned the Decius Mus cycle; he said they were Genoese nobility. Rubens had visited Genoa on several occasions during his eight-year stay in Italy, and also maintained personal con-tacts there later. The contract, dated 9 November 1616, between the Brussels tapestry weavers and merchants Jan Raes and Frans Sweerts and the Genoese merchant Franco Cattaneo has survived. It agreed to the delivery of two series with the same content; it also obliged Rubens to prepare the cartoons, and made him responsible for final checks on the quality of the tapestries themselves. Work had already started on the tapestries by late 1617. The reversed layout of the compositions confirms that the paintings really were intended for this purpose. To the best of our knowledge, Rubens was the first artist to prepare elaborate oil paintings as a basis for tapestries, even though this was not stipulated in his contract. This procedure did not subsequently catch on, however. Of course it is clear that the more detailed the model was, the easier it was to achieve painterly qualities in a textile medium. Tapestry manufactur-ers had already begun in Rubens's day to lay their technically defined design principles aside, and were just beginning to compete

GIOVANNI GIULIANI 1663–1744
Cartouche framing the Decius Muscycle, 1706

PETER PAUL RUBENS 1577–1640
Decius Mus Relating his Dream
VII.1

directly with painting. The two first versions of the Decius Mus series in the elder Jan Raes's Brussels factory were apparently so successful that about twenty more series were woven during the seventeenth century in various studios and various versions. In the nineteenth century, the Princely Collections were fortunate enough to acquire several tapestries, presumably one of the two Editiones principes by Jan Raes.

Confusion was caused by the fact that Giovanni Pietro Bellori in his Vita attributed the paintings to Anthony van Dyck; Johann Adam did in fact buy the series believing them to be masterpieces by van Dyck. The contract and the surviving oil sketches, however, make it clear that the design at least is by Rubens. He had his workshop complete some sections, which is hardly surprising given the cycle's total area of almost 80 square metres. Rubens organized his workshop on the Italian model: the *invenzione*, the invention of a composition, counted as the actual artistic achievement. Trained assistants could then use the master's drawings to complete the work, which Rubens then retouched.

Van Dyck was the only one of Rubens's assistants ever to be mentioned by name. The Decius Mus cycle is the first recorded collaboration between Rubens and van Dyck, who is known to have been working in Rubens's studio while the cycle was in preparation. He must have had to copy the master's own style as it is impossible to identify his own contribution to the pictures. Scholars are thus divid-

ed over the extent to which van Dyck was involved in the execution of this series.

DECIUS MUS RELATING HIS DREAM

The heroic death of the Roman consul Decius Mus is an *exemplum virtutis*, an example of a particularly virtuous act. It is cited on several occasions in Classical literature, but Rubens was the first artist to translate into painting Livy's account of the war between the Romans and the Latins in the year 340 BC (*Ab urbe condita*, Book VII, chapters 6, 9 and 10).

The inhabitants of the plain of Latium had risen against Roman dominance and challenged the Romans to a battle; the Latins had a superior army. The Roman supreme commanders encamped at Capua, the consuls Decius Mus and Titus Manlius, had the same dream: the army whose commander fell in battle would carry the victory. Rubens restricts his narrative to the hero of his sequence of paintings: in the first picture, Decius comes before his army alone to describe his dream. Titus Manlius does not appear until the last picture. The artist shows Decius Mus standing on a pedestal in an imperious pose. Standard-bearers from different units have assembled in front of him in diverse battle-dress. An oil sketch for this painting in the National Gallery, Washington, DC, shows that Rubens

considered enriching the secular story with allusions to the gods of Antiquity by having Jupiter's eagle hover above the consul's head like a divine protector. He chose to omit the mythological touches from the final version, however.

Rubens followed a pictorial formula that was common in Antiquity, the *adlocutio*, in which the commander addresses his legates and tribunes from a raised position. Depictions of this type can be found on triumphal monuments in Rome such as the Arch of Constantine and Trajan's Column. Rubens used relief scenes from the latter as a direct model. He approved of reworking ancient images creatively,

but stressed in his essay "De Imitatio Statuarum" that a sympathetic understanding of the model was also necessary. He went on to say that it was advisable "that judicious use be made of them, that in no way permits the stone to show." Rubens's translation of the relief scene into the medium of painting does retain the frieze-like character, but the symmetrical arrangement of the figures in the ancient model is submitted to a lively variation, involving a large number of movements. The open painterly style provides an additional element of dynamism.

THE INTERPRETATION OF THE VICTIM

According to Livy, shortly before the battle the gods were asked which of the two consuls should sacrifice himself for the sake of Rome. Their fate was to be divined from the entrails of two bulls. Part of the liver of the bull that Decius Mus had sacrificed looked like a severed head. Decius Mus acknowledged that this meant death for him. The moment he realizes this is the subject of the second picture in the series.

Decius Mus recoils from the news in horror and places his hands on his breast to protect himself. His consternation can also be read from the uncertain, unstable position of his legs. Yet the old High Priest (*haruspex*) confirms the judgement by pointing to the bull's liver, leaning forward and fixing the consul's gaze in a way that expresses clearly that this is his destiny. An elaborate sacrificial ceremony is staged around these two principal figures, set outside the commander's tent. An altar has been placed there, and Titus Manlius's bull is just being led up to it. A musician and sacrificial assistants accompany the sacred proceedings. Decius Mus's bull is lying dead on the ground in the foreground, and next to it is a golden bowl, full of the sacrificial creature's blood. The commander's retinue stand by uneasily, watching the events incredulously. The cloaks of the priest and the consul – the bearer of the tidings and the man receiving the news respectively – and the symbolic sacrificial blood are all in red, the strongest colour in the picture.

Clearly Rubens drew on Raphael's handling of a similar subject, *The Bull Sacrificed at Lystra* for his handling of Livy's text. Rubens took the opportunity in Genoa in 1604 to study and copy the famous sequence of cartoons for the tapestries in the Sistine Chapel. Raphael used Antique portrayals of a sacrificial scene here, also including a relief from Trajan's Column in Rome.

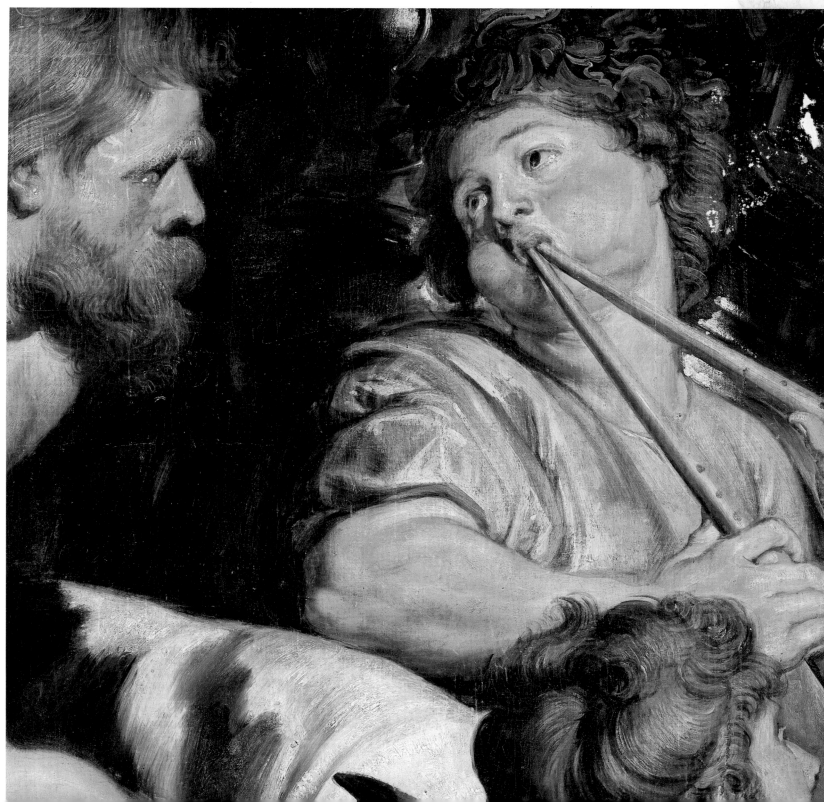

PETER PAUL RUBENS 1577–1640
The consecration of Decius Mus
VII.2

THE CONSECRATION OF DECIUS MUS

After Decius Mus has heard his fate pronounced by the High Priest of Rome, he receives the last rites from him and recites a formulaic prayer for death: "Janus, Jupiter, Father Mars, ye household gods, ye newly adopted gods, ye gods of Rome, ye heavenly ones under whose power we and the enemy stand, and ye gods of the dead, I beg and implore ye: give the people of the city of Rome superior might and victory, but unleash fear, havoc and death on their enemies. As I have expressly promised here, on behalf of the state of Rome, the army and its legions, I now commend the legions of the enemy and myself to the gods of death and to the earth, as sacrifice." The Romans called this solemn rite *devotio*. As was custom, Decius Mus stands with both feet on an arrow and receives the High Priest's blessing, with his voluminous red toga, drawn over his head, emphasizing the devout inclination of his body. The priest's brocade robe, embroidered in gold and gleaming in the light, reinforces the solemnity of the scene. Incidentally, in his depiction of material qualities, Rubens takes up an old Netherlandish tradition here. The poses of the others involved in the scene relate to the two central figures: a witness enveloped in his robe accompanies the priest, while two soldiers lead the commander's war horse in from the right. The horse inclines its head deeply, thus repeating Decius's gesture of humility.

PETER PAUL RUBENS 1577–1640
The Dismissal of the Lictors
VII.5

THE DISMISSAL OF THE LICTORS

"After the prayer for death, Decius Mus ordered his lictors to go to Titus Manlius and immediately to tell his fellow consul that he had commended himself to death on behalf of the army. Then the consul, wrapped in the toga he had slung over his shoulder and fully armed, leaped on to his horse and charged in among the enemy." Livy describes the moment of farewell away from the battle, which is already raging. Rubens chooses not to place the scene in a narrative context, but isolates it.

Rubens based the imposing figure of the hero armed for battle on the Roman statue of *Mars Utor*. The original from the temple of the same name in the Forum Augusteum in Rome is lost, but a Roman copy survives (Museo Capitolino, Rome). Rubens borrowed the basic features of the head, the helmet and armour types. The commander's silhouette stands out impressively against the background. His pose expresses both the present and the future: he stands with his left foot firmly on the ground, dismissing the lictors with an eloquent gesture, but his right hand is already placed on his horse and his right foot is poised to mount. The lictors' inclined heads show that they are reluctant to obey the order; they take a final look over their shoulders to bid farewell to their consul. They bear his emblems of office, the so-called fasces (bundles of rods tied around an axe), away with them. Decius Mus thus also bids farewell to his office as consul before his last service to the people of Rome. The view between the parting figures reveals a landscape that Rubens added as a reminder of his stay in Italy, the ruined Roman Temple of Minerva Medica.

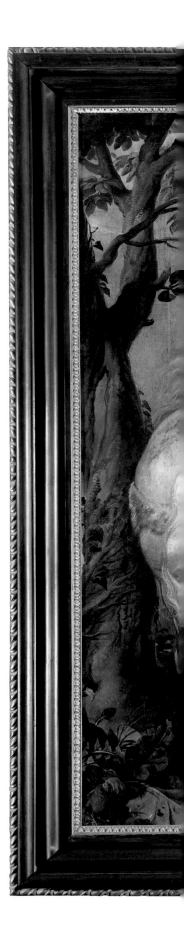

THE DEATH OF DECIUS MUS

The cycle climaxes in the death of Decius Mus, set amidst the Romans' battle against the Latins. Decius Mus allows himself to be run through by a lance before the ranks of the attacking Romans and the fleeing Latins. His white stallion rears as he slips off its back. The animal's elegant pose resembles the levade, a figure in dressage, which was considered a royal art in Rubens's day. The pose thus appears ennobling, underlining the grandeur of the consul's state of mind as expressed in his sacrificial death. His face transfigured, Decius Mus sees the heavens open above him, and rays of divine light touch him as a sign that he is the chosen one. His imminent death is vividly expressed by his sinking to the ground to join the corpses of the fallen lying there.

In an oil sketch for this picture (Museo del Prado, Madrid), Rubens also gave physical form to the idea of being the elect: a genius appears from the clouds, bringing a laurel wreath and a palm branch to the dying man. Yet Rubens decided not to personify the reward of victory in this way in his painting. He staged Decius Mus's sacrificial death as a saint's martyrdom: we are reminded of depictions of the Fall of Saul, in which the saint falls from his horse when dazzled by the sudden blaze of divine light. This fall does not kill Saul, but marks a crucial turning point in his life. The transfigured gaze towards heaven at the moment of death had already been formulated exemplarily by the ancients, as in the Hellenistic sculpture of the *Dying Alexander* in Florence (Uffizi). It was seen as an *exemplum doloris*, an object-lesson in bearing pain heroically at the moment of death. Rubens here fuses Christianity and Antiquity both intellectually and pictorially. This was entirely acceptable to the Catholic Church, especially as St Augustine had expressly singled out the example of Decius Mus as a model for Christians in his treatise *De civitate dei* (V, 18).

The principles underlying the composition of the central group, a dense mass of horses and warriors locked together, and the figure of the white stallion, are derived from the ideas of Leonardo da Vinci. Rubens was able to study textbooks by Leonardo in Arezzo, although he was unable to see the original of the earlier artist's *Battle of Anghiari*, as the fresco was destroyed shortly after its completion. Rubens nonetheless probably saw composition studies or copies of the executed work, which has come down to us in the form of his own drawn copy (Musée du Louvre, Paris). Rubens

adopted the design principle of piling up the corpses of horses on
top of the bodies of the dead warriors, which effectively forms a
base for the group. The structure of the picture, defined by rising
diagonals, is typical of his early work.

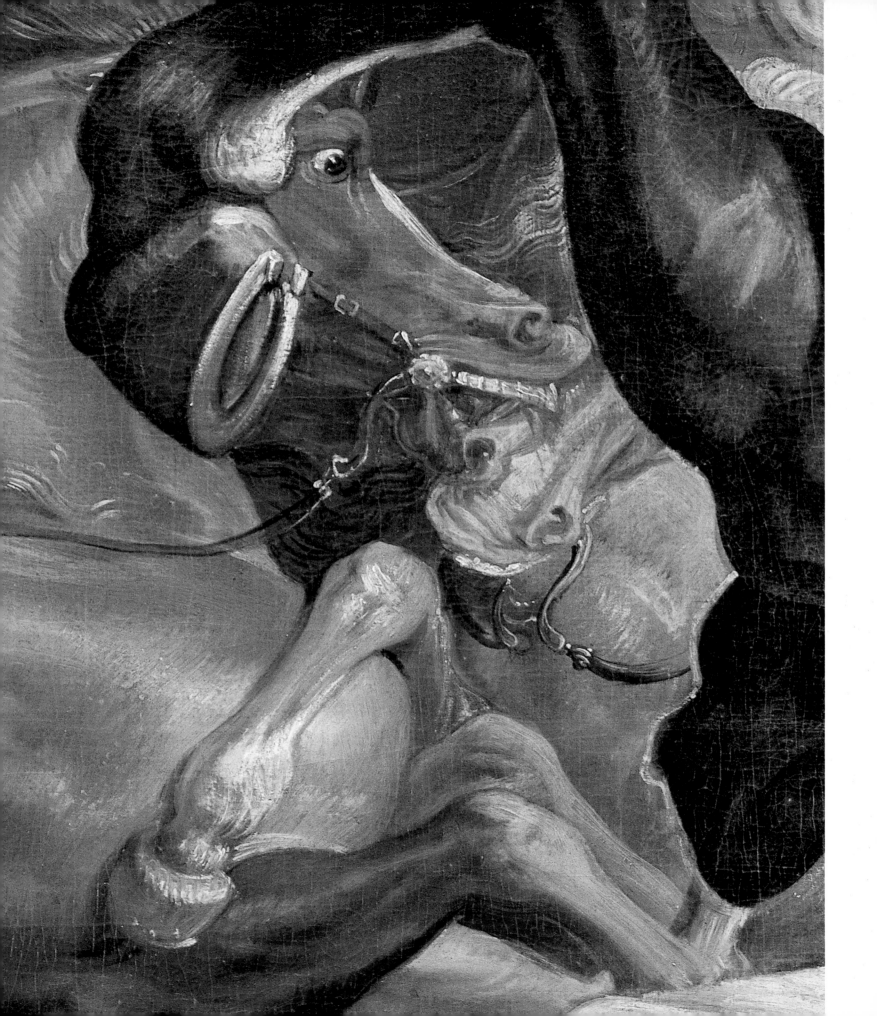

PETER PAUL RUBENS 1577–1640
The Obsequies of Decius Mus
VII.4

THE OBSEQUIES OF DECIUS MUS

Livy reports that the body of Decius Mus was discovered among a pile of the slain enemy the next day, and Titus Manlius then arranged a solemn funeral. He supplies no further detail about the funeral ceremony itself, however. Rubens presents it as a magnificent victory celebration, with Decius Mus lying in the centre of a richly carved, gilded couch. The second consul, whom fate has spared, now appears for the first time: he points to the captured weapons and severed enemy heads being piled up as a sign of victory. Wood for the cremation is being cut to the sound of tubas blown by soldiers in the background, and precious booty in the form of gold and silver vessels and jewellery is being carried in. Humbly bowed, fettered Latins sit in the foreground, their womenfolk dragged in by their hair and clothes. Rubens borrowed these motifs from the *Gemma Austea* (Kunsthistorisches Museum, Vienna), a world-famous and equally valuable ancient cameo showing a Roman victory celebration. Rubens had clearly examined it closely, as evinced by his drawn copy (St. Annen-Museum, Lübeck). In the painting, all this emotionally charged activity is concentrated to provide a contrast with the motionless corpse of Decius Mus in the centre. His red toga, which marks him as consul, has identified him throughout the narrative; it is now also associated with the hero's blood sacrifice.

Detail
VII.4

THE *ENTRE FENÊTRES*

Tapestry series were intended to dress entire rooms. For this reason they often included narrow hangings, so-called *entre fenêtres*, which could be used to cover areas of wall left exposed between windows or at the side of doors. The contract dated 9 November 1616 between Jan Raes the Elder and Franco Cattaneo for the Decius Mus series also lists three narrow hangings of this kind: a trophy and two figures, interpreted as Victoria and Virtus. Rubens placed the last two together in the same picture when drafting the cartoons, and probably left the painting entirely to the workshop. The *entre fenêtres* are not part of the narrative, but comment on the heroic deed of Decius Mus. Virtus is the embodiment of military virtue, the basis for the victory in the form of Victoria.

The Roman custom was to construct a trophy – a tower of captured weapons as a victory monument – on the battlefield itself. It could be that Rubens took his ideas from coins of the imperial period: he piles weapons, armour, battle standards and even as speared enemy head on top of each other. The captured gold, in magnificent vases, is collected in front.

What qualities make the Decius Mus cycle unique? Firstly, the monumentality of the almost life-size figures. As they closely relate to viewers' own proportions, they draw them into the narrative as a matter of course. The actions of the figures in the foreground, and the way the composition opens up to viewers, mean that they almost become part of the dramatic events. The strong colours and the painterly approach, which is very rich in places, intensify our empathy with the unfolding story, told in a sequence of tranquil and turbulent scenes. The fact that the whole cycle is hung in close proximity, literally enclosing viewers, provides a Baroque 'all-round experience' that is not to be found in this form anywhere else in Vienna.

THE ASSUMPTION OF THE VIRGIN
BY PETER PAUL RUBENS

The Assumption of the Virgin was one of the most frequently depicted subjects by Rubens for altarpieces. According to the Apocrypha
and Jacob of Voragine's *Golden Legend*, the Apostles assembled at
the Virgin's empty tomb and witnessed her Assumption. The Church
was interested in representing this tradition pictorially because it
vividly demonstrated physical resurrection, the *assumptio corporis*,
and thus also the immortality of the Virgin's bodily existence.
Protestants denied the cult of the Virgin because they valued the
significance of the Mother of God for the redemption of mankind
less highly than the Roman Catholic Church. The latter responded
by promoting the full worship of the Virgin, seeing images of her
Assumption as a promise to the faithful that they would, like her, be
raised unto the Kingdom of God.

Rubens first addressed the subject in 1611, when a high altarpiece
for Antwerp Cathedral was commissioned from him. The picture
was completed in 1620, and was finally placed in the Jesuit church;
it is now in the Kunsthistorisches Museum in Vienna. The picture in
the Princely Collections is Rubens's last and most monumental version of the Assumption. The circumstances of the commission are
only partly known: the brothers Charles and Johannes Angelus
Schotte ordered the picture for the high altar of the Carthusian
church in Brussels in honour of their parents Theodorus Schotte
and Elisabeth van den Brandt. Their father's death in 1629 and the
publication in 1639 of an engraving of it provide a rough framework
for dating the work. A more precise estimate is gained from seeing
the picture in the context of the artist's oeuvre; a date of around
1637 is suggested.

A Rubens painting of the Assumption is mentioned as being in the
possession of the princes of Liechtenstein as early as 1643; it was
very probably the present one. A short while later, the painting was
in use as a high altarpiece in the Valatice parish church, the seat
of the Liechtenstein family in their extensive estates in south
Moravia. In 1764 the picture was replaced with a copy by the
painter and gallery inspector Vincenzio Fanti, and the original taken
to the new picture gallery in Vienna, where it became one of the
city's major attractions.

This *Assumption*, of which two oil sketches have survived (Courtauld
Institute Galleries, London, and Yale University Art Gallery, New
Haven, CT), differs from earlier compositions in certain formal
aspects, some of which have a bearing on the painting's iconography and content. The Mother of God is now portrayed kneeling,
which seems to express humble joy rather than triumph. The palms
of her hands are turned upwards, which could be interpreted, as in
Raphael's *Transfiguration of Christ*, as a sign of supernatural transformation. This interpretation also accommodates the unusual
choice of the colour white for her dress, which is normally in canonical blue. The colour white symbolizes Christ's transfiguration in
St Mark's Gospel. Rubens uses this symbolic colour here to illustrate Mary's rebirth as she ascends to heaven. He repeats the
Madonna's gesture in the figures of saints Peter and John. Since
Titian's famous *Assunta*, the Assumption of the Virgin (Santa Maria
Gloriosa dei Frari, Venice), those involved in divine events have
raised their arms as an expression of astonishment at such inconceivable happenings. But the parallel gestures used by Rubens also
convey the Apostles' inner involvement.

The bravura painterly approach suggests that Rubens painted the
picture entirely himself. Economical in the use of his painterly
resources, his layers of paint are very thin in some places. We must
remember that the painting, as an altarpiece, was to be seen from
a great distance. The spontaneous, fluent brushwork shows the
enormous certainty the older Rubens had achieved. His admiration
of Titian was no secret, and in fact his handling of paint does reveal
some parallels with the work of the Venetian artist, who even
inspired Rubens's choice of colours. The light palette makes the
Assumption typical of Rubens's late work, before he started to use
darker colours, and to apply paint impatiently, almost hastily, in his
very last years.

PETER PAUL RUBENS 1577–1640
The Assumption of the Virgin, *c.* 1637
VII.8

ANTHONY VAN DYCK AS A FELLOW PAINTER IN RUBENS'S STUDIO

The painting of *St Jerome* came into being at roughly the same time that van Dyck was working in Rubens's studio on the Decius Mus cycle. While related to a composition by Rubens, it also gives an idea of van Dyck's individual painterly approach. Anthony van Dyck (1599–1641) first trained under Hendrik van Balen, then worked in Peter Paul Rubens's studio roughly between 1617 and 1620. The two men must have been close even earlier, as the portrait of Rubens by his younger colleague painted *c.* 1613/15 shows (Kimbell Art Museum, Fort Worth, TX). The two artists became friends at a seminal time for van Dyck. The pupil did indeed follow his mentor's style in the pictures he worked on for Rubens, but he was already starting to develop his distinctively personal approach to portrait painting.

Saint Jerome is depicted here as a hermit in the remote Chalcis desert in Syria, where he was seeking atonement and reflection. His body seems to have been emaciated by the sun; a lavishly billowing coat in the glowing red of his cardinalship envelops him and forms a dramatic contrast with the barren surroundings. The lion that befriended him when he removed a painful thorn from its paw lies beside him on the ground. In undisturbed peace, also symbolized by the sleeping animal, Jerome is shown working on his translation of the Bible that would make his name.

This picture is van Dyck's earliest large-format religious composition. He painted three variations on the subject of Jerome between 1615 and 1618. The painting in the Princely Collections, dating from *c.* 1615/16, takes up Rubens's picture of the penitent Jerome painted shortly before (Gemäldegalerie, Staatliche Sammlungen Dresden), which in its turn forms the basis of a famous sketch by Titian for Santa Maria Nuova in Venice (now Pinacoteca di Brera, Milan). Van Dyck was familiar with this from a copy drawn by Rubens. The young painter combined the two themes of Jerome as a scholar in his study and the penitent saint in the desert by setting the Church Father's translation activities, usually performed in an interior, in the wilderness.

Van Dyck did take the body pose defined by Rubens for the figure of the saint, but distanced himself from the latter's idealized representation by not showing a muscular hero, but a man who was clearly ageing, bowed in the literal sense of the word. He was often compared to Caravaggio with this naturalistic approach. Van Dyck chose an open style of painting that creates a sketchy impression with its apparently spontaneous brushwork, while Rubens inclined towards an enamelled smoothness in his handling of paint. Van Dyck also differs from Rubens in his earthier colours that show the influence on him of Venetian art.

THE BRONZES OF ADRIAEN DE FRIES AND GIOVANNI FRANCESCO SUSINI

The two incomparable, almost life-size figures *Christ in Distress* and *St Sebastian* by Adriaen de Fries (1556–1626) form a distinguished prelude to the Princely Collections. This famous sculptor and draughtsman came from Holland. He first accepted a commission for Emperor Rudolf II (1552–1612) in 1593, and was made official court sculptor in 1601. De Fries worked almost exclusively on bronze sculptures for the emperor, only in exceptional cases accepting private commissions, usually for religious subjects, from court officials in the emperor's immediate entourage. The most important of them was Karl von Liechtenstein (1569–1627). He was appointed to the influential office of Master of the Household shortly after his conversion to Catholicism in 1599, and was made a hereditary prince in 1608.

The first prince of the House of Liechtenstein commissioned the bronze figure of *Christ in Distress* from de Fries in 1607, as an inscription on the plinth states. This impressive, almost life-size devotional statue eloquently expresses a crucial passage in the story of Christ's Passion in which the Son of God has sacrificed himself to redeem mankind. This is identified by a Biblical quotation from Paul's first Epistle to the Corinthians: "EMPTI ESTIS PRETIO MAGNO" (For you are bought dearly). Christ, sitting on a rock, folding his hands and asking for mercy, seems to be waiting for Pilate's men. The suffering to come shows clearly in his face. This sculpture derives its expressive force from the contrast between Christ's suffering features and the classical beauty of his athletic body. The pose with crossed legs goes back to a famous woodcut of the Man of Sorrows by Albrecht Dürer. This choice of model is no coincidence, as Dürer's art was greatly admired again at the imperial court around 1600. But the shape of the sculpture reveals the sculptor's experience of Hellenistic work like the *Belvedere Torso* and the work of Michelangelo, which he had studied in Florence and Rome. Contemporaries took the *Torso* to represent Hercules. As the ancient hero was also interpreted as a prefiguration of Christ, it seemed entirely logical to adopt some formal criteria of his sculptural type when creating a figure of Christ. Rubens presented the Roman consul Decius Mus as a Christian martyr, and here we see this fertile relationship between religious and secular iconography working in the opposite direction.

The thrusting scale of the seated, ultimately highly complicated, pose for the figure of Christ is typical of de Fries, and results from carefully balanced opposing twists of the body. De Fries does not try to make the flesh look natural in his three-dimensional modelling of the body: the arched surface of the athletic chest goes well beyond the natural anatomy of muscles and sinews, forming an almost abstract structure. De Fries exploits the natural qualities of bronze as a material and shows them to their best advantage. A few years after the *Christ in Distress*, de Fries made another statue for the prince, that of *St Sebastian*. It is not known why, or for where, the two statues were made. It is possible that they were intended for the recently built parish church in Valtice, though it was not consecrated until 1671. The sculptures could have stood in the palace chapel in Valtice in the mean time, which was refurbished in 1604. It is probable that the two figures and Rubens's picture for the high altar came to Vienna in 1764, to be shown in the gallery there. Joseph Bauer's exhibition plans dating from 1815 show the bronzes as companion-pieces. A hand-written note identifies the Valtice parish church as the place of provenance for the two figures.

Legend has it that St Sebastian was a captain of the praetorian guard at the imperial court of Diocletian. He ignored an existing ban and adopted the Christian faith, converting many to Christianity. The Roman emperor had him tied to a tree and executed by Numidian archers. De Fries does not show the dramatic climax of the events, but the moment before the saint is martyred. His helplessness is indicated by his bonds and his unprotected nakedness, which again presents an opportunity to show viewers an ideal body. He is seen standing on the ground from which a tree grows. The figure needs the tree for reasons of statics: the figure does not derive its tension solely from its emphatic *contrapposto*, a pose in which one part of a figure twists or turns away from another, but also from the fact that the central part of the body leans forward. One hand is bound above the figure's head, the other behind its back, which lends an S-shaped curve to the whole figure. The three-dimensional modelling of the muscles has been appositely described as a "nervously vibrating surface". This inorganic design principle, which was already becoming apparent in the *Christ in Distress*, is even more strongly in evidence here. The differences between the figure of St Sebastian and the earlier devotional image can be seen as a stylistic development and thus date the saint to the later period between

ADRIAEN DE FRIES 1556–1626
St Sebastian, 1613/15
VII.11

ADRIAEN DE FRIES 1556–1626
Christ in Distress, 1607
VII.10

1613 and 1615. Despite their distance in time, the two works are related in terms of their implications: as a type, the Sebastian is similar to the theme of the *Scourging of Christ*. And as well as this, the two are linked by the representation of an ideal body with an expression of fearful anticipation of suffering to come.

The son and successor of Karl I von Liechtenstein, Prince Karl Eusebius (1611–1684), probably bought the small bronze figure of *St Sebastian* that is first listed in the 1658 inventory: *St Sebastian Tied to a Tree*. The figure adopts an unusual pose, though the sense of absorption in suffering is related to contemporary depictions of the descent from the Cross, thus triggering associations with the suffering of Christ. The composition probably dates from the early seventeenth century and was made in Italy. The bronze in the Princely Collections is probably the earliest of many replicas showing the popularity of this pictorial invention. It stands out from them because of its careful treatment of details and fine chasing. The saint wears a loincloth in most casts, which leads us to assume that the Liechtenstein cast once had one too, though it was separate, and perhaps made of silver. The description of the figure in the inventory also suggests that the saint was bound to the tree-trunk with (silver) cords.

David with the Head of Goliath probably dates from somewhere between 1625 and 1630. It is an independent creation by Susini and Prince Karl Eusebius von Liechtenstein probably acquired it during his visit to Florence in 1636. In contrast to Giambologna's work, with its multiple viewpoints, Susini concentrated on a head view. He followed an Antique model: Susini borrowed the seated motif from the marble statue of Mars Ludovisi, and varied it slightly. His own small bronze copy also shows that he had studied this ancient sculpture. In his interpretation of the theme, Susini highlighted the contrast between the slender boyish youth, with his delicate, even features, and the crude, heavy head of Goliath, which with its wild hair and ungainly forms is an element that represents the whole of the terrifying figure of the giant. David presents his naked, unprotected body in a markedly open pose, thus giving viewers an idea of the danger he faces. The Philistine's enormous sword demonstrates Goliath's physical superiority, overcome by David. The boy seems to be reflecting about his incredible achievement. His melancholy expression is related to Forabosco's painting, which also plays with the contrast between the youth's elegance and the giant's coarseness.

Giovanni Francesco Susini's *Laocoön* is considered to be his most beautiful copy of an Antique work in the Princely Collection. According to Virgil's *Aeneid*, the Trojan priest Laocoön and his sons were killed by two large snakes. The goddess Athena wanted to punish him with death for having warned the Trojans against accepting the gift the Greek, the Wooden Horse of Troy. The Hellenistic marble group of this subject achieved fame after its excavation in Rome in 1506. Even in ancient times the *Laocoön* was considered to be an *exemplum doloris*, a model representation of suffering. In the seventeenth century, the Church recommended that artists use the figure of Laocoön in their depictions of Christ. The ancient bronze reduction was probably also an interpretation of the fragmented original. A characteristic feature of the Liechtenstein group is the narrow base, above which the figures seem to thrust more strongly away from each other, thus enhancing the work's inner tension. The chasing with a red-gold patina gives the surface a rare refinement.

GIOVANNI FRANCESCO SUSINI *c.* 1575–1653
David with the Head of Goliath, 1625/3
VII.32

GIOVANNI FRANCESCO SUSINI *c.* 1575–1653
Laocoön, 2nd quarter of 17th century
after an Antique model
VII.28

Detail
VII.28

GIOVANNI FRANCESCO SUSINI *c.* 1575–1653
The Farnese Bull, 2nd quarter of 17th century
after an Antique model
VII.33

MASSIMILIANO SOLDANI BENZI 1656–1740
Bacchanalia, 1695–97
VII.24

THE BRONZES OF MASSIMILIANO SOLDANI BENZI FOR PRINCE JOHANN ADAM ANDREAS I VON LIECHTENSTEIN

It was probably in 1994 that the architect Domenico Martinelli introduced Massimiliano Soldani Benzi and Prince Johann Adam Andreas I von Liechtenstein to each other. That same year Soldani Benzi made a wax model of a bacchanal for the prince, who wished to have "qualche scherzo bacchanale". Even though this was smashed "into a thousand pieces" while being taken to Vienna, Johann Adam still ordered the relief as a bronze casting in 1695. Bacchus, the god of wine and vegetation, married Ariadne on Naxos. Soldani Benzi shows the two as a loving couple, giving themselves up to the enjoyment of wine amidst their noisy retinue: Silenus, who had been entrusted with Bacchus's education, has drunkenly fallen off his ass among the crowd of scrapping putti. Maenads dance around the statue of Priapus, the god of nature. The whole scene is enriched with symbols of love such as kissing snakes, billing doves etc.

Soldani Benzi himself counted this relief as one of his best works, and indeed the complex composition offers a creative reworking of many ideas from Antique and contemporary sculpture. The denseness of the design achieves almost painterly qualities, and these are shown to particular advantage by Soldani Benzi's sophisticated chasing techniques. The different nuances in the surface structures display considerable virtuosity, resulting in a complex play of light. Soldani Benzi's characteristically translucent, reddish-gold patina makes for the perfect finish.

Also in 1695, Soldani Benzi delivered to Prince Johann Adam the first of nine bronze casts of Antique marble busts of Roman emperors, philosophers and famous women as decoration for his palaces. In the same year he also sent him a wax model of a relief on approval. He recommended to the prince that it should be executed in gilded bronze, and thought that the composition would be a suitable devotional image to be hung near a bed. It is possible that this was the *Christ on the Mount of Olives* of *c.* 1722. The unusual iconography is not based on the gospel: Christ, praying throughout the night on the Mount of Olives, faints into the arms of two angels. The composition relates stylistically to the bronze relief of *Peace Embraces Justice*, the first work by this sculptor that the prince bought for his collection, in 1694. Both compositions are dominated by a dynamic diagonal around which the figures are grouped.

MASSIMILIANO SOLDANI BENZI 1656–1740

The Triumph of Virtue over Vice, *c.* 1701–06

after Giambologna (1529–1608)

VII.34

The Triumph of Virtue over Vice of *c.* 1701–06 is a copy by Soldani Benzi of Giambologna's famous marble group *Florence Triumphs over Pisa*, which stood in the Palazzo Vecchio in Florence. Giambologna designed the group in 1564 for the wedding of Francesco de' Medici as a companion piece to Michelangelo's stone sculpture *The Victory*, which in the seventeenth century was often also called *The Triumph of Virtue over Vice*. Soldani Benzi's bronze was among the twelve copies of the most famous statues of Florence, which he offered to Prince Johann Adam in 1706. The personification of Florence, or an allegory of Virtue, overcomes a man cowering on the ground, and represents either vice or the city of Pisa, according to interpretation. The triumph is expressed by a gesture of physical dominance. In a comparable way, the Roman soldier in *The Obsequies of Decius Mus* reveals his superiority over a captured Latin, whom he pushes to the ground. Thus in both sculpture and painting the theme is interpreted very physically. The violence of the preceding battle can still be discerned in the effort the victor needs to hold his struggling opponent in check.

MASSIMILIANO SOLDANI BENZI 1656–1740

Christ on the Mount of Olives, *c.* 1722

VII.35

MASSIMILIANO SOLDANI BENZI 1656–1740

Time Reveals the Truth, 1695–97

VII.30

MASSIMILIANO SOLDANI BENZI 1656–1740

Peace Embraces Justice, 1694

VII.31

MASSIMILIANO SOLDANI BENZI 1656–1740

Bust of Agrippa

From a series of nine busts after Antique models

VII.13

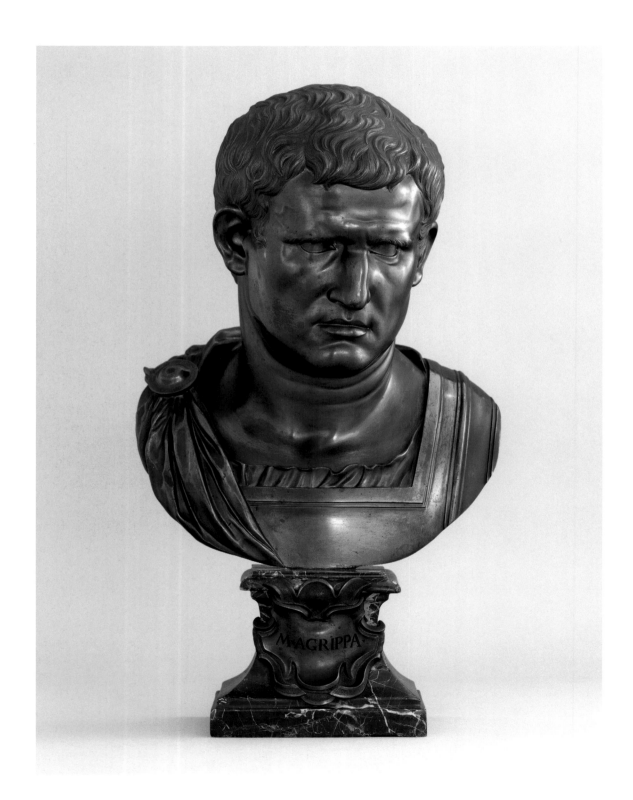

MASSIMILIANO SOLDANI BENZI 1656–1740

Bust of Hadrian

From a series of nine busts after Antique models

VII.18

MASSIMILIANO SOLDANI BENZI 1656–1740

Bust of Vitellius

From a series of nine busts after Antique models

VII.15

MASSIMILIANO SOLDANI BENZI 1656–1740
Bust of Augustus
From a series of nine busts after Antique models
VII.16

MASSIMILIANO SOLDANI BENZI 1656–1740

Bust of Cicero

From a series of nine busts after Antique models

VII.12

MASSIMILIANO SOLDANI BENZI 1656–1740
Bust of Seneca
From a series of nine busts after Antique models
VII.19

MASSIMILIANO SOLDANI BENZI 1656–1740

Bust of Faustina the Younger, 1695

From a series of nine busts after Antique models

VII.17

MASSIMILIANO SOLDANI BENZI 1656–1740

Bust of Marcus Aurelius as a Boy, 1707/12

From a series of twelve busts after Antique models

VII.36

ROBERT LE LORRAIN 1666–1743
Bust of Thetis, *c.* 1710/20
VII.37

ROBERT LE LORRAIN 1666–1743
Bust of Apollo, *c.* 1710/20
VII.38

CLAUDE LE FORT DU PLESSY doc. 1707–1757
Console table, Vienna, *c.* 1717
VII.26

Console table, Bohemia, *c.* 1720/30
VII.20

PAINTINGS

Peter Paul Rubens (1577–1640)
*The Death and Victory of the Roman Consul
Decius Mus*, 1616/17
Provenance: 1616 contract between Peter Paul
Rubens and the tapestry manufacturers Jan Raes
and Frans Sweerts in Brussels and the dealer
Franco Cattaneo from Genoa; 1661 the cycle
falls into the possession of the painter and collector Carel de Witte, Gonzales Conques and Jan
Baptist van Eyck in Antwerp (*The Interpretation
of the Victim* and probably *Trophy* did not come
into their possession until after 1661, both most
likely bear the imperial seal), 1692 in van Eyck's
estate inventory in Antwerp (*The Dismissal of the
Lictors* cannot be traced definitely in the estate
inventory); 1693 acquired by Prince Johann
Adam Andreas I von Liechtenstein from the
dealer Marcus Forchoudt in Antwerp, exhibited
in a gallery in the Liechtenstein City Palace in
Bankgasse in Vienna, from 1807 to 1945 the
cycle has remained in its current location

VII.1 / p. 225
The Consecration of Decius Mus
Oil on canvas; height 294 cm, width 278 cm
Inv. no. GE 47

VII.2 / pp. 232–33
Decius Mus Preparing for Death
Oil on canvas; height 284 cm, width 336 cm
Inv. no. GE 49

VII.3 / pp. 242–43
The Death of Decius Mus
Oil on canvas; height 289 cm, width 518 cm
Inv. no. GE 51

VII.4 / pp. 250–56
The Obsequies of Decius Mus
Oil on canvas; height 289 cm, width 515 cm
Inv. no. GE 52

VII.5 / pp. 236–37
The Dismissal of the Lictors
Oil on canvas; height 286 cm, width 343 cm
Inv. no. GE 50

VII.6 / pp. 228–29
The Interpretation of the Victim
Oil on canvas; height 294 cm, width 412 cm
Inv. no. GE 48

VII.7 / p. 257
The Trophy
Oil on canvas; height 287 cm, width 125 cm
Inv. no. GE 53

VII.8 / p. 260
Peter Paul Rubens (1577–1640)
The Assumption of the Virgin, c. 1637
Oil on canvas; height 501 cm, width 351 cm
Inv. no. GE 80
Provenance: commissioned between 1629 and
1639 by Charles and Johannes Angelus de
Schotte for the high altar of the Carthusian
church in Brussels, before 1643 presumably in
the Carthusian church in Brussels; 1643 acquired
by Prince Karl Eusebius von Liechtenstein, from
1671 altar painting in the Valtice parish church,
1764 moved to the Liechtenstein gallery in the
City Palace in Bankgasse, Vienna, from 1815
to 1945 in the gallery of the Garden Palace at
Rossau

VII.9 / p. 263
Anthony van Dyck (1599–1641)
St Jerome, c. 1615/16
Oil on canvas; height 158 cm, width 131 cm
Inv. no. GE 56
Provenance: 1701 acquired by Prince Johann
Adam I von Liechtenstein from the dealer Marcus
Forchoudt in Antwerp

SCULPTURE AND APPLIED ART

VII.10 / p. 267
Adriaen de Fries (1556–1626)
Christ in Distress, 1607
Bronze with brown natural patina; height 149 cm
Signed and dated on the back of the plinth:
ADRIANUS FRIES HAGENSIS/FECIT 1607
Inscription on the left-hand side of the socle:
EMPTI/ESTIS/PRETIO/MAGNO
Inscription on the back of the socle:
CAROLVS/ALIECHTEN/STEIN. RVD.
II./IMP. CEAS. PE/AUC. SACRI./PALATI/PRAEFEC-
TUS/DEDICAVIT/.AN. P. C. N./MD   VII.
Inv. no. SK 515
Provenance: 1607 commissioned by Prince Karl I
von Liechtenstein, after 1671 with *St Sebastian*
(SK 562), probably placed in the Valtice parish
church, since 1807 in the Liechtenstein Garden
Palace at Rossau

VII.11 / p. 266
Adriaen de Fries (1556–1626)
St Sebastian, 1613/15
Bronze with olive-brown natural patina; height
200 cm
Signed on the side of the base plinth: ADRIANVS
FRIES HAGIENSIS BATAVVS
Inv. no. SK 562
Provenance: 1607 commissioned by Prince Karl I
von Liechtenstein, after 1671 with *Christ in
Distress* (SK 515), probably placed in the Valtice
parish church, since 1807 in the Liechtenstein
Garden Palace at Rossau

Massimiliano Soldano Benzi (1656–1740)
Eight busts after Antique models, 1695
Provenance: 1694/95 acquired by Prince Johann
Adam Andreas I von Liechtenstein as part of the
entire commissioned series

VII.12 / p. 288
Bust of Cicero
Bronze with red-gold lacquer patina;
height 60 cm (including socle)
Inscription on the cartouche: M. CICERO
Inv. no. SK 554

VII.13 / p. 284
Bust of Agrippa
Bronze with red-gold lacquer patina;
height 63 cm (including socle)
Inscription on the cartouche: AGRIPPA
Inv. no. SK 504

VII.14 / not illus.
Bust of Faustina the Elder
Bronze with red-gold lacquer patina;
height 59 cm (including socle)
Inscription on the cartouche: FAVSTINA. SEN.
Inv. no. SK 548

VII.15 / p. 286
Bust of Vitellius
Bronze with red-gold lacquer patina;
height 59 cm (including socle)
Inscription on the cartouche: VITELLIVS
Inv. no. SK 563

VII.16 / p. 287
Bust of Augustus
Bronze with red-gold lacquer patina;
height 62 cm (including socle)
Inscription on the cartouche: AVGVSTVS
Inv. no. SK 513

VII.17 / p. 290
Bust of Faustina the Younger
Red-gold lacquer patina; height 58 cm
(including socle)
Inscription on the cartouche
Inv. no. SK 529

VII.18 / p. 285
Bust of Hadrian
Bronze with red-gold lacquer patina;
height 68 cm (including socle)
Inscription on the cartouche: HADRIANVS
Inv. no. SK 571

VII.19 / p. 289
Bust of Seneca
Bronze with red-gold lacquer patina;
height 60 cm (including socle)
Inscription on the cartouche: SENECA
Inv. no. SK 560

VII.20 / p. 296
Console table, Bohemia, *c.* 1720/30
Lime, poplar, coniferous wood, gilded;
height 71 cm, width 140 cm, depth 81 cm
Inv. no. MO 926
Provenance: *c.* 1930 recorded in the Small
Marble Hall in Valtice Palace

VII.21 / not illus.
Console table, Bohemia, *c.* 1720/30
Lime, poplar, coniferous wood, gilded;
height 71 cm, width 140 cm, depth 81 cm
Inv. no. MO 925
Provenance: 1845 recorded in the Small Marble
Hall in Valtice Palace

VII.22 and VII.23 / not illus.
Two ceremonial vases with lids, 19th century
Porphyry; height 55 cm
Inv. no. SK 812

VII.24 / pp. 274–75
Massimiliano Soldani Benzi (1656–1740)
Bacchanalia, 1695–97
Bronze with red-gold lacquer patina;
height 56 cm, width 78 cm
Inv. no. SK 827
Provenance: 1697 commissioned by Prince
Johann Adam Andreas I von Liechtenstein

VII.25 / p. 277
Massimiliano Soldani Benzi (1656–1740)
Child Bacchante, Clipping Cupid's Wings, 1695
Bronze with brown-black lacquer patina;
height 31 cm, width 35 cm
Inv. no. SK 123
Provenance: 1695 acquired by Prince Johann
Adam Andreas I von Liechtenstein from the artist;
disposed of in the late 19th century; Amelia
Madel in Vienna; 1966 Heim Gallery in London;
1969–73 part of an English private collection
loaned to the Birmingham City Art Gallery; 1976
Heim Gallery in London; 1978 acquired by Prince
Franz Josef II von und zu Liechtenstein

VII.26 / p. 294
Claude le Fort du Plessy (doc. 1707–1757)
Console table, Vienna, *c.* 1717
Walnut, dark brown varnish, marble (top);
height 80 cm, width 148 cm, depth 80 cm
Schönborn-Buchheim Collection, inv. no. M 8
Provenance: since *c.* 1717 in the Garden Room
of Schloss Schönborn in Göllersdorf

VII.27 / not illus.
Claude le Fort du Plessy (doc. 1707–1757)
Console table, Vienna, *c.* 1717
Walnut, dark brown varnish, marble (top);
height 80 cm, width 148 cm, depth 80 cm
Schönborn-Buchheim Collection, inv. no. M 8
Provenance: from *c.* 1717 in the Garden Room
of Schloss Schönborn in Göllersdorf

VII.28 / p. 271
Giovanni Francesco Susini (c. 1575–1653)
Laocoön, 2nd quarter of 17th century
after an Antique model
Bronze, dark red-gold lacquer patina;
height 54 cm, width 44 cm, depth 21 cm
Inv. no. SK 526
Provenance: listed in Prince Karl Eusebius von
Liechtenstein's Quardaroba inventory of 1658

VII.29 / p. 269
Anonymous
St Sebastian, Italy, before 1658
Bronze; height 54 cm
Inv. no. SK 557
Provenance: listed in Prince Karl Eusebius von
Liechtenstein's Quardaroba inventory of 1658

VII.30 / p. 282
Massimiliano Soldani Benzi (1656–1740)
Time Reveals the Truth, 1695–97
Bronze with red-gold lacquer patina;
height 64 cm, width 45 cm
Inv. no. SK 536, companion piece to SK 540
Provenance: 1695 commissioned by Prince
Johann Adam Andreas I von Liechtenstein and
acquired in 1697

VII.31 / p. 283
Massimiliano Soldani Benzi (1656–1740)
Peace Embraces Justice, 1694
Bronze with yellow-brown lacquer patina;
height 62 cm, width 45 cm
Inv. no. SK 540, companion piece to SK 536
Provenance: 1694 acquired by Prince Johann
Adam Andreas I von Liechtenstein from Soldani
Benzi

VII.32 / p. 270
Giovanni Francesco Susini (c. 1575–1653)
David with the Head of Goliath, between 1625/30
Bronze with matt brown varnish on red-gold
patina; height 30 cm
Signed on the left-hand edge and the back
of the stool: FRAN. SVSINI F.
Inv. no. SK 565
Provenance: listed in Prince Karl Eusebius von
Liechtenstein's Quardaroba inventory of 1658

VII.33 / p. 273
Giovanni Francesco Susini (c. 1575–1653)
The Farnese Bull, 2nd quarter of 17th century
after an Antique model
Bronze with red-gold lacquer patina;
height 42 cm, width 38 cm, depth 37 cm
Inv. no. SK 551
Provenance: listed in Prince Karl Eusebius von
Liechtenstein's Quardaroba inventory of 1658

VII.34 / p. 278
Massimiliano Soldani Benzi (1656–1740)
The Triumph of Virtue over Vice, c. 1701–06
after Giambologna (1529–1608)
Bronze, dark brown lacquer patina; height 31 cm
Inv. no. SK 275
Provenance: 1706 offered to Prince Johann
Adam Andreas I von Liechtenstein by Soldani
Benzi; bronze cast in J. Woodward's collection in
Oxford; 1963 Julius Goldschmidt; from 1963 to
1980 in Baron Paul Hatvany's collection; 1980
acquired by Prince Franz Josef II von und zu
Liechtenstein at auction at Christie's in London

VII.35 / p. 280
Massimiliano Soldani Benzi (1656–1740)
Christ on the Mount of Olives, c. 1722
Bronze with golden-brown lacquer patina;
height 65 cm, width 45 cm
Inv. no. SK 912
Provenance: 1695 Soldani Benzi sends a wax
model of the relief to Prince Johann Adam
Andreas I von Liechtenstein; bronze cast in 1722

by the artist, acquired by Filippo Martelli in Florence; 1767 shown in the Santissima Annunziata
in Florence; until 1813 in the possession of the
Martelli family in Florence; 2003 acquired by
Prince Hans-Adam II von und zu Liechtenstein

VII.36 / p. 291
Bust of Marcus Aurelius as a Boy, 1707/12
From a series of twelve busts after Antique models
Red-gold lacquer patina; height 36 cm
Inv. no. SK 523
Provenance: acquired by Prince Johann Adam
Andreas von Liechtenstein

VII.37 / p. 292
Robert le Lorrain (1666–1743)
Bust of Thetis, c. 1710/20
Bronze with dark brown lacquer patina;
height 43 cm
Inv. no. SK 904, companion piece to SK 903
Provenance: before 1889 with *Bust of Apollo*
(SK 903) in the possession of Duc de Talleyrand
at Château de Valency; both acquired in 1899 by
Edouard Chappy at the Talleyrand auction at the
Galerie Georges Petit; 1986 acquired by Prince
Franz Josef II von und zu Liechtenstein

VII.38 / p. 293
Robert le Lorrain (1666–1743)
Bust of Apollo, c. 1710/20
Bronze with dark brown lacquer patina;
height 39 cm
Inv. no. SK 903, companion piece to SK 904
Provenance: before 1889 with *Bust of Thetis*
(SK 904) in the possession of Duc de Talleyrand
at Château de Valency; both acquired in 1899 by
Edouard Chappy at the Talleyrand auction at the
Galerie Georges Petit; 1986 acquired by Prince
Franz Josef II von und zu Liechtenstein

GALLERY VIII

THE EARLY WORK OF PETER PAUL RUBENS

RELIGIOUS SUBJECTS AND HISTORY PAINTING

The Princely Collections hold over thirty paintings by Peter Paul Rubens (1577–1640); they focus on his early work. Rubens's visit to Italy, from which he returned in 1608, represented a hiatus in his creative output. His confrontation with Antiquity is reflected in his monumental compositions with three-dimensional figures. His study of Italian painting was reflected in his powerful colours, which are partly due also to a new painting technique. His pictorial structure is often determined by dynamic diagonals, as in the *Lamentation*. Around this time, Rubens liked to work on mythological and historical themes for which there were no pictorial models and that were seldom depicted after him such as the Decius Mus cycle and *The Discovery of the Infant Ericthonius*, which had never featured in a monumental painting before Rubens. His historical pictures achieve a high degree of authenticity because of his precise knowledge of ancient authors. The following five paintings all date from between 1613 and 1622, and offer a representative cross-section of the Flemish master's early work.

MYTHOLOGICAL SUBJECTS

Peter Paul Rubens presented his *Venus in Front of the Mirror* as the ultimate symbol of beauty. The picture was painted around 1613/14 and shows a rear view of the goddess of love at her toilet. She is aware of the viewer in a mirror that frames her face like a portrait. Great play is made of the sensual reproduction of her skin and silky hair, which is further enlivened by the contrast with the dark-skinned maidservant. The few costly accessories, otherwise decorative additions to elaborate clothing, emphasize the figure's nakedness. The sensual qualities of the painting are created by Rubens's subtle painterly approach. He alternates sketchy brushstrokes, drawn over the ground like a transparent veil, with compact areas, painted in great detail.

One particularly attractive feature of the picture is the contrast between the goddess's encounter with the viewer, which seems to occur almost by chance, and the representation of her beauty, as if conceived for a spectator. The mirror that Cupid holds up for the goddess reveals an additional level of meaning: the reflection of Venus, which reveals her beauty to the viewer, becomes a symbol of painting that competes with nature to produce an image that is as real as possible. Rubens modelled his work on compositions by Titian and Veronese that combine Venus and a mirror, and probably also offered this possible interpretation.

Satyr and Maid with Fruit Basket, a painting from the Schönborn-Buchheim Collection, is Rubens's reply to the question of how we should imagine Baroque *joie de vivre.* Satyrs have a dual nature, meaning they are both human and animal, and thus symbolize a natural, unthinking approach to life that favours intoxicated enjoyment of the moment. They are part of the retinue of Dionysus, the god of wine, and actually play only a peripheral role in ancient myths. Rubens's goat-footed, horned satyr presents the viewer with an overflowing basket of fruit, fixing his opposite number with a diabolical grin. This type of presentation is in the tradition of Caravaggio's *Boy with Grapes* (Galleria Borghese, Rome), even though Rubens did not explore the element of flirting with the viewer as intricately as the earlier painter did. The satyr's direct gaze at the viewer, and his facial type, are reminiscent of the *Head Study of a Bearded Man* in the Princely Collections, which could have been used here. Rubens expresses the sensuality that ancient myths bestowed on satyrs in the sturdy plasticity of the naked torso, emphasized by the light. The expressive face is powerfully modelled with complex shades of colour, the red cheeks indicating how much wine has been enjoyed. At his side is a maid, perhaps a bacchante, a female companion of Bacchus, of a similar nature. With her vine tendril, she seems to be playfully preventing the satyr from reaching the viewer. The colourful quality of the painting is the result of Rubens's visit to Italy, as are the strong contrasts between light and shade, which reflect his study of Caravaggio's work. The picture is thus dated to the period after his return from Italy, around 1615.

Rubens chose a rarely depicted subject for his *Discovery of the Infant Erichthonius*, which he painted in about 1616. A cruel story precedes the erotic depiction of the daughters of Cecrops: Vulcan tried to rape the virgin Minerva who managed to escape, however. The god's semen fell on the ground, impregnating the earth goddess Gaia, who bore the infant Erichthonius who had the form of a serpent. Minerva had to hide this little monster in a basket that she handed over for safekeeping to the daughters of the Athenian king Cecrops, Aglaurus, Herse and Pandrosus who disobeyed the goddess's orders that the basket should not be opened and so uncovered its secret. Rubens followed Ovid, who leaves the daughters'

PETER PAUL RUBENS 1577–1640
Venus in Front of the Mirror, *c.* 1613/14
VIII.1

PETER PAUL RUBENS 1577–1640
Satyr and Maid with Fruit Basket, *c.* 1615
VIII.5

PETER PAUL RUBENS 1577–1640
The Discovery of the Infant Erichthonius, *c.* 1616
VIII.4

curiosity unpunished in his *Metamorphoses*, while other ancient authors report that the disobedient women went mad at their discovery and threw themselves off the Acropolis.

Pictorial elements like the fountain figure of Daphne, the dolphins and the herm of Pan, the god of the fields, are to be read as symbols of fertility and sensuality, and allude to the tale just related and its consequences. For the beauty of Herse, which Ovid describes so eloquently, Rubens went back to Praxiteles's famous statue of Aphrodite (40 BC). Although the original is lost, its form is familiar from countless copies. Its magic lies in the ambivalent expressiveness of her gestures, which make it uncertain whether the goddess is revealing herself or covering herself up. But Rubens also reused his own figures and facial types, which he often took from his head studies: the gracious face of Herse with the almond-shaped, slanting eyes is reminiscent of those of the bacchante in the painting *Maid with Fruit Basket*. The herm of Pan in *The Discovery of the Infant Erichthonius* is in its turn reminiscent of that satyr. Rubens adopted the profile of his *Venus in Front of the Mirror* for Cecrops's daughter Pandrosus.

A little later, in about 1616, Rubens addressed the subject of *Mars and Rhea Silvia*; in this case the Princely Collections own the completed work and also the elaborate oil sketches. According to ancient myth, Mars was attracted to Rhea Silvia, a priestess of Vesta, the goddess of the hearth, who was also worshipped as the protectress of the family, of hospitality and of ordered community life. Ovid reports that Mars overpowered the Vestal while she was asleep. Rubens shifted the scene to the temple. The god has been borne there on a cloud and passionately approaches the priestess, who cringes in horror: as a Vestal, she has sworn an oath of chastity, though possibly not of her own free will. Mars has removed his helmet, and with it his war-like aspirations, for the time being. Cupid, the god of love, acts as pimp, and leads Mars to Rhea. He thus plays a similar formal role to the one in *The Discovery of the Infant Erichthonius*. Virgil records that Mars had twins by Rhea Silvia, Romulus and Remus, who later founded Rome. Vesta's eternal fire, tended by the priestess, burns on the altar on the right. As no images with human faces were made of this goddess, her shrine is marked by a statue of Pallas Athena instead. Rubens demonstrated once more at this point that he was familiar with ancient sources and their contemporary interpretation, as by his friend Justus Lipsius in *De Vesta et Vestalibus Syntagma* (Antwerp, 1605). Rubens

PETER PAUL RUBENS 1577–1640
Mars and Rhea Silvia, *c.* 1616/17
VIII.3

borrowed small details from Roman coins and ancient sarcophagi
like the one in the Palazzo Mattei in Rome.

The fact that the attributes of Mars and Athena are reversed shows
that the painting was used as the basis for a tapestry. It is possible
that it was intended as the first of a series on Romulus, but by
1625 at the latest, when the scene was taken up for the first time
as part of a tapestry for the cycle on the Roman consul Decius
Mus, Rubens had clearly abandoned his ideas for an independent
series.

RELIGIOUS SUBJECTS

Rubens's *Lamentation* appeals to viewers because of the proximity
of the action. They are brought face to face almost frontally with
the ashen body of Christ who lies outstretched on a stone pedestal.
Joseph of Arimathea, who had asked Pilate for the corpse of Christ,
supports his torso as it falls back. The pale-faced Madonna closes
her son's eyes, while St John holds her arm. Mary Magdalene
mourns the dead redeemer with the group of other Marys.
Rubens's interpretation of this subject follows the tradition of
medieval Bible illustration in Italy, which presents Christ lying on the
anointment stone, though the body has not yet been anointed. His
mother is just beginning the cleansing process by gently removing
a thorn from her son's forehead. The ears of corn protruding under
the shroud are probably an allusion to the Eucharistic significance
of Christ's death.

The painting is related to another on the subject by Rubens, one
found in the Kunsthistorisches Museum in Vienna. It is not clear
whether the picture in the Princely Collections was painted before
or after that one, which dates from 1614.

Christ Triumphant over Sin and Death dates from a few years later.
The Bible itself does not describe the Resurrection as an event,
but as a fact, discovered by the Marys at the tomb on the following
day. They find the sarcophagus empty and an angel explains to
them that the redeemer has risen.

A tradition started in the Middle Ages of showing the Risen Christ
standing in the sarcophagus, half visible or just hovering above it.
The scene is often surrounded by soldiers, sometimes sleeping,
sometimes just stirring. It is rare for the Risen Christ to be shown
enthroned on the sarcophagus, as in Rubens's painting, that thus

emphasizes the sacramental character of the tomb. This representation celebrates Christ's victory over death. He is thus dressed in
solemn red, and holds the white flag with a red cross that
announces his Resurrection. Angels bear the symbols of his triumph, the victor's laurel, and signs of his martyrdom, the palm
branches. The skeleton and the snake at Christ's feet stand for
death and sin. The jaws of hell are open to symbolize the downfall
of sin and death, on the right-hand edge of the picture, with flames
flickering out of them. Christ's eyes are wide open and gaze directly
at the viewers, thus conveying to them that the Resurrection of the

Lord also means their redemption. Christ and the angel blowing a
trumpet are taken from Rubens's so-called *Great Last Judgement*
(1616, Alte Pinakothek, Munich).
The painting probably comes from the tomb of the rich Antwerp
citizen Jeremias Cock in the Church of St Walpurgis in Antwerp. It
is known that Cock made purchases for this tomb in 1627, and
that Rubens's painting was associated at an early date with Cock's
entombment in the high choir of the church. The figures are
designed to be seen from below, which also supports the idea
that *Christ Triumphant over Sin and Death* was used as an epitaph

PETER PAUL RUBENS 1577–1640

The Lamentation, *c.* 1613/14

VIII.6

placed at a great height. It is not clear whether the picture was painted for this purpose, or whether Cock selected a picture that Rubens had already completed, as a dating between 1615 and 1622 is entirely plausible on the basis of stylistic criteria.

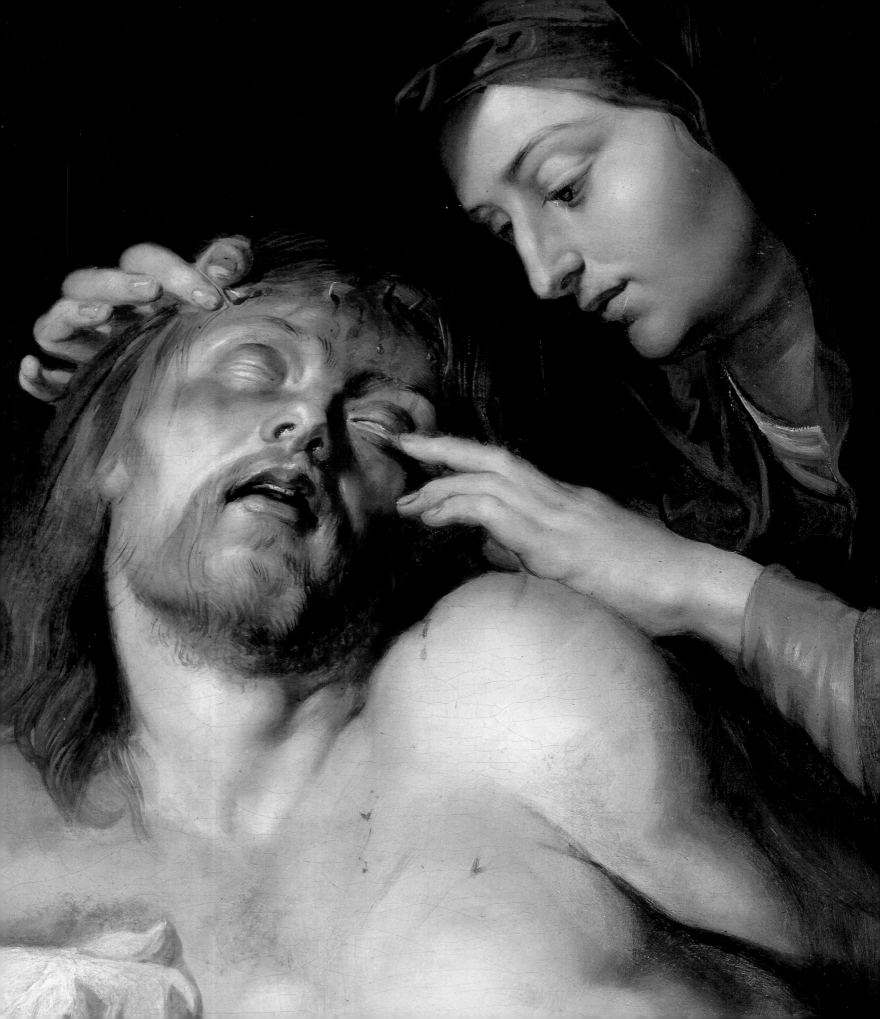

Detail
VIII.6

IDEAL BEAUTY AND THE SENSUAL DELIGHT OF BAROQUE BRONZES

Prince Karl Eusebius travelled from Liechtenstein to Florence in 1636 to make some important art purchases there. It was probably on this visit that he ordered the bronze of *Apollo and Cupid* and the companion piece *Mercury* by François Duquesnoy (1597–1643). The two statuettes are first mentioned in the 1658 inventory of Karl Eusebius's bronzes in Valtice Palace. Both bronzes are conceived as dialogues between the god in question and Cupid. Apollo originally held a bow in his left hand, instructing Cupid, who imitates him, how to shoot an arrow. A figure of Cupid also sat at the feet of Mercury, who was tying a pair of wings to the god's left ankle, so that he could fly through the air. The groups probably date from somewhere between 1635 and 1640. In the eighteenth century these bronzes were thought to be Antique works, as Duquesnoy's authorship had been forgotten. Duquesnoy followed the Antique statue of *Antinous* from the Belvedere for the design of his Mercury. He heightened the figure's *contrapposto* so much that the line of the hip bends through to the side above the figure's centre of gravity. This exaggerated pose is reminiscent of the decorated elegance of Mannerism. Duquesnoy gave his figures a softly chased surface and a subtle modulation that creates a gentle interplay of light and shade.

Two bronzes by Giovanni Francesco Susini (c. 1575–1653) are less elegantly shaped, the figures being somewhat stockier. They are *Venus Burning Cupid's Arrows* and *Venus Chastising Cupid*, which were also acquired by Prince Karl Eusebius and dated 1638. Cupid, son of Venus and god of love, can make both men and gods fall in love with each other at will with his arrows, and thus embodies unbridled passion. His mother Venus is also among his victims, as he instigated a liaison between her and Mars, the god of war, in his usual way. She was caught out by the Olympian gods and ridiculed. As a punishment, Venus burned his arrows, tied him to a myrtle tree and whipped him with rose twigs. Figuratively, the theme here is the subjugation of passion. Susini took ideas for his creation of Venus for both groups of figures from Giambologna (1529–1608) – from his sculptures of *Fortuna* or *Fiorenza* – but adapted them to his style: instead of the multiple viewpoint adopted for their models, Susini concentrated on the front view for these compositions.

Karl Eusebius's acquisitions also include Susini's *Kneeling Woman Bathing*. The model for this was one of Giambologna's most frequently cited compositions, which he had developed from the Antique *Crouching Venus* by Doidalses. The figure's complicated pose is attractive to look at from all sides, and as a *figura serpentinata*, an upwardly spiralling form akin to a snake, it is typical of the Flemish sculptor. Giambologna gradually began to focus on depicting beauty by means of a multiple viewpoint rather than on the content of the work. Even among admirers of his work, iconography was of secondary importance. The princely inventory of 1658 identifies the figure as "a small woman, titivating and washing herself". The use of multiple viewpoints was also popular in contemporary painting: in his *Venus*, Rubens used the trick of the mirror to reveal the attractive face of the goddess whose back is turned to the viewer, and in *The Discovery of the Infant Erichthonius* the beauty of the sisters is celebrated in the pose they adopt in relation to the viewer. In 1695, Prince Johann Adam Andreas I was approached by Massimiliano Soldani Benzi (1656–1740) with an offer to copy in bronze *Bacchus* by Michelangelo (1475–1564). The Grand Duke Francesco de' Medici had acquired the sculpture in 1570, and exhibited it along with the famous antiquities in his collection in the new Uffizi gallery in Florence. This was a clear statement of the particular esteem in which this figure, now famous, was held. After the French King Louis XIV had also had a copy made, the prince accepted the suggestion, at the same time ordering copies of two other famous Florentine antiquities, the *Medici Venus* and the *Dancing Faun*. Possibly it was not a good idea to retain the scale, as Michelangelo's modelling, entirely appropriate to the fifteenth-century tradition, did not satisfy the patron in Soldani Benzi's faithfully executed bronze version. The prince, who appreciated the aesthetic of Antique sculpture, made no secret of his disappointment, and called the figure "a badly designed work … in an ugly pose, very bad idea, also dry". Leaving this princely displeasure aside, Soldani Benzi's bronze offers an interesting counterpoint to Rubens's satyr. The elegant design and reticent gesture of the Renaissance copy, which again depends on an Antique model, blend with the Baroque figure's opulent physicality and aggressive expression.

FRANÇOIS DUQUESNOY 1597–1643
Apollo and Cupid, *c.* 1635/40
VIII.13

FRANÇOIS DUQUESNOY 1597–1643
Mercury, *c.* 1630/40
VIII.14

GIOVANNI FRANCESCO SUSINI *c.* 1575–1653
Venus Chastising Cupid, 1638
VIII.10

GIOVANNI FRANCESCO SUSINI *c.* 1575–1653
Venus Burning Cupid's Arrows, 1638
VIII.11

GIOVANNI FRANCESCO SUSINI *c.* 1575–1653
Kneeling Woman Bathing, 2nd quarter of
17th century, after Giambologna (1529–1608)
VIII.9

MASSIMILIANO SOLDANI BENZI 1656–1740
Bacchus, 1699–1701
after Michelangelo Buonarroti (1475–1564)
VIII.8

PAINTINGS

VIII.1 / p. 305
Peter Paul Rubens (1577–1640)
Venus in Front of the Mirror, c. 1613/14
Oil on panel; height 123 cm, width 98 cm
Inv. no. GE 120
Provenance: presumably acquired by Prince Johann
Adam Andreas I von Liechtenstein from the art
dealer Pieter van Hecke in Antwerp

VIII.2 / p. 316
Peter Paul Rubens (1577–1640)
Oil sketch of *Mars and Rhea Silvia*, c. 1616/17
Oil on canvas; height 46 cm, width 66 cm
Inv. no. GE 115
Provenance: Prince Ourasoff; E. W. Edwards
Collection in Cincinnati, OH, 1976 auction of the
estate of Eleonore Edwards at Christie's in London;
1977 acquired by Prince Franz Josef II von und
zu Liechtenstein

VIII.3 / pp. 314–15
Peter Paul Rubens (1577–1640)
Mars and Rhea Silvia, c. 1616/17
Oil on canvas; height 208 cm, width 272 cm
Inv. no. GE 122
Provenance: 1710 acquired by Prince Johann
Adam Andreas I von Liechtenstein from the art
dealer Jean Pierre Bredael in Antwerp

VIII.4 / pp. 308–09
Peter Paul Rubens (1577–1640)
The Discovery of the Infant Erichthonius, c. 1616
Oil on canvas; height 218 cm, width 317 cm
Inv. no. GE 111
Provenance: 1704 acquired by Prince Johann
Adam Andreas I von Liechtenstein from the art
dealer Marcus Forchoudt in Antwerp

VIII.5 / p. 306
Peter Paul Rubens (1577–1640)
Satyr and Maid with Fruit Basket, c. 1615
Oil on canvas; 113 x 71 cm
Schönborn-Buchheim Collection, inv. no. G 006
Provenance: first recorded in 1830 in the
Schönborn-Buchheim Collection

VIII.6 / p. 317
Peter Paul Rubens (1577–1640)
The Lamentation, c. 1613/14
Oil on canvas; height 151 cm, width 204 cm
Inv. no. GE 62
Provenance: 1710 acquired by Prince Johann Adam
Andreas I von Liechtenstein from the art dealer
Justus Forchoudt in Vienna

VIII.7 / p. 319
Peter Paul Rubens (1577–1640)
Christ Triumphant over Sin and Death, 1615/22
Oil on canvas; height 182 cm, width 230 cm
Inv. no. GE 270
Provenance: 1627 probably commissioned by
Jeremias Cock for his tomb in the Church of
St Walburga in Antwerp; 1813/14 acquired by J. F.
Wolschot at the Vink de Wesel auction in Antwerp;
1831/32 probably came into the possession of
George Watson Taylor; presumably owned by Sir
William Knighton at Blindworth Lodge, Hampshire;
1897 art dealer C. Sedelmeyer in Paris; 1925
Sarens auction in Brussels; from 1956 in the
collection of J. Declercq in Antwerp; 2002 acquired
by Prince Hans-Adam II von und zu Liechtenstein

SCULPTURE AND APPLIED ART

VIII.8 / p. 327
Massimiliano Soldani Benzi (1656–1740)
Bacchus, 1699–1701
after Michelangelo Buonarroti (1475–1564)
Bronze with red-brown lacquer patina;
height 198 cm
Inv. no. SK 573
Provenance: 1695 commissioned by Prince Johann
Adam Andreas I von Liechtenstein from Soldani
Benzi; 1703 acquired by the same prince

VIII.9 / p. 326
Giovanni Francesco Susini (c. 1575–1653)
Kneeling Woman Bathing, 2nd quarter of
17th century, after Giambologna (1529–1608)
Bronze with gold-brown lacquer patina;
height 26 cm
Inv. no. SK 569
Provenance: listed in Prince Karl Eusebius von
Liechtenstein's Quardaroba inventory of 1658

VIII.10 / p. 324
Giovanni Francesco Susini (c. 1575–1653)
Venus Chastising Cupid, 1638
Bronze with gold-brown patina, traces of dark
brown lacquer; height 58 cm
Signed and dated on the tree-trunk:
IO.FR.SVSINI.FLOR.FAC. / MDCXXXVIII
Inv. no. SK 542, companion piece to SK 543
Provenance: listed in Prince Karl Eusebius von
Liechtenstein's Quardaroba inventory of 1658
with *Venus Burning Cupid's Arrows* (SK 543)

VIII.11 / p. 325
Giovanni Francesco Susini (c. 1575–1653)
Venus Burning Cupid's Arrows, 1638
Bronze with gold-brown patina, traces of dark
brown lacquer; height 56 cm
Signed and dated on a quiver:
IO.FR.SVSINI.FLOR.F. / MDCXXXVIII
Inv. no. SK 543, companion piece to SK 542
Provenance: listed in Prince Karl Eusebius von
Liechtenstein's Quardaroba inventory of 1658
with *Venus Chastising Cupid* (SK 542)

VIII.13 / p. 322
François Duquesnoy (1597–1643)
Apollo and Cupid, c. 1635/40
Bronze with light brown lacquer patina; height 66
cm, width 27
Inv. no. SK 610, companion piece to SK 611
Provenance: with *Mercury* (SK 611) listed in Prince
Karl Eusebius von Liechtenstein's Quardaroba
inventory of 1658

VIII.14 / p. 323
François Duquesnoy (1597–1643)
Mercury, c. 1630/40
Bronze with light brown lacquer patina;
height 63 cm, width 28 cm
Inv. no. SK 611, companion piece to SK 610
Provenance: with *Apollo and Cupid* (SK 610)
listed in Prince Karl Eusebius von Liechtenstein's
Quardaroba inventory of 1658

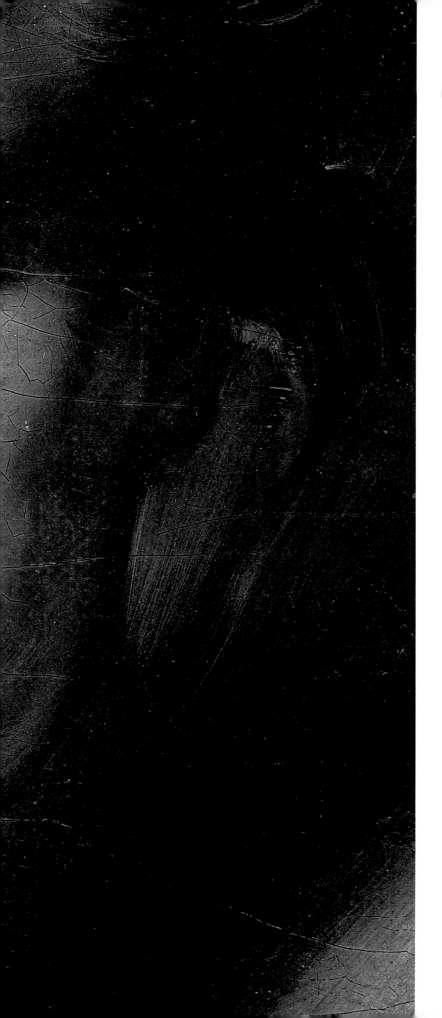

GALLERY IX

SEVENTEENTH-CENTURY FLEMISH AND DUTCH PORTRAIT PAINTING

EARLY PORTRAITS BY PETER PAUL RUBENS

The seventeenth century is seen as the Golden Age of Flemish and Dutch painting because of the wide range of innovative achievements and also the high level of artistic productivity. The genre of picture that was apparently most in demand was the portrait: in the first half of the century, more portraits were painted even than religious subjects. Portraits were not highly thought of in art theory, however. The requirement that the image should resemble the sitter was feared to be a curb on artistic feeling, and anyway it was impossible to beat nature at her own game. In addition, patrons' expectations restricted the range of creative possibilities to pictorial types that had changed very little since the sixteenth century. Despite all this, the greatest artists of the day, like Peter Paul Rubens, successfully rose to the challenge. And the fame of Anthony van Dyck and Frans Hals is based exclusively on their unique portraiture.

Rubens (1577–1640) also found himself faced with conservative schemes in the portrait genre. Patrons wanted to be portrayed in three-quarter length. The model usually posed upright, looking directly at the viewer. There is also little variety available in terms of pose: reticent body language, with the hands held close to the body, was seen as refined and appropriate. Attributes indicated social status or alluded to the subject's biography. The artist's scope lay in the psychologically insightful reproduction of the features and in the effective use of the painterly resources available to him.

On returning from Italy, Rubens convincingly demonstrated that he had these qualities when he received his first major portrait commissions from the governor of the Spanish Netherlands and his wife. The *Portrait of Jan Vermoelen* (1589–1656) also dates from this period. Vermoelen came from an old, influential Antwerp family. The portrait dates from 1616, and captures the young man at the age of twenty-seven, in other words before the start of his successful career, which saw him become General Commissioner and Admiral of the Spanish fleet. Vermoelen appears in black clothing against a dark background in which a magnificent armchair – a frequently recurring motif in the Flemish master's portraits – sets a colourful accent. Rubens reproduces the matt, golden-brown embossed texture of the leather by omitting its ornamental forms, thus allowing the ground to show through at these points. He thus created an

illusion of the embossed pattern. This shows a certain mastery in handling paint, and an economical approach. The ochre ground that appears here gives the whole picture a gentle warmth. Fashionable dress of the time included a white, stiff ruff that framed the face. Rubens modelled the features powerfully by accentuating the flesh tones with his typical red and blue notes. And he applied paint thickly, to create accents that structured areas of uniform colour; thus the black robe stood out from the background, which was also black.

Rubens was able to break away from the genre's rigidly schematic approach in his intimate family portraits. The *Portrait of Clara Serena Rubens*, painted c. 1616, is one of the most touching child portraits in the history of European art. It shows Rubens's five-year-old daughter from his marriage to Isabella Brant. Her resemblance to her mother is clear. The disarming directness with which the child looks at the viewer is not typical of contemporary portrait painting, but expresses the intimate relationship between father and daughter. Rubens uses colour with great skill to capture her face. The warm colouring of the flesh tones makes a particular impact against the grey-green ground and the child's clothing. The strong red of the cheeks and the highlights on her nose and forehead convey an impression of intense life. The painting is trimmed on all four sides, and looks incomplete at first because the clothing is hastily painted. Detailed work on these parts, however, cannot have been his intention as the portrait was probably destined for private use and not for sale. Rubens obviously concentrated on the key aspect of the portrayal, his daughter's face.

Rubens captured his sons Albert and Nikolaus Rubens in a double portrait in c. 1626/27. These two children were both from his first marriage, to Isabella Brant, and were around thirteen and nine years old respectively at the time. Nikolaus (1618–1655), the younger, still seems quite uninhibited. He ignores the viewer and is preoccupied with his goldfinch which he has tethered to a ribbon, a popular children's game. In contrast to his younger brother, Albert (1614–1657) seems serious, almost adult, and a little precocious, not least because of his distinguished clothing and the casual elegance of his pose. His father encouraged him to read and furthered his classical education. The boy published his first poem in Latin at the age of thirteen; the book in his hand definitely refers to his scholarly nature. Albert Rubens ultimately became one of the most highly respected scholars of the Graeco-Roman world of his day.

PETER PAUL RUBENS 1577–1640
Portrait of Clara Serena Rubens, *c.* 1616
IX.1

PETER PAUL RUBENS 1577–1640
Double Portrait of Albert and Nikolaus Rubens, *c.* 1626/27
IX.2

The contrast between the two brothers may be due to their different ages and characters. Possibly yet another level of meaning is concealed in the picture: in his treatise on the most famous Greek painters, Pliny wrote that Parrhasius, the master of eloquent expression, painted two boys embodying the tranquillity of nature (*securitas*) and also the innocence (*simplicitas*) of that age. Perhaps Rubens was trying to imply this theme in his portrait of his sons.

EARLY PORTRAITS BY ANTHONY VAN DYCK: A KEY FEATURE OF THE PRINCELY COLLECTIONS

The Princely Collections have one of the world's largest holdings of early portraits by Anthony van Dyck (1599–1641). The *Portrait of an Old Man* dates from *c.* 1618, presumably during the period when van Dyck was working in Peter Paul Rubens's studio. The young artist, who was already a master-member of the Guild of St Luke, was an outstanding portrait painter even then, even though in his early work his style is so close to Rubens's own that it is sometimes difficult to distinguish between them. The painting in the Princely Collections is considered to be a masterpiece among van Dyck's early portraiture. As in most of the early portraits, van Dyck remains true to convention in the pose adopted by his subject, for example. Here the clothing and accessories are not sufficient to show whether this is a member of the nobility or the bourgeoisie. In the seventeenth century, in particular, prestigious portraits served to demonstrate the Antwerp citizenry's claims to recognition, and approbation and differences in status did not necessarily show in the way individuals presented themselves. An inscription on the back of the picture gives the subject's age as fifty-five. The elegant armchair was a frequently encountered, conservative motif in this genre. This specimen, in gold-embossed leather, is astonishingly similar to the one in Rubens's *Portrait of Jan Vermoelen*. That picture in fact was a model for this 1618 portrait by van Dyck not just in this detail, but generally. Though harmonizing with Rubens's work in terms of the colour concept, van Dyck's blacks have a cool tinge of grey, deriving from the white-grey ground. The younger artist's more open brushwork becomes apparent in the treatment of the clothing, though the individual brushstrokes do exhibit a certain stiffness. Despite this painterly freedom, van Dyck does seem to value emphasizing individual characteristics more highly when

Detail
IX.2

PETER PAUL RUBENS 1577–1640
Portrait of Jan Vermoelen, 1616
IX.7

Detail
IX.7

reproducing facial features: the expression on his subject's face seems to be more precisely observed than that of Rubens's model. The bravura modelling of the ruff also shows richer variation than is the case with Rubens.

The *Portrait of a Man* and *Portrait of a Woman*, conceived as companion pieces, show the same characteristics of this early period. They date from 1618, and are the earliest dated paintings in van Dyck's oeuvre. The portrait of the married couple, with the two sitters facing each other symmetrically, clearly reveals its origins in the diptych, whose wings were actually connected to each other. Portraits of this type were seen mainly as a record of marital status, and did not express emotional commitment. The conventional

black clothing with white, stiff ruffs, a Netherlandish fashion that was sometimes influential abroad, helps to support the sense of emotional distance between them. Van Dyck enlivens the monotony of the clothing, a particular challenge for every painter, with thickly applied accents to ornament and folds, and gives the ruff almost physical substance in this way. The pictures do not seem to have been painted at the same time: the woman's portrait is more secure in the use of painterly resources than its counterpart. Van Dyck's hasty, open brushwork is apparent particularly in the subject's left hand, where the painter lays broad black lines over the flesh tones of the fingertips to suggest the hand plunging into the darkness of the room.

Detail
IX.6

ANTHONY VAN DYCK 1599–1641
Portrait of a Woman, *c.* 1618
Portrait of a Man, *c.* 1630/32
IX.9 and IX.11

ANTHONY VAN DYCK 1599–1641 >
Portrait of a Genoese Nobleman, 1624
Portrait of Maria de Tassis, *c.* 1629/30
IX.3 and IX.12

The *Portrait of a Genoese Nobleman* of 1624 marks a clear stylistic break in van Dyck's oeuvre. The artist had spent several months in England, where he was to work in his later years, in 1620/21 at the invitation of James I. A subsequent visit to Italy lasting several years took him to what were the most important artistic centres. In his study of his great Renaissance predecessors, he was fascinated above all by Venetian painting, and here particularly by Titian, who lastingly changed his approach to painting and pictorial structure, as the works in the Princely Collections show. Van Dyck's first long stay was in Genoa, which as a port and major trading centre had long had close ties with Antwerp, and he always ended up there after his journeys around Italy. Rubens had successfully introduced the Flemish portrait here, prepared an engraving of the Genoese

palaces and was indebted to the city for important commissions such as the Decius Mus cycle. Van Dyck was certainly able to benefit from his contacts here, and became a great success as a portrait painter. According to the inscription, the portrait shows a 32-year-old man, and was painted while van Dyck was in Genoa. It differs from those in the earlier phase in that the body language is more lively and the pose opens up to the viewer. The colour tones are now more saturated, owing their basic warmth to a red ground. The painting is also more refined, with soft transitions. Titian's influence can be seen in these characteristics. Van Dyck's Italian sketchbook shows that he studied the earlier artist's work with particular care.

Van Dyck returned to Antwerp in 1627. The next five years were seen as the high point of his creative life. He worked for the Church and the nobility, princes and merchants in Flanders and well beyond its borders. The Archduchess and Governor Isabella Clara Eugenia appointed him court painter in 1630 in recognition of his achievements. His lively portraits continued to challenge the statuesque quality of the portrait and its rigid schemes, and introduced ever more subtle variations. Enriched by an incomparable painterly refinement, van Dyck's portraits made a major contribution to seventeenth-century work in this genre.

It is not least this painterly refinement that makes the *Portrait of Maria de Tassis*, c. 1629/30, one of van Dyck's masterpieces. It entered the Princely Collections at the same time as the *Portrait of Antonio de Tassis* (1584–1651) of 1634 through the offices of Prince Johann Adam Andreas I von Liechtenstein. The subjects' family came from Bergamo, and developed the first postal system in Europe in the late fifteenth century. Maria came from the Antwerp branch of the family, which traditionally provided the imperial postmaster. The portrait shows her at the age of about nineteen. She wears a magnificent silk dress, fully in tune with contemporary French fashion in its emphasis on *décolleté* and hip. It is artfully trimmed with gold braid, and much puffed and pleated, all of which creates a lively play of light, showing the costly shimmer of the fine material to full advantage. Van Dyck painted the robe and ostrich feather fan with great attention to detail and a rich tonal quality reminiscent of Titian. The woman's youthful features are framed with a broad collar in the most delicate lace. She regards the viewer with a hint of a smile. Her unaffected charisma and charm bring the distinguished pose to life.

In 1632, van Dyck entered the service of King Charles I, probably the greatest collector and most refined art connoisseur of all British monarchs. His portraits of members of the royal family and the court pointed the way ahead for portraiture in England, where Titian's approach was so highly regarded. The *Portrait of Antonio de Tassis* was painted during a short stay in Antwerp in 1634. It shows Maria's father at the age of fifty, as an inscription points out. The brother of the imperial postmaster fought in the army of the Spanish Netherlands against the States General, losing his left arm. He later turned to the spiritual life, and took holy orders in 1629. From 1630 he worked as a canon in Antwerp Cathedral, and van Dyck's portrait shows him in this role. His wide garment conceals the miss-

ing arm, while the right hand holding the book features prominently as a sign of scholarship. The obliquely incident light emphasizes his serious, concentrated gaze at the viewer, bringing the right eye into the foreground, while the left-hand half of the face is plunged into shadow. Van Dyck owed this commission for the portrait, and probably also for the one of his daughter, to de Tassis's connoisseurship in art. He left one of the most remarkable art collections in Flanders when he died in 1651. His portrait was engraved in the 1656 *Iconography*, which published portraits of major military commanders, rulers, artists and clerics based on work by van Dyck.
The paintings of father and daughter are probably not to be regarded as companion pieces, as stylistic reasons suggest that the portrait of Maria de Tassis was painted some years before her father's, which is dated 1634. Also different dimensions – a piece has been added to the male portrait – and the different settings suggest they were not intended as a double portrait, which in any case would be unusual in the father-daughter combination.

PORTRAITS BY FRANS HALS

The portraits of Frans Hals (1580/85–1666) have a different appeal from those of van Dyck. His contemporaries liked his frequently unconventional portraits because of their intensity of life. It was felt that they were painted in a way that made them seem to live and breathe. Little is known about the artist's life. Hals was apprenticed to the Flemish painter and art theoretician Karel van Mander in Haarlem. He accepted his first major commissions in 1616, the year he also visited Rubens and van Dyck in Antwerp. The municipal bourgeoisie had become the politically dominant force in the northern Netherlands. Hals painted the archers' and musketeers' guilds in groups, and also portraits of preachers, men of letters, scholars, painters and Haarlem's affluent burghers.
The *Portrait of Willem van Heythuysen* (d. 1650) of c. 1625/30 was an attraction in the Princely Collections for almost 150 years. It was sold in 1969, and is now in the Alte Pinakothek in Munich. It was painted at the time of an economic upswing in Haarlem. Heythuysen had accrued great wealth through the prosperous textile trade, and so was a typical representative of the Golden Age. In addition to beer brewing, textile production was the region's most important industry. Hals presents the new self-confidence of the region's burgers in a work resembling a state portrait, a full-length picture of monumental dimensions; it was to remain his only one of this type. Heythuysen strikes a theatrical pose, dressed of course in the finest cloth – so-called Dutch satin – and bears his ornamental German sword more as a ceremonial baton than a weapon. The niche behind him is hung with lavish drapery and forms an appropriate background for his arrogant display of wealth. The rose branch and the loving couple in the background are *vanitas* symbols, indicating the transience of this earthly splendour. The fluent painting, using accentuated brushstrokes, suggests a date somewhere in the mid-1620s.
After the deaths of Peter Paul Rubens (1640) and Anthony van Dyck (1641), Frans Hals became the most important portrait painter in the Netherlands. He now received major public commissions, which established his international reputation, in addition to private ones. Haarlem's economic boom came to an end in the 1650s, however, because many dealers, merchants and artists moved to Amsterdam, the wealthiest city in Europe. The number of commissions for Frans Hals also dropped. Around this time, he painted portraits that

ANTHONY VAN DYCK 1599–1641

Portrait of a Man, 1618

IX.4

ÆT. 57.

FRANS HALS 1580/85–1666
Portrait of a Man, 1650/52
IX.10

did not rely on lavish displays of prestige and status. These late portraits became famous because of Hals's ability to capture the subject's character in a complex, highly nuanced facial expression. The *Portrait of a Man* painted in 1650/52 is a typical picture of this period. An unknown man looks out at us roguishly from under the broad brim of his black hat. The raised eyebrows and hint of a smile make the picture seem like a snapshot. Hals concentrates on the head and hands as expressive devices. The rest of the painted area is sparingly formed. In the course of his career the artist reduced his colour range to dark shades of black, brown and grey. Only the faces stand out from the darkness now. The painting becomes increasingly sketchy, which in turn lends it life. In some parts the

free brushstrokes seem to dissolve the forms, which are executed with strong, dark lines. This approach suggests that Hals probably worked his pictures out directly on canvas, as no preparatory sketches for his portraits have survived.

APPLIED ART OF THE BAROQUE PERIOD

The cabinet, made in Antwerp shortly after 1650, consists of two parts: the actual cabinet and the table with Tuscan columns supporting it. The architectural articulation of the table-top and its drawers makes it seem like the entablature of a columned hall. The central section of the cabinet itself takes the form of a cupboard whose doors are flanked and separated in the middle by three herm atlantes. It opens to reveal an elaborately mirrored piece of miniature interior architecture, framed in colour, behind which is a painted garden landscape in perspective. The outside of the cabinet is almost completely covered with tortoiseshell and ornamented in gilded bronze. Sheets from the shell of the loggerhead turtle were used to surface furniture in Antwerp in particular. Although tortoiseshell is a hard, brittle material, it is easy to work. It can be sawn into translucent sheets, and also bent and compressed when warm. The yellowish, flamed sheets were underlaid with red paint to intensify their colours.

Prince Johann Adam Andreas I von Liechtenstein acquired a resplendent tankard by Matthias Rauchmiller (1645–1686), whose work he particularly admired, in 1707. This magnificent specimen, dated 1676, is considered to be the most important piece of German Baroque ivory because of its outstanding artistic quality and the complexity of its iconographic content. It is also the only work of art in ivory bearing Rauchmiller's signature. The artist placed his very personal interpretation of the rape of the Sabine women on the walls of the tankard. Contemporary painting usually presented the subject in a very elegant form, thus playing it down, but Rauchmiller depicts the narrative as a violent event, despite the beautiful lines of the bodies and draperies. The frieze with figures winds around the vessel in violent movement, with both attackers and victims linked in a variety of ways. The carvings on the figured frieze reach a depth of up to 23 millimetres, so that the deeply undercut figures seem to stand out freely in three dimensions. Despite the fragility of these often wafer-thin details, the tankard has survived in excellent condition. Rauchmiller worked the lid and the handle in ivory. He shaped the latter from a double-headed female herm and even gave a figured form to structural parts like the hinge, which is shaped like a dolphin's head.

In 1636, Prince Karl Eusebius von Liechtenstein acquired a jasper table from the Florentine studio of Giuliano di Piero Pandolfini (doc. 1615–1637). This is probably identical with the *pietra dura* table-top in the Princely Collections, whose centre is also decorated with the prince's arms. In contrast to the earlier one that Karl I commissioned from the imperial gem-cutting workshop in Prague, this table no longer consists of individual pictorial panels, but has a uniformly dark background of black marble, into which the coloured motifs are inlaid with lapis-lazuli, chalcedony and various kinds of jasper. The shape of the flowers, animals and cartouches, and the inlay technique, suggest Florence as the place of provenance. The candelabra vases drew on ancient grotesque motifs as models. Symmetrical articulation and mirror-image repetition structure the wealth of forms.

Giuliani di Piero Pandolfini took over the Prague workshop in 1615, with his brother-in-law Cosimo di Giovanni Castrucci. After their patron, Emperor Rudolf II, had long been dead, they accepted an invitation from the Medici to establish a new workshop in Florence.

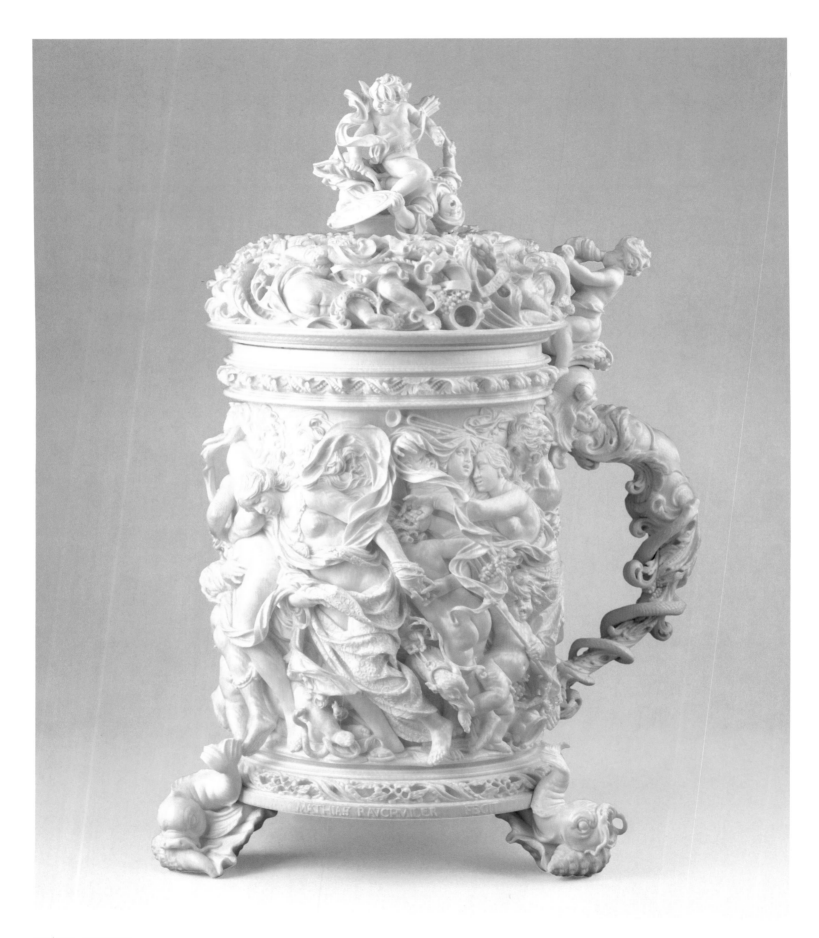

MATTHIAS RAUCHMILLER 1645–1686
Resplendent tankard, 1676
IX.21

JOSEPH BERGLER 1718–1788
The Sacrifice of Abraham, 1753
IX.17

GIOVANNI FRANCESCO SUSINI *c.* 1575–1653
Striding Horse, mid-17th century
IX.19

GIOVANNI FRANCESCO SUSINI *c.* 1575–1653
Striding Bull, mid-17th century
IX.20

GIULIANO DI PIERO PANDOLFINI doc. 1615–1637
Pietra dura table-top, 1636
IX.14

Cabinet, Antwerp, shortly after 1650 >
IX.16

PAINTINGS

IX.1 / p. 334
Peter Paul Rubens (1577–1640)
Portrait of Clara Serena Rubens, c. 1616
Oil on canvas, mounted on panel; height 37 cm,
width 27 cm
Inv. no. GE 105
Provenance: 1639 presumably in the estate of
Jan Brant, Rubens's father-in-law; 1656 in the
possession of Archduke Leopold Wilhelm of
Austria; estate inventory of Prince Johann Adam
Andreas I von Liechtenstein in 1712; 1733
identified by seal as entail

IX.2 / p. 335
Peter Paul Rubens (1577–1640)
Double Portrait of Albert and Nikolaus Rubens,
c. 1626/27
Oil on panel; height 157 cm, width 93 cm
Inv. no. GE 114
Provenance: after 1640 in the possession of
Albert Rubens; 1733 identified by seal as entail

IX.3 / p. 344
Anthony van Dyck (1599–1641)
Portrait of a Genoese Nobleman, 1624
Oil on canvas; height 131 cm, width 101 cm
Inscribed and dated bottom right:
AE. Ts.32.1624
Inv. no. GE 61
Provenance: 1733 identified by seal as entail

IX.4 / p. 350
Anthony van Dyck (1599–1641)
Portrait of a Man, 1618
Oil on panel; height 106 cm, width 74 cm
Dated top left: Ao 1618.
Inscription top right: AET.57.
Inv. no. GE 70, companion piece to GE 71
Provenance: 1733 identified by seal as entail

IX.5 / not illus.
Anthony van Dyck (1599–1641)
Portrait of a Woman, 1618
Oil on panel; height 105 cm, width 76 cm
Dated top left: Ao 1618.
Inscription top right: AET.58.
Inv. no. GE 71, companion piece to GE 70
Provenance: 1733 identified by seal as entail

IX.6 / p. 341
Anthony van Dyck (1599–1641)
Portrait of an Old Man, c. 1618
Oil on panel; height 107 cm, width 74 cm
Inscription on front: 26
Inscription on reverse: oudt 55 Jaren
Inv. no. GE 95
Provenance: 1733 identified by seal as entail

IX.7 / p. 339
Peter Paul Rubens (1577–1640)
Portrait of Jan Vermoelen, 1616
Oil on panel; height 126 cm, width 96 cm
Dated top left: AETATIS SVE Ao 1616
Inv. no. GE 87
Provenance: presumably from 1656 in the pos-
session of Peter Vermoelen, son of Jan Vermoe-
len; before 1805 acquired by Prince Alois I von
Liechtenstein (mentioned as "purchased" in
Dallinger's 1805 catalogue of the collection)

IX.8 / p. 349
Anthony van Dyck (1599–1641)
Portrait of Antonio de Tassis, 1634
Oil on canvas; height 126 cm, width 89 cm
Inscription top right: AETATIS 50 ANNO.16.
Inv. no. GE 73
Provenance: after 1651 with the *Portrait of Maria
de Tassis* (GE 58) in the possession of Catharina
de Tassis, Antonio's eldest daughter, subsequent-
ly both in the possession of Maria Anna de Tas-
sis, Antonio's granddaughter, and later Countess
Cryckenborch; 1658 sold together from Maria
Anna de Tassis's effects in Antwerp; 1710 both
acquired by Prince Johann Adam Andreas I von
Liechtenstein from the art dealer Jan Peeter van
Bredal in Antwerp

IX.9 / p. 343
Anthony van Dyck (1599–1641)
Portrait of a Woman, c. 1618
Oil on canvas; height 105 cm, width 82 cm
Inv. no. GE 63
Provenance: 1733 identified by seal as entail

IX.10 / p. 352
Frans Hals (1580/85–1666)
Portrait of a Man, 1650/52
Oil on canvas; height 108 cm, width 80 cm
Inv. no. GE 235
Provenance: before 1868 J. H. Cremer Collection
in Brussels; 1868 auctioned by le Roy in Brussels; 1868 art dealer C. Sedelmeyer in Paris;
c. 1870 Gustav Ritter von Eppstein in Vienna;
before 1871 F. J. Gsell in Vienna; 1872 auctioned by Plack in Vienna; 1872 Löscher in Vienna; 1898 art dealer C. Sedelmeyer in Paris;
1898 Albert Baron von Rothschild in Vienna;
1938 requisitioned from Louis Baron von Rothschild in Vienna for the Linz "Führermuseum";
from 1948 in the Kunsthistorisches Museum in
Vienna; 1998 restored to Albert and Nathaniel
Barons von Rothschild; 1999 auctioned at
Christie's in London; 1999 in a private collection;
2003 auctioned by Sotheby's in New York; 2003
purchased by Prince Hans-Adam II von und zu
Liechtenstein

IX.11 / p. 343
Anthony van Dyck (1599–1641)
Portrait of a Man, c. 1630/32
Oil on canvas; height 105 cm, width 81 cm
Inv. no. GE 65
Provenance: 1733 identified by seal as entail

IX.12 / p. 345
Anthony van Dyck (1599–1641)
Portrait of Maria de Tassis, c. 1629/30
Oil on canvas; height 128 cm, width 92 cm
Inv. no. GE 58
Provenance: after 1651 with the *Portrait of Antonio de Tassis* (GE 73)
in the possession of Catharina de Tassis, Antonio's eldest daughter, subsequently both in the
possession of Maria Anna de Tassis, Antonio's
granddaughter, and later Countess Cryckenborch;
1658 sold together from Maria Anna de Tassis's
effects in Antwerp; 1710 both acquired by Prince
Johann Adam Andreas I von Liechtenstein from
the art dealer Jan Peeter van Bredal in Antwerp

IX.13 / p. 19
Frans Hals (1580/85–1666)
Portrait of Willem van Heythuysen, c. 1625/30
Oil on canvas; height 205 cm, width 135 cm
Bayerische Staatsgemäldesammlung, Alte
Pinakothek, Munich
Inv. no. 14101
Provenance: 1789 in the possession of G. W. van
Oosten de Bryn; 1821 acquired by Prince Johann
I von Liechtenstein from the Huybens art dealer-
ship; 1969 sold to the Bayerische Staats-
gemäldesammlung

SCULPTURE AND APPLIED ART

IX.14 / pp. 360–61
Giuliano di Piero Pandolfini (doc. 1615–1637)
Pietra dura table-top, 1636
with the coat of arms of Prince Karl Eusebius von
Liechtenstein
Comessi de pietre dure and gilt bronze; height
129 cm, width 94 cm
Inv. no. SK 1402
Provenance: 1636 commissioned by Prince Karl
Eusebius von Liechtenstein

IX.15 / not illus.
Giovanni Giuliani (1663–1744)
Wooden base for the *pietra dura* table-top by
Piero Pandolfini (IX.14), 1711
Carved lime, in 1847 the original green bronze
gilding heavily gilded and silver gilt; height
82 cm, width 113 cm, depth 95 cm
Inv. no. MO 1566
Provenance: 1711 commissioned by Prince
Johann Adam Andreas I von Liechtenstein for the
pietra dura table-top (SK 1402)

IX.16 / p. 362
Cabinet, Antwerp, shortly after 1650
Panel, tortoiseshell with red underlay, bronze gild-
ed, enamel, mirror-glass; height 178 cm, width
153 cm, depth 56 cm
Inv. no. MO 11
Provenance: before 1940 in the possession of
Oscar Hamel in Vienna; 1940 acquired by Prince
Franz Josef II von und zu Liechtenstein

IX.17 / p. 357
Joseph Bergler (1718–1788)
The Sacrifice of Abraham, 1753
Alabaster; height 62 cm, width 41 cm, depth
42 cm
Signed and dated on tree-trunk: JOSEPH
BERGLER F. 1753
Inv. no. SK 906

Provenance: before 1823 in the possession of
Joseph Bergler the Younger, Joseph Bergler's
son; 1823 acquired by Prince Rudolf von Kinsky,
until 1986 in the Palais Kinsky in Vienna, sold
to private collection; 2002 acquired by Prince
Hans-Adam II von und zu Liechtenstein

IX.18 / not illus.
Console table, Bohemia, c. 1720
Gilt panel; height 76 cm, width 96 cm,
depth 73 cm
Inv. no. MO 1571

IX.19 / p. 358
Giovanni Francesco Susini (c. 1575–1653)
Striding Horse, mid-17th century after
Giambologna (1529–1608), after 1593
Bronze, red-brown lacquer patina;
height 37 cm (including socle)
Inv. no. SK 550
Provenance: 1652 probably in the collection of
Jan van Meurs in Antwerp together with Striding
Horse (SK550); both acquired by Prince Johann
Adam Andreas von Liechtenstein in 1696 as a
work by Giambologna from the art dealer Marcus
Forchoudt in Antwerp

IX.20 / p. 359
Giovanni Francesco Susini (c. 1575–1653)
Striding Bull, mid-17th century
after follower of Giambologna
Bronze, red-brown lacquer patina; height 37 cm
Inv. no. SK 553
Provenance: 1652 probably in the collection of
Jan van Meurs in Antwerp together with Striding
Horse (SK550); both acquired by Prince Johann
Adam Andreas von Liechtenstein in 1696 as a
work by Giambologna from the art dealer Marcus
Forchoudt in Antwerp

IX.21 / p. 356
Matthias Rauchmiller (1645–1686)
Resplendent tankard, 1676
Ivory, silver cup inside; height 34.9 cm
Inscription on bands: MARS STERNIT PRATA
VICTOR A PART A
Signed and dated lower edge: ANNO 1676
MATHIAS RAVCHMILLER FECIT
Stamped on the bottom of the silver vessel: E B
(in the horizontal oval)
Inv. no. SK 326
Provenance: 1707 acquired by Prince Johann
Adam Andreas I von Liechtenstein from the Rec-
tor of Vienna University, Wolfgang Karl Lebzelter

IX.22 / not illus.
Anonymous, The Netherlands, 17th century
Table, table-top with schwarzlot painting
Ebony, ivory; height 80 cm, width 85 cm,
depth 59 cm
Inv. no. MO 1580

GALLERY X

LANDSCAPE, STILL LIFE, GENRE PAINTING AND PORTRAITURE

VARIETY IN SEVENTEENTH-CENTURY DUTCH PAINTING

Seventeenth-century Dutch painting is known for its unique of genres. It developed around 1600 in both Holland and Flanders, and – making its influence felt across Europe – contributed crucially to the emergence of specialist fields for artists. History painting was seen as the most complex genre in terms of content, and the most demanding artistically, and was thus the most highly rated. Its formal structure became increasingly complex, and individual elements like landscape, still life and genre scenes became subjects in their own right. At the same time, patrons began to develop more sophisticated tastes in art. The new motifs reveal the shift in the significance of paintings from being symbolic vehicles for religious or moral instruction to technically perfected objects to be viewed mainly as aesthetic objects. This also reflects changes in artistic patronage away from the Church and court to the prosperous merchant class that had acquired wealth by trading in a flourishing economy and political power. By collecting art, this new élite was keen to demonstrate its wealth and refinement. Art delighted the eye and the senses, but it was also often bought speculatively. The commercialized market was driven by supply and demand, which meant artists became less dependent on patrons.

LANDSCAPE

Landscape as a genre is a sixteenth-century invention. In the Middle Ages, it merely provided a backdrop for scenes with figures, and realism was of no importance. When landscape became fashionable as a background in altarpieces and portraits, it gradually developed into a subject worthy of treatment. It established itself as a genre in its own right around 1520, though early examples made no attempt to identify a particular setting. They were not painted outdoors as a landscape portrait, but created in the studio as fantasy landscapes comprising individual elements. Landscape specialization started around 1600. The Princely Collections embrace the whole spectrum: cliff and mountain landscapes, forest, village, river, lake and seaside settings. Jan Brueghel the Elder (1568–1625) was the youngest son of Pieter Brueghel the Elder (c. 1526/30–1569) who had revolutionized Flemish landscape painting. He moved beyond Joachim Patinir's panoramic landscapes and in his work achieved

continuous three-dimensional depth for the first time. Along with Peter Paul Rubens, Jan was one of the favourite painters of the Spanish monarchs Albert and Isabella Clara Eugenia. Versatile in all genres, he was much in demand by Rubens, Joos de Momper and others to help produce special commissions such as landscapes and still lifes, and their subordinate figures and animals. Dated 1598, his *Landscape with the Young Tobias* shows a merry com-pany in an imaginary riverside setting. In its crowded midst, the religious scene can scarcely be seen: Tobais, on the advice of his companion, the Archangel Raphael, pulls a fish out of the water. He will use its gall to cure his father's blindness. The real subject here, however, is the meticulously painted landscape into whose depths the composition leads the viewer's gaze. The break in the forest and the course of the river lead one's gaze to the centre of the picture. Beyond it, reality fades into the atmospheric distance. The impression of depth is achieved by the considered use of colour: it gradually diminishes in intensity as it moves away from the colourful figures in the brown foreground via the green forested area in the middle distance to terminate in the blue haze into which the mountains disappear.

Around 1595, Jan Brueghel was the first artist to paint a forest landscape (Galleria Ambrosia, Milan). Taking it as his starting-point, Gillis van Coninxloo (1544–1607) created his *Forest Landscape*, in which one of the highlights of Flemish landscape painting. In it, the viewer has a close-up view of a dense forest. He appears to be standing at a bend in the stream flowing out of the impenetrable wood towards him. In the middle, the stream runs around an island on which a traveller is encamped. The banks of the stream lend a sense of depth as they wend their way into the background. This, too, is a carefully composed landscape. In this type of forest painting, the artist does not show the open sky that otherwise is important in creating an impression of spatial breadth and depth. This painting, dated 1598, achieves great painterly intensity and an increasingly atmospheric quality in its fine shades of brown and green. Breaking through the mighty treetops, the light is reflected in the water and, against a background of impenetrable darkness, transforms the island on which the traveller is lying into an agreeable place. Through its accentuated handling of light, the forest landscape becomes highly atmospheric and seems to be positively charged with emotion. In a further development, the forest – penetrated by a single clearing – becomes a world through which a lone

JAN BRUEGHEL THE ELDER 1568–1625
Landscape with the Young Tobias, 1598
X.1

figure passes (Coninxloo, *Forest Landscape*, Kunsthistorisches Museum, Vienna).

Joos de Momper the Younger (1564–1635) specialized exclusively in landscapes. His large workshop in Antwerp was as productive as that of Rubens. The *Large Mountain Landscape* was probably paint-ed *c.* 1620 during Momper's most active phase when he was expanding his repertoire in which mountain landscape played a cru-cial role. His landscapes featured mostly Alpine ranges and some Scandinavian ones, too. There is no record of whether Momper, like most of his fellow artists, ever visited Italy, but many motifs in his

work suggest that he did. The sense of space and form in his moun-tain views appears to bear all the marks of a journey across the Alps. Momper models himself on the work of Pieter Brueghel the Elder, who tended to stick more closely to nature, but his treatment of his observation of nature is freer. In the paintings he executed from memory, he combined at will any elements he had observed. The viewer occupies a high vantage point; a path leads uphill beside steep, wooded slopes; the travellers walking along it emphasize the way it falls back down into the depths. There is a striking contrast between the tiny figures – so small as to be considered accessories

GILLIS VAN CONINXLOO 1544–1607
Forest Landscape, 1598
X.3

(staffage), and thus probably the work of Hans Jordaens III (c. 1595–1643) – and the massive rock formations.

The inequality between them may well be intended to symbolize the power of nature over man. Yet nature here is artificial: the mountains appear fantastically stylized, which means that issues of statics and tectonics are not addressed, which in turn means even more scope for a wealth of invention. Essentially it amounts to an accumulation of generalized observations. Most of Momper's landscapes have something fantastic about them: abnormally strong contrasts between light and dark are not the product of the fall of

the light, and his tones become progressively lighter and cooler towards the back and distinguish individual zones. These observations apply essentially to the *Landscape with a Mountain Pass*, which is on a somewhat smaller scale and was probably painted c. 1600/1610.

Antwerp's cultural heyday came to an end with the decline of trade around mid-century. Following the foundation of the Academy of Art in Paris, Antwerp lost its role in northern Europe's artistic vanguard to the French capital. In the Netherlands, Amsterdam had now become the main commercial centre. *The Rhine at Arnhem* of 1645

JOOS DE MOMPER THE YOUNGER 1564–1635
Landscape with a Mountain Pass, *c.* 1600/1610
X.2

by Jan van Goyen (1596–1656) dates from this period of radical change, and it represents a new view of landscape. The aim now was to capture the features of a particular area and to achieve recognizability. The fields of the province were a popular motif, although paintings like van Goyen's one are not characterized by accurate topography. Artists usually contented themselves with views of unmistakable landmarks. The new affinity for nature that is being expressed here is also reflected in a growing interest in cartography and travel. Large numbers of van Goyen's sketchbook sheets have survived, and they reveal a great deal about his work-

ing methods. When travelling through the Dutch provinces, he had captured landscape motifs in countless drawings, which were then used as the basis of his compositions in his studio. (Painting out-of-doors did not become common until the nineteenth century.) In *The Rhine at Arnhem*, mist enshrouds the town. Its landmarks – the massive bulk of the Groote Kerk with its 100-metre-high tower and the older, smaller Church of St Walpurgis with its Gothic twin-towered façade – rise out of the rapidly sketched sea of houses. This motif is typical of the artist's late work in which towns amidst a wide expanse of land stand out against the horizon. In his method of

JOOS DE MOMPER THE YOUNGER 1564–1635

Large Mountain Landscape, *c.* 1620

Figures presumably by Hans Jordaens III (*c.* 1595–1643)

X.7

working, van Goyen first divided his paintings into light and dark areas, thus defining light and space. In a second step, he added individual landscape motifs, an approach that clearly shows how atmosphere was more important to him than topographical accuracy. By dispensing with local colours, he adds to a sense of atmosphere in which shades of grey, brown, ochre and green predominate. Van Goyen's hasty brushwork further accentuates the atmospheric quality of his work.

Philips Wouwerman (1619–1668) specialized mainly in equestrian scenes and history paintings. His *Landscape with Bathers* of *c.* 1660 takes up a theme that was popular above all in Italian painting. The

seventeenth century is familiar with this motif from mythological portrayals, e.g. Diana and Actaeon, with the young man surprising the goddess and her companions as they bathe. Artists like Pieter van Laer (*c.* 1592/95–1642) and others also make it a subject in its own right. In contemporary cycles of the seasons, young bathers symbolize the spring. Bathing outdoors was probably something of a spring ritual that was not just for washing, but also expressed delight at rising temperatures. This certainly applies to the exclusively male bathers in Wouwerman's painting: one happily removes his warm winter clothing, another washes himself while a third plays in the water with a dog. This merry company is in open countryside,

JAN VAN GOYEN 1596–1656
The Rhine at Arnhem, 1645
X.6

and is being watched with amusement by passing travellers. Yet the theme of bathers is not used here merely to create skilful variations on ideal types. On the contrary, the figures are modelled very much from life in a way that allows us to apply Karel van Mander's remark about Dutch painting's "lamentable" nudes to this painting too. The landscape itself is neither Dutch nor Italian. The sight of the brick buildings at the water's edge first brings Central Europe to mind. Wouwerman never in fact went to Italy, but owes the warm light in his painting to the example of the so-called Italianizers, Dutch

artists like Pieter van Laer who returned home with a preference for southern landscapes and themes such as life in the streets and squares of Rome.

A new and popular motif in Dutch painting was seascapes and ships. As an expression of Holland as a wealthy trading nation and maritime power, it was especially appropriate and reflected the importance of shipping to the country both in times of war and peace. Willem van de Velde the Younger (1633–1707) specialized in this genre. His father was a marine draughtsman who captured the

activities of the Dutch fleet in pictures whose motifs were accurate in every detail. Willem often borrowed them for his own inventive compositions – as in the proportions and execution of his painting *Ships off the Coast*. We see a crew rowing away from the great ship of state, and fishing boats striking sail while a Dutch merchant ship is being beached. The scene may be crowded with people, but their bustling activity creates no sense of unrest. Van de Velde has carefully composed apparently random elements: ships' hulls, masts and sails set balanced horizontal and vertical accents, lending the

picture a harmonious feel. Paintings like this were not highly prized merely for their subject matter, however; their charm also lay in their atmospheric mood. The light from the low sun causes the clouds to glow, shimmers on the surface of the water and lends the sails a warm sheen. It places the individual ships' portraits in a natural setting, creating a situation that seems removed from everyday life. The painting is dated 1672, the year in which van de Velde moved to England. With the state yacht flying the Dutch flag, this must be one of the last pictures that van de Velde painted in Amsterdam.

WILLEM VAN DE VELDE THE YOUNGER 1633–1707

Ships off the Coast, 1672

X.5

STILL LIFE

The term still life comes from the Dutch *stilleven* and, as the origin of the name suggests, the Dutch were masters of this genre, too. The expression appears in inventories from about 1650. The genre, in fact, came into being in Europe in the sixteenth cen-tury, but was not fashionable until the seventeenth century. It, too, reflected the specialization that was widespread at the time. Either on their own, arranged on breakfast tables or as part of market or kitchen scenes, flowers, fruit, game, fish, hunting trophies, weapons and musical instruments were reproduced in great detail and with metic-ulous skill. The artist's intention was to produce an utterly life-like painting. Modern viewers are impressed above all by the aesthetic presentation and the naturalistic way objects are portrayed. Yet when they were painted, these everyday objects had a second, moralistic meaning that today we can decipher only with difficulty. Still life came last in the hierarchy of genres because it depicted the least noble things in creation. This did not in any way diminish its popularity, however. On the one hand, still life was a suitable subject for sophisticated decorative serial paintings such as Franz Werner Tamm's (1658–1724) *Flowers, Fruit and Poultry* of 1707. Prince Johann Adam Andreas I von Liechtenstein bought a whole series of such still lifes from about 1706 for installation above the doorways of his palaces in Vienna and Valtice, where the monumen-tal, lavishly painted, colourful pictures created a powerful decora-tive effect. On the other hand, small-format still lifes became popu-lar cabinet pieces that were executed with the greatest precision. The high prices that these works commanded and the fact that they were collected by the greatest art connoisseurs and art lovers indicates the high esteem in which they were held.

Still lifes with flowers and fruit were the most popular works. *Fruit Still Life with a Silver Beaker* of 1648 by Jan Davidsz. de Heem (1606–1684) is a particularly finely executed collector's piece. One of the most important still life painters of the seventeenth century, de Heem acquired the role of mediator between Dutch and Flemish art. After moving in 1635/35 from Leiden to Antwerp, he began

JAN DAVIDSZ. DE HEEM 1606–1684

Fruit Still Life with a Silver Beaker, 1648

X.28

ROELANT SAVERY 1576–1639

Bouquet of Flowers, the so-called Liechtenstein Bouquet, 1612

X.30

to enliven his originally monochrome palette with more powerful colours. Flemish painting inspired him to switch to larger, wider formats and more lavish arrangements, but his motifs remained intimate and his compositions more placid than those of his Flemish contemporaries. This applies to the painting on display, in which de Heem adapted a composition by the Haarlem painters Pieter Claesz. (1597–1661) and Willem Claesz. (1594–1680) Heda. An arrangement of tableware and fruit is displayed on a wooden table with a green tablecloth gathered into deep folds. The sunlight, clearly entering through a side window, animates the objects whose

matt, shiny and reflecting surfaces suggest their tactile qualities. Down to the last detail, de Heem achieves remarkable realism in depicting the fruit and tableware, for example in the drops of water on the grapes that reflect the light. In his *Teutsche Academie*, published in 1675, Joachim von Sandrart, a contemporary of the artist, claimed that de Heem moved to Antwerp specially because "there one could have strange fruits of all manner of great plums, peaches, apricots, bitter oranges, lemons, grapes, and others, in better perfection and greater numbers, so that the same could be counterfeited from life". Patrons also valued de Heem's creative ability that

was allied to the complex symbolism of the objects he painted. This still life might relate to the sacrament of marriage, as suggested by the walnuts, vine tendrils and the silver beaker that since Antiquity had played a role in wedding rites. This picture from the Princely Collections may well have been the perfect wedding present for somebody.

Flower paintings developed as a genre in their own right around 1600. During the Renaissance, science – including botany – again flourished, and the resulting observation of nature was certainly advantageous for the development of the genre. Exotic plants and flowers also became established in Europe after their discovery in "new" continents.

The meticulous attention to detail in the *Bouquet of Flowers* by Roelant Savery (1576–1639) reveals the painting's origins in botanical studies. This quality appealed to his patron Emperor Rudolf II at whose court Savery was employed when he painted the picture and whose gardens he certainly had access to. Savery used oil paint with the refinement and precision of drawing, and his work is thus

related to the achievements of the famous miniaturist Georg Hoefnagel (1542–1600), who also worked in Prague. His colourful arrangement is symmetrical and composed in an orderly fashion, though the abundance of flowers is a misleading element here. In the foreground, he lines up a mouse, a grasshopper, a salamander and a bee, apparently offering them to the viewer as objects for scientific study. Apart from the pleasure derived from the beauty of the pictures, viewers at the time also took particular delight in the secondary levels of meaning in flower still lifes: here, the mouse and the flower that has fallen off can be seen as symbolizing earth; the bee, air; and the salamander, fire. Together with the water in the vase, this arrangement represents an allegory of the four elements. The flowers, which bloom at different times of the year, symbolize the four seasons. Cut flowers, which retain their beauty only over a few days, also stand for the transience of human life. Savery's painting entered the collection of Count Wrschowetz around 1700. He had Johann Adalbert Angermayer (1674–1740) produce a companion piece that is now also held in the Princely Collections.

JOHANN ADALBERT ANGERMAYER 1674–1740
Bouquet of Flowers with Animals, 1704
X.32

AMBROSIUS BOSSCHAERT THE ELDER 1573–1621

Bouquet of Flowers in a Niche

X.26

JAN VAN HUYSUM 1682–1749
Bouquet of Flowers
X.27

In its symmetrical composition and scientific precision, *Bouquet of Flowers in a Niche* by Ambrosius Bosschaert the Elder (157– 1621) represents the same degree of sophistication. Bosschaert the Elder was one of the first painters in Holland to specialize in flower paintings.

Jan van Huysum (1682–1749) was one of the leading still life painters in the first half of the eighteenth century. In the refinement and meticulousness with which he paints the flowers, leaves, fruit and creatures in his *Bouquet of Flowers*, he is very much the equal of his predecessors. His pictures are characterized by a draughts-man-like approach that was the perfect vehicle for his precise attention to detail. Like the painting in the Princely Collections, they are all technically brilliant and so most of them have survived in good condition. Despite the realistic presentation, Huysum's dense arrangement still has an ornamental quality and the composition is intended to produce an effect on the canvas. The principal element of its structure is a slightly oblique vertical axis with the objects grouped around it. Emphasis on decorative qualities and the pastel tones reflect the Rococo style. Van Huysum was a direct heir to the tradition of flower painting that Willem van Aelst (1627–1687) had established in Amsterdam in the 1650s and which remained the defining type well into the eighteenth century. Many years spent in Italy and France had influenced Aelst who introduced the Dutch to ornamental compositions. Van Huysum's work in its turn served as a model for several generations of still life painters in the eighteenth and nineteenth centuries.

Delight in glorious flower arrangements was expressed not only in painted still lifes, however. Gem-cutters, too, strove to capture the beauty of nature using their precious materials. Bouquets of flowers were cut from various agates and displayed in *Maienkrüge*, usually lidless vessels used as vases. Prince Karl Eusebius von Liechtenstein's *Maienkrug* was carved from a 35-pound block of smoky quartz cut by Dionysio Miseroni (c. 1607–1661); the prince's contract with him is dated 10 September 1638. Miseroni, whose first documented piece of work this is, was to produce "a vessel in the form of a *Maienkrug*, as large as the stone will bear". This explains the vase's unusual hexagonal shape: it corresponds to the natural shape of the quartz so that as little of the costly material as possible was lost in cutting. Miseroni worked on it for a year, creating, in terms of form and decoration, a new style that set a precedent. The prince was able to have the vase mounted by Tobias Vogt in Breslau as early as 1639. The mount, which was lost in the Napoleonic Wars, was described in the 1678 inventory of the Silver Vault. The goldsmith made a golden base that he fastened to the body of the vessel with four clasps in the form of lizards. He also made two handles shaped like curved lizards. The *Maienkrug* was re-mounted in 1810. The vase, bearing the emblem of the House of Liechtenstein and the shield of the Duchy of Troppau, is an art object created exclusively for representative purposes. In his *Werk von der Architektur* (Treatise on Architecture), Karl Eusebius argued that costly vessels were worthy of a prince on account of the rarity of the stone.

FRANS SNYDERS 1579–1657
The Lioness
X.23

GENRE PAINTING

Genre painting involves depicting the customs and traditions of particular classes or professions. It does not deal with religious, mythological or historical events, but addresses everyday pastimes and typical activities in the lives of noblemen, townsfolk, artisans and peasants, for example the courtly hunt, a feast in an inn, village fairs, gambling, peasant weddings and harvesting. Incidentals are also depicted in great detail, which means that these pictures also reveal much about social history. As in still life, genre painting conceals another level of meaning that goes beyond mere superficial realism; with their symbolism, everyday objects lend scenes a moralizing context. With origins in the grotesque ornamentation and miniatures of the Middle Ages, genre painting reached its apex in seventeenth-century Dutch art. In panel painting, everyday scenes were usually associated with religious themes before they (everyday scenes) developed into subjects in their own right during the sixteenth century.

Pieter de Bloot (1601–1658) painted numerous landscapes and peasant scenes. In his picture *Christ in the House of Mary and Martha*, he combined the religious scene with a kitchen still life in the foreground. Going back to mid-sixteenth-century compositions by Pieter Aertsen (1507/08–1575), this type was already obsolete when the picture was painted in 1637. While the religious scene is supplanted, it does not mean that interest in faith and its message was declining. On the contrary: this arrangement symbolizes the dualism of human life. Human beings usually take more interest in their physical well-being, represented by the still life of magnificent fruit, vegetables etc., than their spiritual salvation and their belief in God. The challenge, therefore, is to overcome the temptations

offered by everyday pleasures so that the soul can be saved
through devotion to the true values of life. Here, Mary and Martha,
with their different characters, represent the two possible ways of
serving God: book in hand, Mary denotes the *vita contemplativa*, a
life of study and meditation. With her apron and rolled-up sleeves,
Martha signifies the *vita activa*, the way of good deeds. The sensual
aspect of the lavish arrangement of delicacies on the kitchen table
is an allusion to sexuality: the cat eating the fish, birds, eggs and
onions were all considered to be erotic symbols.

Dating from the late 1630s, *The King Drinks* by Jan Miense
Molenaer (1610–1668) is also concerned with physical pleasures.
Molinaer was first and foremost a genre painter, and his religious
scenes, too, largely relate to peasant life. The painting in the
Princely Collections depicts the customs observed on a church
holiday: from the sixteenth century, Epiphany was celebrated in
Holland with farcical comedies presented by amateur actors.
Another traditional element of the festivities was the king's cake,
or bean cake: the person who found a bean hidden in their piece
of cake was king or queen for the day. Molenaer's painting clearly

MATTHIAS STOM(ER) *c.* 1600 – after 1650
The Adoration of the Shepherds, *c.* 1640/50
X.17

MATTHIAS STOM(ER) *c.* 1600 – after 1650
The Lutenist and the Flautist, 1640s
X.24

shows such a merry company. With a paper crown dangling from the back of her chair, the old woman is the elected queen. Contorted and grinning faces show that much beer has been drunk. Yet a moralizing tone underlines the unbridled merriment: a young man drinking greedily from a tankard had been an allegory of gluttony, one of the seven deadly sins, from the fifteenth and sixteenth centuries. The bean feast is by no means an unusual subject in Dutch art. Numerous paintings by Jacob Jordaens (1593–1678) on this theme have survived, and an engraved copy of one of them is inscribed with a quotation from the Bible: "Do not try to prove your strength by wine-drinking, for wine has destroyed many" (Sirach 31, 25 [Apocrypha]).

Celebratory customs were not just the province of genre painting. *The Saccomazzone Players* by Giovanni Francesco Susini (*c.* 1575–1653) is based on a design by Orazio Mochi (d. 1625) for the Boboli Gardens in Florence, which he executed with the assistance of Romolo Ferrucci del Tadda (d. 1621). Mochi translated a typical genre scene into the medium of sculpture. *Saccomazzone* literally means a bundle of sacks, and is the name of a noisy interlude in country dances. Two players had to keep one hand on a stone placed between them. Both were blindfolded and had to try to hit the other with a knotted cloth or a sack in his hand, and both ducked to avoid the blows, which required a great deal of agility. Susini chose a very narrow oval plinth for his bronze cast, so the players' wild thrashing in the air is shown to better advantage. Jan Steen (1626–1679) was the most famous painter of the lives of ordinary people. His style is narrative and often embellished with anecdotal detail. His paintings often made use of figures from the theatre. The class who commissioned paintings tended to have a humanistic education, and so enjoyed the inventive moralizing concealed in his portrayals of frivolity and extravagance, the subject also of *The Fat Kitchen*. Steen gave the man of the house, who is carving the ham, his own features, and the housewife in the comfortable armchair is his wife Margareta. Steen frequently incorporated this family portrait in his genre scenes, meaning that the painting can be dated to the late 1660s. Its earthy monochrome tones accord with the colour schemes of contemporary landscapes. Its affinity with the work of van Goyen, in particular, very probably stems from the time Steen spent as a young pupil of Goyen's in The Hague. Another popular subject was music-making. *The Lutenist and the Flautist* (Schönborn Collection, Vienna) by Matthias Stom(er)

(*c.* 1600–after 1650) is an example of the Caravaggesque style associated with the city of Utrecht. It is no coincidence that this night piece was for a long time attributed to Gerrit van Honthorst (1592–1656), as thematically it clearly shows his influence in its half-length portraits of musicians, and stylistically in its extreme light and dark contrasts. Stom(er), however, chose a warmer light, often with a reddish tone, and his faces, with their exaggerated modelling, can easily be distinguished from Honthorst's smoother ones. Also in the painting in the Schönborn-Buchheim Collection depicting a lute player and a flutist, candlelight draws the figures out of the darkness; placed low, the weak light source casts characteristic shadows over the musicians' kindly faces. The same effects can be seen in *The Adoration of the Shepherds* in the Princely Collections. This painting dates from the same period, the 1640s in Italy where Stom(er) spent most of his life.

There is a coarser element in a comparable scene by Joos van Craesbeeck (*c.* 1605–before 1661). He trained as a baker, but met Adrian Brouwer (1605/06–1650), who was a prisoner in Craesbeeck's place of work, the citadel in Antwerp. Brouwer taught him to paint, and Craesbeeck's entire oeuvre clearly reveals his teacher's influence. He did not start to use more luminous colours until after Brouwer's death, a development we can see in *The Lute Concert* of *c.* 1650. Here, two women, supported by an old couple who are bawling rather than singing, try to entertain a cavalier with their lute playing, but he is already semi-conscious with drink. The women are unable to impress him despite their fashionable attire, which makes it possible to date the picture to the early 1650s. Brouwer's influence can be seen in the grimacing old couple and the slumped man. Yet Craesbeeck also assimilated some innovations from Dutch painting: the young woman with her back to the viewer, who appears as a dark silhouette, and the soft, atmospheric light suggest some knowledge of Rembrandt's work. His execution seems rather careless, but suits his crude treatment of the motif. David Teniers the Younger (1610–1690) interpreted the same theme with a more kindly eye for the lower orders to which his *Peasants Making Music* belong. The setting is based on Brouwer's work in the 1630s, but here the peasants' merriment does not end in excess. Teniers depicts peasant life as seen in an idealized view by the urban middle class and aristocratic landowners, and has little to do with reality. The refined way in which the young man holds his wine glass is reminiscent of high society. No moralizing tone is evi-

JOOS VAN CRAESBEECK *c.* 1605–before 1661
The Lute Concert, *c.* 1650
X.18

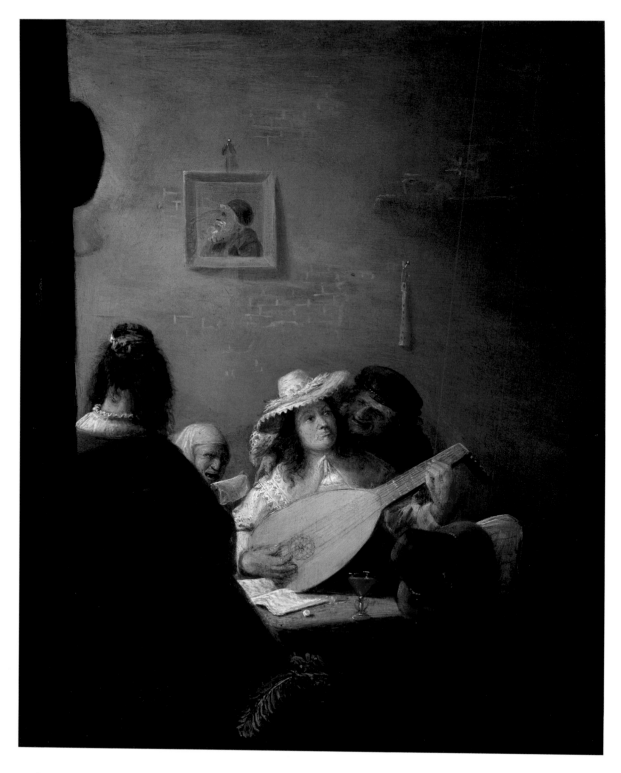

DAVID TENIERS THE YOUNGER 1610–1690

Peasants Making Music, *c.* 1650

X.19

GERRIT DOU 1613–1675
The Violin Player, 1653
X.25

dent in Teniers's innocent depiction of this merry company. In the work of Brouwer or Craesbeeck, the impression would be given that the old woman, looking in through the door unnoticed, was checking to see that the young folk were not behaving indecently, but here there is no suggestion of that. On the contrary: music-making symbolizes the virtue of moderation, and indeed the jug of wine has been set aside on the windowsill here, and there is a jug of water on the table in its place. Teniers was one of the seventeenth century's most popular artists. He worked for Archduke Leopold Wilhelm, both as court painter and administrator of his art collections. The painting in the Princely Collections dates from *c.* 1650, and was owned by Leopold Wilhelm, the governor of the Netherlands.

The Violin Player of 1653 by Gerrit Dou (1613–1675), signed and dated 1653, shows a man leaning comfortably out of the window while playing his violin and gazing into the distance. Here Dou follows a composition by Gerrit van Honthorst, though he has transferred it to a smaller format. This refined painting style was very highly regarded by collectors because it was so exquisitely executed, and it also commanded very high prices. Dou was the son of a glass engraver, and was first trained in his father's profession, which had a lasting effect on his technique. His gift for accurate observation is revealed in the sheet music blowing about in the wind and the richly ornamented carpet hanging over the parapet. His smoothly applied paint shows no sign of brushstrokes.

REMBRANDT HARMENSZ. VAN RIJN 1606–1669

Cupid with the Soap Bubble, 1634

X.12

Gentle lighting effects, a subtle use of light and dark areas and his soft modelling reveal the influence of his teacher Rembrandt. The viewer looks through the window into a painter's workshop where a young man is grinding pigments. The relief under the parapet is a reference to this and shows, among other things, a putto holding a mask in front of his face, an act symbolizing painting. The musician himself could be the artist: portraying artists as musicians was a common theme in Dutch painting. Here, Dou was probably taking music as an inspiration for artists as his theme.

Dou's famous teacher Rembrandt Harmensz. van Rijn (1607–1669) is represented in the Princely Collections by an early work, the *Cupid with the Soap Bubble* of 1634. Supported by a plumped-up cushion, the god of love reclines on a bed covered with red fabric. Using a straw, he has blown a bubble in a shell. This motif is a famil-

EGLON VAN DER NEER 1634–1703
Young Woman at Breakfast, 1665
X.11

iar *vanitas* symbol in seventeenth-century Dutch art, but the notion of the transience of life is not usually associated with Cupid. In his usual manner, Rembrandt finds a creative solution by creating an association with mythology, making the fragile soap bubble a symbol of love's fragility. Certainly, it is true that the matches made by Cupid with his arrows rarely lasted any time. It is possible that Rembrandt borrowed the motif from a copperplate engraving by Hendrick Goltzius (1558–1617). The picture is dated 1634, and has survived in very good condition; in its painterly qualities, it is a typical early work by Rembrandt. The composition based on diagonals, the strong, raking light that still leaves the background dark and the glowing colours are typical features of his work from the early 1630s. Interior scenes of the homes of the upper-middle-classes were popular in Dutch genre painting. Moralizing or didactic messages were concealed within domestic scenes or everyday tasks. Henrik Gerritsz. Pot (*c.* 1585–1657) was one of the first exponents of 'merry company' genre scenes. In his *Portrait of a Young Woman* of *c.* 1635, the boundaries between genre and portraiture are blurred. A second glance reveals it to be a portrait in the way it is so casually integrated into an everyday scene. As there is an obvious companion piece to the woman, *Portrait of a Man*, the connection makes it clear that these are indeed portraits, and not random models. This type is actually of Flemish origin. The Dutch adaptation is in fact a bourgeois version of the full-length portrait of an aristocrat, as introduced to Dutch painting by Rubens and van Dyck. Van Dyck's *Portrait of a Genoese Nobleman*, for example, is a notable forerunner of this style of painting. In Pot's picture, a woman sits at a table with songbooks open in front of her. Her fashionable dress with its wide lace collar and her coiffure, with a narrow bonnet, suggest the painting was done in the mid-1630s. Both the music and the lapdog symbolize sensual love. Her husband, in contrast, is shown in his study surrounded by the signs of his scholarship.

Young Woman at Breakfast by Eglon van de Neer (1634–1703) appears at first glance to be of the same type, but this painting should be classed more as a genre piece. Van der Neer painted numerous pictures of young women sitting at tables performing everyday tasks. The elegant young woman in this painting holds a tin plate with oysters and a peeled lemon on it. A knife, bread and a silver tray with a wine glass and a white jug are on the table in front of her. In van der Neer's paintings, these still-life-like arrangements are usually symbolic. Here, the oyster, which was considered to be an aphrodisiac, appears to allude to sensuality and lust. Depicted in all its detail, the woman's expensive dress is visually sensuous. Van der Neer has reproduced the fullness and silky sheen of the red dress with great virtuosity. The white satin bodice with its slit sleeves is a work of art in itself. The colourful impression is enhanced by the three harmonious shades of red in the upholstery, the dress and the sleeve lining. With such characteristics, the picture, which dates from 1665, is typical of the last phase of genre painting in the seventeenth century in which artists were more concerned with technical perfection in their work than they had been before. During this conservative phase, there was a preference for old picture styles that were enlivened by their refinement. As the sumptuous quality of the objects comes to the fore, their symbolic meaning becomes noticeably less significant.

PORTRAITURE

The portrait was the genre most in demand in the Netherlands in the first half of the seventeenth century. As well as several portraits by Rubens, Hals and van Dyck, the Princely Collections also hold a number of works by Rembrandt and his pupils. Some of them are direct successors to the great master, while others succeeded in distancing themselves from his influence. The *Self-portrait* by Samuel van Hoogstraaten (1627–1678) was painted in 1645 when the artist was an apprentice in Rembrandt's workshop. Rembrandt had examined his own features carefully in many self-portraits, and probably encouraged his pupils to reproduce facial features and expressions in this way. Hoogstraaten painted himself at the age of eighteen, with a degree of seriousness and dignity that are unusual for his age. This impression is also underlined by the gold chain, which occurs in several Rembrandt self-portraits and was probably available as a prop in the workshop. Since Cesare Ripa's *Iconologia*, the gold chain had been considered an important attribute in painting. Its links symbolize the continuity of the artistic tradition, while the costly metal represents painting's high rank to which the artist, too, should aspire. The soft, atmospheric light that draws the figure out of the darkness, and which seems to come from the figure itself rather than from another source, is very akin to Rembrandt's own creative ideas.

Portrait of a Youth by Pieter de Grebber (*c.* 1600–1652/53) was thought for a time to be a work of the Rembrandt school and was attributed both to Jan Lievens (1607–1674) and Aert de Gelder (1645–1727). Even though there is now agreement on who produced it, the old attributions are understandable. Numerous studies of young men in theatrical poses and clad imaginatively in fur and gold chains have survived in the work of Rembrandt and his pupils, but in its idealization of the figure and soft brushwork, de Grebber's painting differs from the style of Rembrandt.

Godfried Schalcken (1643–1706) was trained by two pupils of Rembrandt: firstly van Hoogstraten, and then Gerrit Dou, who considerably influenced his style. The technical perfection of Schalcken's *Self-portrait* and the portrait of his wife, the *Portrait of Françoise van Diemen*, follow Dou's model. In these paintings, which are on copper and in very good condition, the fashionable silks, brocades and Venetian lace are portrayed in loving and meticulous detail. The couple's elegant attire and pose, and the distinguished setting lend the portraits a noble aura. As the hand-on-heart gesture is associated with marriage vows, this double portrait was probably painted for the couple's wedding in 1679. The works of art in the background of these portraits testify to the moral standards that seventeenth-century Dutch society applied to marriage. Hanging behind Schalcken is a painting of a sleeping Venus, seen by his contemporaries as a motif symbolizing suppressed sexual desire. Similarly, his wife's portrait shows a sculpture of the virgin goddess Diana, who in images of married women symbolized chastity. For modern viewers, the portrait thus acquires the value of a sociological study.

PIETER DE GREBBER *c.* 1600–1652/53

Portrait of a Youth

X.15

SAMUEL VAN HOOGSTRATEN 1627–1678
Self-portrait, 1645   Detail
X.14   X.10

GODFRIED SCHALCKEN 1643–1706

Self-portrait, 1679

X.9

GODFRIED SCHALCKEN 1643–1706
Portrait of Françoise van Diemen, 1679
X.10

DIONYSIO MISERONI *c.* 1607–1661
Vase with lid (*Maienkrug*), 1639/40
X.35

GIOVANNI FRANCESCO SUSINI *c.* 1575–1653
The Saccomazzone Players, 2nd quarter of 17th century
X.36

Pietra dura table-top, Florence, mid- to 2nd half of 17th century
X.33

PAINTINGS

X.1 / p. 371
Jan Brueghel the Elder (1568–1625)
Landscape with the Young Tobias, 1598
Oil on copper; height 36 cm, width 55 cm
Signed and dated bottom left: BRVEGHEL, 1598
Inv. no. GE 477
Provenance: 1787 acquired by Prince Alois I von
Liechtenstein from the collection of his librarian,
Abbé Valentin Lucchini, in Vienna

X.2 / p. 373
Joos de Momper the Younger (1564–1635)
Landscape with a Mountain Pass, c. 1600/1610
Oil on panel; height 45 cm, width 66 cm
Inv. no. GE 1789
Provenance: between 1674 and 1680 acquired
by Prince Karl Eusebius von Liechtenstein from
the art dealer Peter Bousin in Vienna

X.3 / p. 372
Gillis van Coninxloo (1544–1607)
Forest Landscape, 1598
Oil on panel; height 42 cm, width 61 cm
Signed and dated bottom left: G V CONINCXLOO
1598
Inv. no. GE 751
Provenance: 1820 acquired by Prince Johann I
von Liechtenstein at the auction of Prince Wenzel
Anton von Kaunitz's collection in Vienna

X.4 / not illus.
Jan Griffier the Elder (1645–1718)
Rhine Landscape
Oil on panel; height 51 cm, width 69 cm
Signed bottom left: Griffier
Schönborn-Buchheim Collection, inv. no. G 046
Provenance: first recorded in 1830 in the
Schönborn-Buchheim Collection

X.5 / p. 378
Willem van de Velde the Younger (1633–1707)
Ships off the Coast, 1672
Oil on canvas; height 45 cm, width 55 cm
Signed and dated bottom centre on a slat:
W. V. Velde 1672
Inv. no. GE 918
Provenance: 1881 acquired in Paris by Prince
Johann II von Liechtenstein as a work by J. van
de Cappelle

X.6 / p. 376
Jan van Goyen (1596–1656)
The Rhine at Arnhem, 1645
Oil on panel; height 65 cm, width 97 cm
Signed and dated on the ferry-boat: VG 1645
Inv. no. GE 902
Provenance: probably 1776 auction at Soeter-
woude near Leiden; probably 1828 auction at
Baranowsky in Vienna; before 1880 acquired
by Prince Johann II von Liechtenstein

X.7 / p. 374
Joos de Momper the Younger (1564–1635)
Large Mountain Landscape, c. 1620
Figures presumably by Hans Jordaens III
(c. 1595–1643)
Oil on canvas; height 226 cm, width 327 cm
Inv. no. GE 730
Provenance: before 1655 collection of Don Diego
de Mexia Marquéz de Leganés, Spanish ambassador in Brussels; 1655 left to Conde de Altamira, until 1820 collection of the 8th Conde de
Altamira; 1820 sold to Marquéz de Salamanca
in Madrid; 1985 auction at Sotheby's in London;
1986 purchased by Prince Franz Josef II von
und zu Liechtenstein

X.8 / p. 377
Philips Wouwerman (1619–1668)
Landscape with Bathers, c. 1660
Oil on canvas; height 59 cm, width 81 cm
Signed bottom right: PHILS. W.
Inv. no. GE 432
Provenance: 1733 identified by seal as entail

X.9 / p. 414
Godfried Schalcken (1643–1706)
Self-portrait, 1679
Oil on copper; height 43 cm, width 32 cm
Signed bottom right: G. schalcken
Inv. no. 584, companion piece to GE 588
Provenance: 1821 acquired with the *Portrait of
Françoise van Diemen* (GE 588) by Prince Johann
I von Liechtenstein from the art dealer Huybens in
Vienna

X.10 / p. 415
Godfried Schalcken (1643–1706)
Portrait of Françoise van Diemen, 1679
Oil on copper; height 43 cm, width 32 cm
Signed bottom right: G. schalcken (not authentic)
Inv. no. 588, companion piece to GE 584
Provenance: 1821 acquired with the *Self-portrait*
(GE 584) by Prince Johann I von Liechtenstein
from the art dealer Huybens in Vienna

X.11 / p. 406
Eglon van der Neer (1634–1703)
Young Woman at Breakfast, 1665
Oil on panel; height 31 cm, width 27 cm
Signed and dated right on the table-top:
E. van der Neer 1665f
Inv. no. GE 475
Provenance: recorded from 1720 in the Princely
Collections

X.12 / p. 404
Rembrandt Harmensz. van Rijn (1606–1669)
Cupid with the Soap Bubble, 1634
Oil on canvas; height 75 cm, width 93 cm
Signed and dated bottom right: Rembrandt/
f:. 1634
Inv. no. GE 880
Provenance: 1923 in private Russian collection in
Berlin; before 1930 in private collection in Hol-
land; 1930 Goudstikker art dealership in Amster-
dam; from 1930 in Baron Heinrich Thyssen-
Bornemisza's collection in Schloss Rohoncz, from
1949 in the possession of his heiress, Baronesse
Gabrielle Bentinck-Thyssen in Lugano; 1995
acquired by Prince Hans-Adam II von und zu
Liechtenstein at the auction of the Bentinck-
Thyssen Collection at Sotheby's in London

X.13 / p. 405
Hendrik Gerritsz. Pot (c. 1585–1657)
Portrait of a Young Woman, c. 1635
Oil on panel; height 44 cm, width 34 cm
Inv. no. GE 901, whereabouts of companion
piece unknown
Provenance: 1894 acquired by Prince Johann II
von Liechtenstein as a work by Antonie
Palamedesz at auction at Adrian Hope in London

X.14 / p. 412
Samuel van Hoogstraten (1627–1678)
Self-portrait, 1645
Oil on panel; height 54 cm, width 45 cm
Signed and dated right at shoulder height:
S.v.H. 1645
Inv. no. GE 107
Provenance: first mentioned in V. Fanti's 1767
collection catalogue (as a work by Rembrandt)

X.15 / p. 410
Pieter de Grebber (c. 1600–1652/53)
Portrait of a Youth
Oil on panel; height 79 cm, width 62 cm
Signed bottom left: G
Inv. no. GE 89
Provenance: 1674 acquired by Prince Karl
Eusebius von Liechtenstein from the art dealer
Marcus Forchoudt in Antwerp

X.16 / not illus.
Adrian van Ostade (1610–1685)
The Hermit, c. 1636/37
Oil on panel; height 67 cm, width 58 cm
Signed bottom right: Ar. ostade
Inv. no. GE 906
Provenance: 1688 in the Weber Collection in
Amsterdam; 1912 acquired by Prince Johann II
von Liechtenstein at the Weber auction in Berlin

X.17 / pp. 396–97
Matthias Stom(er) (c. 1600–after 1650)
The Adoration of the Shepherds, c. 1640/50
Oil on canvas; height 117 cm, width 166 cm
Inv. no. GE 110
Provenance: first mentioned in Dallinger's 1805
collection catalogue (as a work by Honthorst)

X.18 / p. 400
Joos van Craesbeek (c. 1605–before 1661)
The Lute Concert, c. 1650
Oil on panel; height 30 cm, width 23 cm
Signed bottom on bench: CB
Inv. no. GE 476
Provenance: 1671 acquired by Prince Karl
Eusebius von Liechtenstein from the art dealer
Marcus Forchoudt in Antwerp

X.19 / p. 401
David Teniers the Younger (1610–1690)
Peasants Making Music, c. 1650
Oil on panel; height 37 cm, width 28 cm
Signed bottom right: D. TENIERp.FEC
Inv. no. GE 525
Provenance: 1656 in the collection of Archduke
Leopold Wilhelm of Austria; 1676 acquired by
Prince Karl Eusebius von Liechtenstein from the
art dealer Marcus Forchoudt in Antwerp

X.20 / p. 393
Pieter de Bloot (1601–1658)
Christ in the House of Mary and Martha, 1637
Oil on panel; height 47 cm, width 66 cm
Signed and dated bottom right on a piece of
paper in the stone niche: P. de Bloot/1637
Inv. no. GE 663
Provenance: 1787 acquired by Prince Alois I von
Liechtenstein with the collection of his librarian,
Abbé Valentin Lucchini, in Vienna

X.21 / p. 394
Jan Miense Molenaer (1610–1668)
The King Drinks, late 1630s
Oil on panel; height 42 cm, width 56 cm
Signed left, on the woman's chair: J. minsen
molenaer
Inv. no. GE 447
Provenance: recorded in the Princely Collctions
from 1780

X.22 / p. 395
Jan Steen (1626–1679)
The Fat Kitchen, late 1660s
Oil on panel; height 36 cm, width 45 cm
Signed bottom left: JSteen
Inv. no. GE 907
Provenance: 1787 at auction by the Chevalier
Lambert in Paris; 1886 acquired by Prince
Johann II von Liechtenstein at the Keil-Grote
auction in Cologne

X.23 / p. 392
Frans Snyders (1579–1657)
The Lioness
Oil on canvas; height 111 cm, width 198 cm
Inv. no. GE 2135
Provenance: before 1809 in the possession of
Amman de Schwamberg in The Hague; 1809
auctioned in Paris; before 1823 in the posses-
sion of George Watson Taylor in London; 1823
acquired by the 2nd Earl of Normanton at an auc-
tion at Christie's in London; 2004 purchased by
Prince Hans-Adam II von und zu Liechtenstein

X.24 / p. 399
Matthias Stom(er) (c. 1600–after 1650)
The Lautenist and the Flautist, 1640s
Oil on canvas; height 90 cm, width 79 cm
Schönborn-Buchheim Collection
Inv. no. GE 065
Provenance: recorded in the Schönborn-Buchheim
Collection as a work by Gerrit van Honthorst since
1830

X.25 / p. 403
Gerrit Dou (1613–1675)
The Violin Player, 1653
Oil on canvas; height 32 cm, width 20 cm
Signed and dated bottom centre: Gdov 1653
Inv. no. GE 150
Provenance: 1727 the collection of Philippe Duc
d'Orléans in Paris, subsequently Louis Philippe
Joseph Duc d'Orléans in Paris; 1792 in the
Thomas Moore Slade Collection in London; prob-
ably 1793 auction of the Moore Slade Collection
in Pall Mall in London; 1793 John Davenport Col-
lection; 1801 auction of the Davenport Collection
at Christie's in London, purchase by Meyers; after
1801 Richard Walker Collection in Liverpool;
1803 auction of the Walker Collection at
Christie's in London, purchased by Birch; probably 1815 auctioned at Philipps in London; Charles
Duc de Berry Collection in Paris; 1837 auction by
the Duchesse de Berry in the Palais de l'Elysée in
Paris, purchased by Demidoff; Baron Alphonse de

Rothschild Collection in Paris; Alex Wengraf in
London; 1980 Joseph Ritmann in Amsterdam;
1980 E. Speelman art dealership in London;
Nordmann Gallerie in Maastricht and London; pri-
vate collection in Maastricht; 1999 acquired by
Prince Hans-Adam II von und zu Liechtenstein

X.26 / p. 387
Ambrosius Bosschaert the Elder (1573–1621)
Bouquet of Flowers in a Niche
Oil on panel; height 35 cm, width 23 cm
Signed bottom left: AB
Inv. no. GE 57
Provenance: before 1923 in the possession of
Charles Seer in Bournemouth, from 1923 Walter
Seer Collection in Bournemouth, 1956 auction of
the Seer Collection at Christie's in London; art
dealer Duits in London; in the possession of Sid-
ney J. van den Bergh in Wassenaar; art dealer
Speelman in London; before 2000 private collec-
tion in the United States; 2000 acquired by
Prince Hans-Adam II von und zu Liechtenstein

X.27 / p. 388
Jan van Huysum (1682–1749)
Bouquet of Flowers
Oil on canvas; height 89 cm, width 71 cm
Signed bottom: Jan van Huysum fecit.
Inv. no. GE 540
Provenance: 1819 acquired by Prince Johann I
von Liechtenstein from the estate of Wilhelm Graf
von und zu Sickingen in Vienna; 1950 sold to
private collection; 2002 re-acquired, by Prince
Hans-Adam II von und zu Liechtenstein

X.28 / p. 392
Jan Davidsz. de Heem (1606–1684)
Fruit Still Life with a Silver Beaker, 1648
Oil on panel; height 46 cm, width 65 cm
Signed and dated top left: J. D. Heem f.A 1648
Inv. no. G 778
Provenance: 1733 identified by seal as entail

X.30 / p. 383
Roelant Savery (1576–1639)
Bouquet of Flowers, the so-called *Liechtenstein
Bouquet* 1612
Oil on panel; height 49 cm, width 34 cm
Signed and dated: R. SAVERY. 1612
Inv. no. GE 789
Provenance: c. 1700 Felix Sekerka von Sedèic
Count Wrschowetz Collection in Prague, 1723
sold from the estate of Count Wrschowetz; 1787
acquired by Prince Alois I von Liechtenstein with
the collection of his librarian, Abbé Valentin Luc-
chini, in Vienna

X.31 / pp. 380–81
Franz Werner Tamm (1658–1724)
Flowers, Fruit and Poultry, 1707
Oil on canvas; height 104 cm, width 211 cm
Signed and dated on reverse: Fr. V. Tamm. 1707
Inv. no. GE 1262
Provenance: probably commissioned by Prince
Johann Adam Andreas I von Liechtenstein

X.32 / p. 386
Johann Adalbert Angermayer (1674–1740)
Bouquet of Flowers with Animals, 1704
Oil on panel; height 50 cm, width 34 cm
Signed and dated bottom right: I. A. Angermayer.
F. Ao 1704
Inv. no. GE 787
Provenance: commissioned by Felix Sekerka von
Sedèic Graf Wrschowetz in Prague as companion
piece to Savery's *Bouquet of Flowers* (GE 789),
1723 sold from the estate of Graf Wrschowetz;
1787 acquired by Prince Alois I von Liechtenstein
with the collection of his librarian, Abbé Valentin
Lucchini, in Vienna

SCULPTURE AND APPLIED ART

X.33 / p. 419
Pietra dura table-top, Florence, mid- to 2nd half
of 17th century
Commessi di pietre dure, gilt bronze; height
64 cm, width 108 cm
Inv. no. SK 1403

X.34 / not illus.
Wooden base for the *pietra dura* table-top, 1711
Lime, in 1847 the original green bronze gilding
was heavily gilt and silver gilt; height 82 cm,
width 103 cm, depth 63 cm
Inv. no. MO 1567
Provenance: 1711 commissioned by Prince
Johann Adam Andreas I von Liechtenstein for the
pietra dura table-top (SK 1402)

X.35 / pp. 416–17
Dionysio Miseroni (c. 1607–1661)
Vase with lid (*Maienkrug*), 1639/40
with the coat of arms of the House of Liechtenstein and the Duchy of Troppau
Smoky crystal, mounted in gilt bronze and silver
gilt, partly enamelled; height 38 cm, width
20 cm, original base by Tobias Vogt, Breslau
(1640); new setting by Kremnitzer, Vienna (1810)
Inv. no. SK 310
Provenance: 1638 purchase of a smoky topaz
by Prince Karl Eusebius von Liechtenstein; 1639
cut by Miseroni for Prince Karl Eusebius von
Liechtenstein

X.36 / p. 418
Giovanni Francesco Susini (c. 1575–1653)
The Saccomazzone Players, 2nd quarter
of 17th century
after Orazio Mochi (d. 1625) and Romolo
Ferrucci del Tadda (d. 1621)
Bronze, golden-brown lacquer patina; height
42 cm (including socle)
Inv. no. SK 602
Provenance: before 1658 acquired by Prince
Karl Eusebius von Liechtenstein

APPENDIX

SELECTED BIBLIOGRAPHY

COLLECTION CATALOGUES AND MUSEUM GUIDES

Fanti, Vincenzio: *Descrizzione completa di tutto cio che ritrovasi nella galleria di pittura e scultura di Sua Altezza Giuseppe Wenceslao del S.R.I. principe regnante della casa di Lichtenstein*, Vienna 1767.

Dallinger von Dalling, Johann: *Description des tableaux, et des piéces de sculpture, que renferme la gallerie de son altesse Francois Joseph chef et prince Regnant de la maison de Liechtenstein*, Vienna 1780.

Falke, Jacob: *Katalog der Fürstlich Liechtensteinischen Bilder-Galerie im Gartenpalais der Rossau zu Wien*, Vienna 1873.

Hanfstaengl's Galerie-Publikationen (ed.): *Die Fürstlich Liechtensteinische Gemälde-Galerie zu Vienna*, Munich/London/New York 1895.

Bode, Wilhelm: *Die Fürstlich Liechtenstein'sche Galerie in Wien*, Vienna 1896.

Tietze-Conrat, E.: *Die Bronzen der fürstlich Liechtensteinschen Kunstkammer*, Vienna 1918.

Grünstein, Leo: *Die Wiener Liechtenstein-Galerie*, Braunschweig 1918.

Glück, Gustav: *Die fürstlich Liechtensteinsche Bildergalerie*, Vienna 1923.

Kronfeld, Adolf: *Führer durch die Fürstlich Liechtensteinsche Gemäldegalerie in Wien*, Vienna 1931.

Stix, Alfred/Strohmer, Erich V.: *Die Fürstlich Liechtensteinische Gemäldegalerie in Wien*, Vienna 1938.

Baumstark, Reinhold: *Meisterwerke der Sammlungen des Fürsten von Liechtenstein. Gemälde*, Zurich 1980.

Wieczorek, Uwe (ed.) issued by the Kunststiftung der LGT Bank in Liechtenstein *Meisterwerke der Sammlungen des Fürsten von Liechtenstein – Skulpturen, Kunsthandwerk, Waffen* (with texts by Maraike Bückling, Dirk Syndram, Johannes Ramharter), Berne 1996.

EXHIBITION CATALOGUES AND OTHER PUBLICATIONS ON THE COLLECTIONS

Exh. cat. *Meisterwerke aus den Sammlungen des Fürsten von Liechtenstein*, by Gustav Wilhelm and Paul Hilber, Kunstmuseum Luzern, Lucerne 1948.

Exh. cat. *Wiener Biedermeier-Maler und Carl Spitzweg. Aus den Sammlungen des Fürsten von Liechtenstein*, by Gustav Wilhelm, Kunstmuseum Luzern, Lucerne 1950.

Exh. cat. *Waffen aus vier Jahrhunderten. Ausstellung aus den Sammlungen Seiner Durchlaucht des Fürsten von Liechtenstein*, by S.D. Prinz Constantin von und zu Liechtenstein and Gustav Wilhelm, Kunstausstellungen in Liechtenstein, Vaduz 1952/53.

Exh. cat. *Flämische Malerei im 17. Jahrhundert. Ausstellung aus den Sammlungen Seiner Durchlaucht des Fürsten von Liechtenstein*, by S.D. Prinz Constantin von und zu Liechtenstein and Gustav Wilhelm, Kunstausstellungen in Liechtenstein, Vaduz 1955.

Exh. cat. *Holländische Maler des 17. Jahrhunderts. Sammlungen des Fürsten von Liechtenstein*, by Gustav Wilhelm, Vaduz 1970.

Exh. cat. *Die Jagd in der bildenden Kunst. Aus Beständen der Sammlungen des Fürsten von Liechtenstein*, by Gustav Wilhelm and Erwin Heinzle, Palais Liechtenstein Feldkirch, Bregenz 1971.

Wilhelm, Gustav: *Das Werden der Fürst-Liechtensteinischen Gemäldegalerie*, St Gall 1976 (Schriftenreihe der Gesellschaft Schweiz-Liechtenstein no.2).

Exh. cat. *Der Goldene Wagen des Fürsten Joseph Wenzel von Liechtenstein*, by Rudolf H. Wackernagel, Herbert Haupt and Georg Kugler, Kunsthistorisches Museum Wien – Wagenburg, Vienna 1977.

Exh. cat. *Venezianische Kunst in der Schweiz und in Liechtenstein*, issued by the Schweizerische Stiftung Pro Venezia Zürich und Schweizerisches Institut für Kunstwissenschaft Zürich (with contributions by André Corboz, Eduard Hüttinger, Mauro Natale, Werner Oechslin, Hugo Schneider u.a.), Seedamm-Kulturzentrum Pfäffikon/Musée d'art et d'histoire Geneva, Milan/Zurich 1978.

Exh. cat. *Wiener Biedermeier. Gemälde aus den Sammlungen des Regierenden Fürsten von Liechtenstein*, by Reinhold Baumstark, Staatliche Kunstsammlung Vaduz, Vaduz 1983.

Exh. cat. *Deutsche Malerei 15.–19. Jahrhundert. Aus den Sammlungen des Regierenden Fürsten von Liechtenstein*, by Reinhold Baumstark, Staatliche Kunstsammlung Vaduz, Vaduz 1979.

Exh. cat. *Peter Paul Rubens. Aus den Sammlungen des Fürsten von Liechtenstein*, by Gustav Wilhelm, Staatliche Kunstsammlung Vaduz, Vaduz 1974.

Exh. cat. *Liechtenstein – The Princely Collections*, issued by the Metropolitan Museum of Art, Washington, DC and the Princely Collections, Vaduz (with contributions by Reinhold Baumstark, James D. Draper, Georg Kugler, Sir John Pope-Hennessy, Olga Raggio, Dominique Thiébaut etc.), Metropolitan Museum of Art New York, New York 1985.

Supplements:
Kugler, Georg: *The Golden Carriage of Prince Joseph Wenzel von Liechtenstein*, New York 1985.

Pyhrr, Stuart W.: *Firearms from the Collections of the Prince of Liechtenstein*, New York 1985.

Baumstark, Reinhold: *Peter Paul Rubens. The Decius Mus Cycle*, New York 1985.

Lorenz, Hellmut: *Liechtenstein Palaces in Vienna from the age of the Baroque*, New York 1985.

Exh. cat. *Die Bronzen der Fürstlichen Sammlung Liechtenstein,* issued by the Liebighaus – Museum alter Plastik, Frankfurt am Main and the Princely Collections, Vaduz (with contributions by Reinhold Baumstark, Martin Büchsel, Brita von Götz-Mohr, Sabine Schulze etc.), Liebighaus – Museum alter Plastik in der Schirn Kunsthalle Frankfurt am Main, Frankfurt am Main 1986.

Exh. cat. *Im Lichte Hollands. Holländische Malerei des 17. Jahrhunderts aus den Sammlungen des Fürsten von Liechtenstein und aus Schweizer Besitz,* issued by the Öffentlichen Kunstsammlungen Basel and the Schweizerischen Institut für Kunstwissenschaft (with contributions by Reinhold Baumstark, Paul H. Boerlin, Eduard Hüttinger, Marcel Röthlisberger, Petra ten-Doesschate Chu etc.), Kunstmuseum Basle, Zurich 1987.

Exh. cat. *Peter Paul Rubens – Tod und Sieg des römischen Konsuls Decius Mus,* by Reinhold Baumstark, Staatliche Kunstsammlung Vaduz, Vaduz 1988.

Exh. cat. *Fünf Jahrhunderte italienische Kunst aus den Sammlungen des Fürsten von Liechtenstein,* von Uwe Wieczorek (with further contributions by Michaela Herrmann and Volker Krahn), Staatliche Kunstsammlung Vaduz, Berne 1994.

Exh. cat. *Princely Taste. Treasures from great Private Collections*, by Alexis Gregory, Israel Museum Jerusalem, Jerusalem 1995.

Exh. cat. *Collections du Prince de Liechtenstein,* issued by the Musée national d'histoire et d'art Luxembourg (with contributions by Uwe Wieczorek, Reinhold Baumstark, Philippe de Montebello), Ville Européenne de la Culture Luxembourg, Luxembourg 1995.

Smola, Franz: *Die Fürstlich Liechtenstein'sche Kunstsammlung. Rechtsfragen zur Verbringung der Sammlung von Wien nach Vaduz in den Jahren 1944/45*, Frankfurt am Main/Berlin/Berne/New York/Paris/Vienna 1999 (Rechtshistorische vol. 197).

Exh. cat. *"Götter wandelten einst ..." – Antiker Mythos im Spiegel alter Meister aus den Sammlungen des Fürsten von Liechtenstein,* by Uwe Wieczorek, Staatliche Kunstsammlung Vaduz, Berne 1998.

Lack, Hans Walter: *Ein Garten für die Ewigkeit – Der Codex Liechtenstein*, Berne 1999.

Divo, Jean-Paul: *Die Münzen und Medaillen der Fürsten von Liechtenstein*, Zurich 2000.

THE HOUSE OF LIECHTENSTEIN

Falke, Jacob: *Geschichte des fürstlichen Hauses Liechtenstein*, 3 vols., Vienna 1868/1877/1882.

Wilhelm, Gustav: *Stammtafel des Fürstlichen Hauses von und zu Liechtenstein*, Vaduz n .d.

Stekl, Hannes: *Österreichs Aristokratie im Vormärz. Herrschaftsstil und Lebensformen der Fürstenhäuser Liechtenstein und Schwarzenberg*, Vienna 1973 (Sozial- und wirtschaftshistorische Studien).

Martin, Georges: *Histoire et genealogie de la maison de Liechtenstein. Histoire de la principaute*, La Ricamarie 1976.

Wilhelm, Gustav: *Die Fürsten von Liechtenstein und ihre Beziehungen zu Kunst und Wissenschaft*, Schaan 1976 (Sonderdruck aus dem Jahrbuch der Liechtensteinischen Kunstgesellschaft).

Press, Volker/Willoweit, Dietmar (eds.): *Liechtenstein – Fürstliches Haus und staatliche Ordnung. Geschichtliche Grundlagen und moderne Perspektiven*, Vaduz/Munich/Vienna 1987.

Oberhammer, Evelin (ed.): *"Der ganzen Welt ein Lob und Spiegel". Das Fürstenhaus Liechtenstein in der frühen Neuzeit* (with contributions by Evelin Oberhammer, Gernot Heiss, Hellmut Lorenz, Herbert Haupt etc.), Vienna 1990.

Polleross, Friedrich B.: "'Dem Adl und fürstlichen Standt gemes Curiosi'. Die Fürsten von Liechtenstein und die barocke Kunst"; in: *Frühneuzeit-Info*, vol. 4 (1993), no. 2, pp. 174–185.

Die Sammlungen des Fürsten von Liechtenstein (with contributions by Uwe Wieczorek, Evelin Oberhammer, Karl Schütz, Manfred Leithe-Jasper, Walter Koschatzky, Christian Witt-Doerring, Hellmut Lorenz, Wolfgang Prohaska), special issue of Parnass, vol. 15 (1995), no. 11.

Wagner, Harald: *Die Regierenden Fürsten von Liechtenstein*, Triesen 1995.

Schöpfer, Gerald: *Klar und fest. Geschichte des Hauses Liechtenstein*, Riegersburg 1996.

Dotson, Samuel C.: *Genealogie des Fürstlichen Hauses Liechtenstein seit Hartmann II. (1544–1585)*, Falköpning 2003.

Pečar, Andreas: *Die Ökonomie der Ehre. Höfischer Adel am Kaiserhof Karl VI. 1711–1740*, Darmstadt 2003.

MONOGRAPHS

Pezzl, Johann: *Lebensbeschreibung des Fürsten Raimund Montekukuli, des Fürsten Wenzel Liechtenstein, des Hofraths Ignatz von Born samt einem Portraite*, Vienna 1792.

Lowy. A. M. D.: *Alois Fürst von und zu Liechtenstein. Ein Totengedächtnis*, Vienna 1859.

Wolf, Adam: *Fürstin Eleonore Liechtenstein. 1745–1812. Nach Briefen und Memoiren ihrer Zeit*, Vienna 1875.

Criste, Oskar: *Feldmarschall Johannes Fürst von Liechtenstein. Eine Biographie*, Vienna 1905.

Höss, Karl: *Fürst Johann II. von Liechtenstein und die Bildende Kunst*, Vienna 1908.

Fleischer, Victor: *Fürst Karl Eusebius von Liechtenstein. Als Bauherr und Kunstsammler (1611–1684)*, Vienna/Leipzig 1910.

Reichel, Eduard: *Johann II. Fürst von und zu Liechtenstein. Sein Leben und Wirken*, Lednice 1932.

Norbert, Jansen: *Franz Joseph II. – regierender Fürst von und zu Liechtenstein. Ein Portrait. Mit einer kurzgefaßten Geschichte des Landes und des Hauses Liechtenstein*, Vaduz 1978.

Wakounig, Marija: *Die Mission von Franz Liechtenstein in St. Petersburg 1894–1898. Ein Grandseigneur in der Diplomatie*, abilitationsschrift, Universität Wien, Vienna 1996.

Froschauer, Irmtraut: *Dr. Eduard Prinz von und zu Liechtenstein. Das vielseitige Wirken eines altösterreichischen Beamten*, Salzburg 1981.

Exh. cat. *Joseph Wenzel von Liechtenstein – Fürst und Diplomat im Europa des 18. Jahrhunderts*, issued by the Reinhold Baumstark (with contributions by Herbert Haupt, Georg Kugler, Hellmut Lorenz and Volker Press), Staatliche Kunstsammlung Vaduz, Einsiedeln 1990.

Banauch, Maria: *Prinz Aloys von und zu Liechtenstein. Stationen im Leben eines ungewöhnlichen Politikers*, Diplomarbeit, Universität Wien, Vienna 1997.

Sulzbacher, Cornelia: *Die außenpolitische Gesandtschaftstätigkeit des liechtensteinischen Gesandten in Österreich Dr. Eduard Prinz von und zu Liechtenstein*, Diplomarbeit, Universität Salzburg 1997.

Haupt, Herbert: *Fürst Karl I. von Liechtenstein. Obersthofmeister Kaiser Rudolfs II. und Vizekönig von Böhmen. Hofstaat und Sammlungstätigkeit*, 2 vols (sources and main text), Vienna/Cologne/Graz 1983 (Quellen und Studien zur Geschichte des Fürstenhauses Liechtenstein I./1 und 2).

Haupt, Herbert: *Von der Leidenschaft zum Schönen. Fürst Karl Eusebius von Liechtenstein (1611–1684)*, Source, Vienna/Cologne/Graz 1998. (Quellen and Studien zur Geschichte des Fürstenhauses Liechtenstein II./2).

Langer, Stephanie: *Das "Werk von der Architektur" des Fürsten Karl Eusebius von Liechtenstein*, Magisterarbeit, Freie Universität Berlin 1999.

Winkelbauer, Thomas: *Fürst und Fürstendiener. Gundaker von Liechtenstein. Ein österreichischer Aristokrat des konfessionellen Zeitalters*, Vienna/Munich 1999 (Mitteilungen des Instituts für Österreichische Geschichtsforschung, suppl. vol.).

Exh. cat. *Johann II. von und zu Liechtenstein. Ein Fürst beschenkt Wien*, von Renata Kassal-Mikula, Historisches Museum der Stadt Wien, Vienna 2003.

Körner, Stefan: *Die Gärten des Fürsten Aloys Joseph I. von Liechtenstein in Eisgrub, Feldsberg und Wien. Gartenkunst um 1800 zwischen Ästhetik und Ökonomie*, Magisterarbeit, Freie Universität Berlin 2004.

IN-HOUSE ARCHIVES AND LIBRARY

Bohatta, Hanns: *Liechtensteinische Bibliographie*, 2 vols. (vol. 1: I. Das Geschlecht der österreichischen Liechtensteine, II. Das Fürstentum Liechtenstein; vol. 2: III. Die österreichischen Besitzungen des fürstlichen Hauses), Buchs-Werdenberg n.d.

Bohatta, Hanns: *Katalog der in den Bibliotheken der regierenden Linie des fürstlichen Hauses von und zu Liechtenstein befindlichen Bücher aus dem 16.–20. Jahrhundert*, 3 vols., Vienna 1931.

Stundner, Franz/Eggendorfer, Anton: "Handschriften des fürstlich Liechtensteinischen Archives zu Vaduz"; in: *Mitteilungen aus dem Niederösterreichischen Landesarchiv*, vol. 2 (1978), pp. 70–80 and vol. 3 (1979), pp. 48–65.

Oberhammer, Evelin: "Das Hausarchiv der regierenden Fürsten von Liechtenstein"; in: *Scrinium. Zeitschrift des Verbandes österreichischer Archivare*, vol. 24 (1981), pp. 165–84.

Oberhammer, Evelin: "Die Fürstlich Liechtensteinische Fideikommissbibliothek"; in: Cox-Indestege, Elly/Jacobs, Erna (eds.): "De Privébibliotheken van de Regerende Vorstenhuizen in Europa", pp. 181–89, in: *Archives et Bibliothèques de Belgique*, vol. LXIII (1992), no. 1–4, pp. 3–320.

THE HISTORY OF THE CONSTRUCTION AND DECORATION OF THE LIECHTENSTEIN GARDEN PALACE AT ROSSAU

Tietze, Hans: *Andrea Pozzo und die Fürsten Liechtenstein*, in: Festschrift des Vereines für Landeskunde von Niederösterreich, Vienna 1914.

Baum, Elfriede: *Giovanni Giuliani*, Vienna/ Munich 1964.

Knopp, Norbert: *Das Garten-Belvedere. Das Belvedere Liechtenstein und die Bedeutung von Ausblick und Prospektbau für die Gartenkunst*, Berlin 1966 (Kunstwissenschaftliche Studien vol. XXXVI).

Lorenz, Hellmut: "Das 'Lustgebäude' Fischers von Erlach – Variationen eines architektonischen Themas"; in: *Wiener Jahrbuch für Kunstgeschichte*, vol. 32 (1979), pp. 59–76.

Lorenz, Hellmut/Rizzi, Wilhelm Georg: "Domenico Egidio Rossis Originalpläne für das Wiener Garten-palais Liechtenstein"; in: *Wiener Jahrbuch für Kunstgeschichte*, vol. 33 (1980), pp. 177–79.

Lorenz, Hellmut: "Ergänzungen zu Fischers 'Belvedere Liechtenstein'"; in: *Wiener Jahrbuch für Kunstgeschichte*, vol. 38 (1985), pp. 233–38.

Lorenz, Hellmut: "Ein 'exemplum' fürstlichen Mäze-natentums der Barockzeit. Bau und Ausstattung des Gartenpalais Liechtenstein in Wien"; in: *Zeitschrift des deutschen Vereins für Kunstwissen-schaft*, vol. 43 (1989), pp. 7–24.

Lorenz, Hellmut: "Zu Rottmayrs Treppenhaus-fresken im Wiener Gartenpalast Liechtenstein"; in: *Acta Historiae Artium Hungariae*, vol. 34 (1989), pp. 137–144.

Lorenz, Hellmut: *Domenico Martinelli und die österreichische Barockarchitektur*, Vienna 1991 (Österreichische Akademie der Wissenschaften. Philosophisch-historische Klasse. Denkschriften, vol. 218).

Miller, Dwight C.: *Marcantonio Franceschini and the Liechtensteins. Prince Johann Adam Andreas and the Decoration of the Liechtenstein Garden Palace at Rossau-Vienna*, Cambridge/New York/ Melbourne/Sidney/Port Chester 1991 (Cambridge Studies in the History of Art).

Miller, Dwight C.: *Marcantonio Franceschini (1648–1729)*, Turin 2001.

Werner, Jakob: *Santino Bussi 1664–1736*, Diplomarbeit, Universität Wien, Vienna 1992.

Polleross, Friedrich B.: "'Utilità, virtù e bellezza'. Fürst Johann Adam Andreas von Liechtenstein und sein Wiener Palast in der Roßau"; in: *Öster-reichische Zeitschrift für Kunst und Denkmalpflege*, vol. 47 (1993), pp. 36–52.

Magani, Fabrizio: *Antonio Bellucci. Catalogo Ragio-nato*, Rimini 1995.

Reuss, Matthias: *Antonio Belluccis Gemäldefolge für das Stadtpalais Liechtenstein in Wien*, Hildes-heim/Zurich/New York 1998 (Studien zur Kunst-geschichte, vol. 126).

INDEX OF NAMES

PHOTOGRAPHIC ACKNOWLEDGEMENTS

The illustrations come from the collections of
the Prince of Liechtenstein in Vaduz with the
exception of:

Bayerische Staatsgemäldesammlung,
Alte Pinakothek, Munich © Joachim Blauel –
ARTOTHEK Alte Pinakothek, Munich, p. 19
MAK – Österreichisches Museum für angewandte
Kunst/Gegenwartskunst, Vienna: p. 31 (top)
Civiche Raccolte d'Arte – Gabinetto dei disegni –
Castello Sforzesco – Milan, Commune di Milano –
tutti i diritti die legge riservati: p. 33 (top and
bottom)
National Gallery of Scotland, Edinburgh: p. 34
Kunstbibliothek, Staatliche Museen zu Berlin:
Preussischer Kulturbesitz, Berlin: p. 35
Graphische Sammlung Albertina, Vienna: pp. 36, 37
National and University Library, Zagreb:
p. 39 (left and right)
Akademie der bildenden Künste, Vienna, Copper
Engraving Room: pp. 40 (top and bottom), 41
Zisterzienabtei Stift Heiligenkreuz,
Stiftsmuseum: p. 50
Private collection, Bergamo: pp. 74–75
Private collection, Vaduz: pp. 84–85
Schönborn-Buchheim Collection: pp. 150, 191, 294,
295, 306, 307, 399

This volume is published to accompany the opening of the LIECHTENSTEIN MUSEUM VIENNA on 28 March 2004.

CONTRIBUTIONS by Johann Kräftner, Andrea Stockhammer

EDITORIAL AND ACADEMIC ASSISTANT
Stefan Körner

PICTURE EDITOR Michael Schweller

PHOTOGRAPHS Atelier Kräftner, Vienna, image industry, Brno/Geb.; Photostudio Preute, Vaduz; Collections of the Prince von und zu Liechtenstein, Vaduz

REPRO Alexander Dillinger and Christian Ziegler at Grasl Druck & Neue Medien 2450 Bad Vöslau, Austria

CONCEPT AND DESIGN Johann Kräftner

PUBLICITY Alexandra Hanzl

REGISTRAR, FIT-UP, CO-ORDINATION
Michael Schweller

RESTORATION Robert Wald, Helga Musner, Ruth Weiss-Klebel and Tanja Neuhorn

© 2004 Prestel Verlag,
   Munich · Berlin · London · New York

The Deutsche Bibliothek lists this publication in the Deutsche Nationalbibliografie; detailed biographical data can be called up on the internet at http://dnb.ddb.de

Front cover illustration Peter Paul Rubens, *Venus in Front of the Mirror*, *c.* 1613/14 (detail; cf. p. 305)
Back cover illustration: Roelant Savery, *Bouquet of Flowers*, so-called *Liechtenstein Bouquet*, 1612 (detail; cf. p. 383)
Frontispiece: Peter Paul Rubens, *Double Portrait of Albert and Nikolaus Rubens*, *c.* 1626/27 (cf. p. 335)
pp. 8–9: Hyacinthe Rigaud, *Portrait of Prince Joseph Wenzel I von Liechtenstein*, 1740
p. 10: Coat of arms of Prince Karl I of Liechtenstein from the "Arms Book"of Esaias Jessenski von Gross Jessen, 1615
pp. 26–27: Bernardo Bellotto, *The Liechtenstein Garden Palace in Vienna Seen from its Belvedere*, 1759/60 (detail; cf. p. 45)
pp. 84–85: Raimund Stillfried von Rathenitz, Grand Gallery of the Liechtenstein Garden Palace at Rossau, 1815
pp. 96–97: Marco Basaiti, *Madonna and Child*, *c.* 1500 (detail; cf. p. 155)
pp. 134–35: Francesco di Cristofano, called Franciabigio, *Portrait of a Man*, 1517 (detail; cf. p. 155)
pp. 176–77: Sebastiano Ricci, *Battle of the Romans and the Sabines*, *c.* 1700 (detail; cf. p. 192)
pp. 220–21: Peter Paul Rubens, *Decius Mus Relating his Dream*, 1616/17 (detail; cf. p. 225)
pp. 300–301: Peter Paul Rubens, *Mars and Rhea Silvia*, *c.* 1616/17 (detail; cf. pp. 314–15)
pp. 330–31: Peter Paul Rubens, *Portrait of Clara Serena Rubens*, *c.* 1616 (detail; cf. p. 334)
pp. 366–67: Jan Davidz. de Heem, *Fruit Still Life with a Silver Beaker*, 1648 (detail; cf. p. 382)
pp. 424–25: Marcantonio Franceschini, *The Transformation of the Dead Adonis*, 1692–1700

Prestel books are avaiable worldwide. Please contact your nearest bookseller or one of the following Prestel offices for information concerning your local distributor:

Prestel Verlag
Königinstrasse 9, 80539 Munich
Tel. +49 (89) 38 17 09-0; Fax +49 (89) 38 17 09-35

Prestel Publishing Ltd.
4 Bloomsbury Place, London WC1A 2QA
Tel. +44 (20) 7323-5004; Fax +44 (20) 7636-8004

Prestel Publishing
900 Broadway, Suite 603, New York, NY 10003
Tel. +1 (212) 995-2720; Fax +1 (212) 995-2733

www.prestel.com

The Library of Congress Cataloguing-in-Publication data is available; British Library Cataloguing-in-Publication Data: a catalogue record for this book is available from the British Library; Deutsche Bibliothek holds a record of this publication in the Deutsche Nationalbibliografie; detailed bibliographical data ca be found under: http://dnb.ddb.de

PROJECT CO-ORDINATION
Victoria Salley

EDITING
Stephen Telfer

TRANSLATION
Michael Robinson

DESIGN
WIEN NORD PILZ Werbeagentur, Vienna, and sk grafikbüro, Munich

PRODUCTION AND TYPESETTING
sk grafikbüro, Munich

REPRO, PRINTING AND BINDING
Grasl Druck & Neue Medien, 2450 Bad Vöslau, Austria

Printed in Austria on acid-free paper

ISBN 3-7913-3143-4 (English edition)
ISBN 3-7913-3142-6 (German trade edition)
ISBN 3-7913-3144-2 (Italian edition)